THE SOUTHERN BELLE
in the
AMERICAN NOVEL

THE SOUTHERN BELLE

in the

AMERICAN NOVEL

Kathryn Lee Seidel

university presses of florida
University of South Florida Press
Tampa

UNIVERSITY PRESSES OF FLORIDA is the central agency for scholarly publishing of the State of Florida's university system, producing books selected for publication by the faculty editorial committees of Florida's nine public universities: Florida A&M University (Tallahassee), Florida Atlantic University (Boca Raton), Florida International University (Miami), Florida State University (Tallahassee), University of Central Florida (Orlando), University of Florida (Gainesville), University of North Florida (Jacksonville), University of South Florida (Tampa), University of West Florida (Pensacola).

ORDERS for books published by all member presses of University Presses of Florida should be addressed to University Presses of Florida, 15 NW 15th Street, Gainesville, FL 32603.

To my mother and father

CONTENTS

ACKNOWLEDGMENTS

I could not have completed this project without the help and encouragement of colleagues and friends. The intellectual progenitor of this book is Lewis Lawson, who remarked more than ten years ago that Temple Drake has many sisters. He and Jackson Bryer at the University of Maryland have provided continued support and advice. At a time when I needed to write full time, the General Research Board of the University of Maryland provided a summer grant and the English Department allowed a semester of reduced teaching load. Barbara Bowman, Annabel Patterson, and Anne Goodwyn Jones read the manuscript and gave candid and ultimately fruitful advice. Terence Hoagwood helped proofread the manuscript. The work of Anne Goodwyn Jones, Catherine Clinton, Lucinda MacKethan, and Bertram Wyatt-Brown appeared as I was writing and thus saved me the problem of having to write in depth about biographical issues, historical realities, the Eden motif, and southern honor. Any errors are of course my own.

The encouragement, caring, and inspiration of a steadfast group of friends provided a constant sense of an audience, those intelligent and sensitive readers whom I want to understand the book; Joyce Rothschild, Kathleen Hickok, Barbara Bowman, Martha Wulfsberg, and Joseph Arden are my ideal readers.

A seven-year-old girl has helped me understand that, while much of her personality is innate, my culture and I can choose which traits to endorse. This girl is my daughter Leslie, at my side as I wrote, daily reminding me why this topic is important. Most of all, I thank Carl and Elinor Seidel, my parents, who read the manuscript, typed it, proofed it, mailed it, fretted over it, and never doubted for an instant that it would be published.

INTRODUCTION

The Goddess in the Southern Pantheon:
Madonna or Magdalen?

And such girls! . . . more grace, more elegance, more refinement, more guileless purity, were never found in the whole world over, in any age, not even that of the halcyon . . . so happy was our peculiar social system—there was about these country girls . . . mischief . . . spirit . . . fire . . . archness, coquetry, and bright winsomeness—tendrils these of a stock that was strong and true as heart could wish or nature frame; for in the essentials their character was based upon a confiding, trusting, loving, unselfish devotion—a complete, immaculate world of womanly virtue and home piety was theirs, the like of which . . . was . . . never excelled, since the Almighty made man in his own image . . . young gentleman, hold off, . . . lay not so much as a finger-tip lightly upon her, for she is sacred.[1]

She did not move. Her eyes began to grow darker and darker, lifting into her skull above a half moon of white, without focus, with the blank rigidity of a statue's eyes. She began to say Ah-ah-ah-ah in an expiring voice, her body arching slowly backward as though faced by an exquisite torture. When he touched her she sprang like a bow, hurling herself upon him, her mouth gaped and ugly like that of a dying fish as she writhed her loins against him.[2]

The quotation from George W. Bagby's *The Old Virginia Gentleman* (1885) presents the southern belle "on her pedestal" in a typical nineteenth-century description. The quotation from William Faulkner's *Sanctuary* (1931) describes the lurid nymphomania of Temple Drake, the most extreme example of the fate of the modern southern belle. The metamorphosis began abruptly, about 1914, and continued until

1939; it was during this period that the southern belle as a character in fiction discarded her cloak of gentility and purity to reveal depravity, destructiveness, rebellion, or neurosis. Milly, in Ellen Glasgow's *They Stooped to Folly*, bears an illegitimate child; Jenny Blair, in Glasgow's *The Sheltered Life*, precipitates the murder of the married man she loves and drives his wife to insanity; Miss Habersham, in Isa Glenn's *Southern Charm*, survives her rape and thrives as a successful career woman in New York; Caddie Compson, in William Faulkner's *The Sound and the Fury*, becomes the mistress of a Nazi general; Temple Drake becomes a prostitute. For that matter, more recently this "wicked" belle figure has herself become a stereotype, lacking even the warmth, love, and intelligence that characterized many of the fallen belles of the 1920s and 1930s. For example, in Kyle Onstott's *Mandingo*, the belle is a nymphomaniac whose first affair was with her brother. Missy Anne in Alex Haley's *Roots* is a caricature of the traditional belle; she is simpering, silly, and ultimately destructive in her relationship with her friend Kizzy.

Bagby's portrait of the nineteenth-century belle, however, is the one that is still probably most familiar to readers, even today. The traditional southern assumptions about men and women—and indeed many of the other components of the southern milieu—are familiar to a broad range of readers: the colonel with his mint juleps, the white-columned verandas peopled with belles in flouncing ruffled gowns, the slim, aristocratic young swains proposing marriage on bended knee, the mammy, the faithful black retainer. These remnants of plantation life form a whole system of stereotypes that is apparently at home in the popular imagination. Francis P. Gaines, often quoted for his excellent summary of the plantation novel of the nineteenth century, points out that popular songs, popular magazines, and popular culture keep alive the traditions.[3] Stereotypical southern characters abound in cinema, fiction, and nonfiction, although they are often viewed unfavorably and replaced with a new set of stereotypes: the beautiful but damned belle, the strong black woman, the proud, defiant black man, the sadistic overseer, the dissipated young master, the ineffectual mistress, and the enervated master. Florence King devotes a chapter to several of these stereotypes in *Southern Ladies and Gentlemen*. Amusing but exaggerated accounts of today's southern women are found in Sharon McKern's *Redneck Mothers, Good Ol' Girls and Other Southern Belles*. Shown on television, *Gone with the*

Wind drew one of the largest television audiences in history. *Mandingo* and its sequel, *Drum*, substitute the stereotypes of weak whites and proud blacks for the proud whites and childlike blacks of earlier works. Drugstore best-sellers include gothic romances set on plantations—*Glorious Angel*, by Joanna Lindsey, *Poinciana*, by Phyllis Whitney, *Delta Blood*, by Barbara Terry Johnson, and the Falconhurst novels by Lance Horner and Kyle Onstott. One can also find more serious current fiction set in the plantation South, such as *Jubilee*, by Margaret Walker, *Beulah Land*, by Lonnie Coleman (which became a television miniseries), and of course *Gone with the Wind*, by Margaret Mitchell, never out of print since it was published in 1936. Television brought Alex Haley's semifictional *Roots* to millions of viewers, who then bought the book and probably many other plantation novels in order to satisfy their curiosity about "how it really was" in the Old South.

How can we account for the two types of belle? The stunning transition of the belle figure from a representative of the virtues of southern society to an embodiment of its vices took about a hundred years—from 1832 to 1939, the range of this study. The meaning of the belle figure changes dramatically in the 150 novels I have studied, but there are crucial similarities.

The belle's personality traits and the plot or life story an author invents are roughly reflective of the author's attitude toward the South itself. Moreover, the seeming disparity between nineteenth-century belles, such as Bagby's, and twentieth-century belles, such as Temple Drake, evaporates because modern authors show that traditional personality traits can manifest themselves in two clusters that are apparently opposed but are really equal parts of the self-image that the belle's milieu has encouraged her to adopt. The belle defined by Bagby is in her late teens, a daughter of a rich plantation owner; we meet her usually at that moment of her life when she is most marriageable, and her short career as a belle ends with marriage. As early as 1910 Emily Putnam wrote in *The Lady*: "The woman of Southern romance is the young girl; the social intercourse of the little Southern cities consisted chiefly of balls and dances at which young girls might be seen by young men. When she was married, her husband carried her to his plantation and there she lived in isolation . . . for [her] the dance was over."[4] But what of her childhood, and what happens to her after marriage? How are the traits that make her a successful belle, with hordes of suitors, useful (or not) after she marries or after she reaches her twenties still unmarried? These are the questions writers of our century ask, and their answers are fascinating.

This study begins with the apparent contradiction between the ideal nineteenth-century and the "fallen" twentieth-century belles. Where one is sweet, the other is sensual; where one is praised for her virtue and beauty, the other is narcissistic and vice-ridden. I propose that both belles are drawn from one consistent image. The nineteenth-century belle has within her the seeds for her own literary meta-morphosis, since she has been taught by her society to repress instincts and displace emotions that linger in her unconscious, awaiting release. Thanks to their changed milieu, writers of the Southern Renaissance (1914–39) were able to find the means to dismantle the nineteenth-century myth of the southern belle within the belle figure herself.

I also argue that from the earliest novels to the most recent, the southern belle is the symbol of the South itself. Early on, writers saw the belle as their ideal South, pure and noble. More self-conscious and critical modern southern writers use the "darker" side of the belle—the repressed narcissism, etc.—to indict the Old South or to describe the New.

The reasons for these changes are both cultural and psychological. When the traditional southern mythos clashed with the forces set loose by World War I, the South's fantasies about itself no longer provided the sanctuary of values that had been sufficient for sixty years after the Civil War. Artists, always the creators of order, had to begin to reorder their world. Breaking up the idols of the old order is usually the first step for the artist of the new. Thus the demythologizing began in poetry, in fiction, in histories, in scholarship, for, as Mircea Eliade writes, "the tendency to demythologize is a destruction of the world to create another."[5] Simply by presenting the actual situation of the black on the plantation, the historian could dispel claims that the "darkies" were childlike, happy creatures, singing all day under the protective eye of their benevolent masters. Simply by revealing that the South was not founded by blue-blooded relatives of dukes and earls, Thomas J. Wertenbaker could identify the yeoman farmer as the principal southern ancestor.[6] An artist, by dramatizing any one of the fragments of the myth, could reveal the truth or falsity of the southern gentleman, of southern history, of the Civil War, of the southern belle.

As yet, however, there has been no thorough investigation of the goddess in the southern pantheon, the belle.[7] But artists have found that creating the psychology of the belle is surprisingly easy. Myths do not have to be overturned but rather pursued relentlessly. There is indeed a consistency in the traditional and the modern belle: the girl George W. Bagby describes in the quotation at the beginning of this introduction *is* Temple Drake in the second quotation. The reason for this equivalence lies in the authors' perception that the cultural and psychological demands placed upon southern women predisposed them to adopt certain modes of behavior rather than others. The writers I have chosen for this study depict the belle as they do because they perceive in various ways that the traits of the nineteenth-century belle are sufficient cause of the motives and actions of the modern belle. The Old South wanted its women to be pure, chaste ideals of spirituality, but this demand can produce women who repress their sexual needs, who denigrate and deny the physical, and whose behavior therefore exhibits the tensions that such repression causes—a tendency to be "high-strung," nervous, "hysterical," hypochondriacal—as repressed instincts are displaced into other forms of behavior. An entire society that boasts of its women as the most splendid examples of feminine pulchritude, rivaled perhaps only by the fair Dianas of Greece, produces a woman whose appearance is emphasized from babyhood, to the detriment of her intellect, personality, and talents. The girl who is told, in effect, to become a lovely object can become a narcissist, self-admiring as well as admired for her lovely shell. Simone de Beauvoir, however, shows the ease with which male anxiety has been projected onto the "empty shell."[8] Karen Horney, a psychoanalyst of the 1920s and 1930s whose work is only now becoming widely known, emphasizes the tendency of the narcissistic woman, treated as an object, to see herself as an object and to expect this treatment from others, often in ways that dehumanize the woman in order to obtain the requisite objectness.

As Sandra M. Gilbert and Susan Gubar show in their fine work, *The Madwoman in the Attic*, this sense of woman as object corresponds with the identification of the object or work of art with the female.[9] As I shall show, the southern belle is the designated object or work of art of her culture; the emblem of her as a statue on a pedestal represents the projection of her society's attitudes toward women and sexuality, toward blacks and guilt, toward itself and its weakness and loss.

A society that prefers its lovely women to be charming and flirtatious coquettes who never yield their purity can create a situation of impossible tension for the belle: she is asked to exhibit herself as sexually desirable to the appropriate males, yet she must not herself respond sexually. She must be as alluring as the Dark Lady, yet as pure as the White Maiden. The literature in which the belle appears reveals that such a juxtaposition within one personality is too much for some of the modern belles to bear. Nineteenth-century belles, whose Victorian milieu reinforces the southern dicta for feminine behavior, are more successful. After World War I, the basic conflicts in the personality of the belle become the central emphasis in literature that depicts the belle.

My method unites textual analyses with historical, cultural, and psychological insights in order to show the connections between southern women's experience, southern cultural mythology, and southern writers' imaginative unification of the two. I am most interested in the belle as a character in literature, but since she so often reflects the concerns of her society, I attempt to account for the social and historical forces that influence her portrayal. The work of Karen Horney has been most helpful to this study because she strives to explain the relationship between personality and culture. More as an anthropologist than as a psychologist, Horney identifies a number of personality disorders that result not from a childhood trauma but from a cultural expectation or tendency.

Jean Baker Miller points out that because our society has defined men as dominant and women as subordinate, whole sets of personality traits are endorsed as "normal" or "abnormal." As I will show, the personality traits deemed normal for southern ladies were both benign and destructive, so that a girl could be sweet and pure, yet narcissistic and masochistic.

The emphasis in each chapter, however, is on close reading of several novels by important or influential authors. The distinction between "important" and "influential" explains why authors such as Faulkner, whose work is of the highest quality, and less well known authors such as Thomas Dixon, Jr., indeed Colonel William Falkner, Faulkner's great-grandfather, are all discussed in this book. My principle of selection has been to include (1) those works that were most representative of their period's portraits of belles, (2) those that proved extraordinarily influential to other writers' portraits of belles, and (3) those that are of the best literary merit and are usually both representative and influential yet have the further distinction of transcending the stereotypes in some unique way. The quality of a novel is discussed if that is an issue. In several cases, some background on more or less unknown authors is given, and occasionally a plot synopsis of a relatively unfamiliar novel is necessary. Otherwise, this study attempts to present a literary history of the belle figure by closely analyzing the belle in novels that follow the conventions of the time; to examine the psychology of the belle in novels that focus on her motivations (and oftentimes defy convention to do so); and to ponder the mythic significance of the belle in southern fiction and culture.

I / Genre and Convention

I

The Belle as an Antebellum Ideal

In 1936, when Margaret Mitchell told the reader that "Scarlett O'Hara was not beautiful," but that "men seldom realized it when caught by her charm,"[1] she was continuing a long tradition in the physical description and personality of the southern belle. A hundred years earlier, in 1832, John Pendleton Kennedy described Bel Tracy, heroine of *Swallow Barn*, as "headlong and thoughtless, with quick impulses, that gave her the charm of agreeable expression, although her features are irregular, and would not stand a critical examination. Her skin is not altogether clear; her mouth is large, and her eyes of a dark gray hue."[2] Like Scarlett, Bel is a girl with whom any feminine reader can identify; she is not a born beauty but a beauty by virtue of her passionate and vigorous personality. Kennedy implies that there is hope for even the unattractive reader, a crucial message since an increasing part of the reading audience between 1820 and 1850 were women whom prosperity had blessed with leisure time in which to read, and who were interested in reading about the situation of other women, like themselves, whose sphere was essentially the home and whose lives were absorbed with marriage and children.[3]

What is a southern belle? What are her circumstances and attributes? Bel Tracy, although the first southern belle in a novel, already had most of the attributes that are popularly associated with the belle figure. The belle is the young, unmarried daughter of a landed (and thus aristocratic) family, who lives on a great plantation. She is of marriageable age, ready to be courted. Although she may be only sixteen or seventeen, she is regarded as being at the zenith of her life. The first fictional belle, Bel Tracy, is motherless and has a father who dotes on her. She is exuberant, a bit vain, and rather naive. She is talented as a horsewoman and skilled in music. Proud of her aristocratic heritage, she has one flaw, "a vein of romance in her composition"; she desires not just a man but a "gallant cavalier,"[4] perhaps from the novels of Sir Walter Scott. Sheltered by her father, she has no mother to instruct her about what to expect from life. She is finally rescued from her fantasies by a stalwart lad, and the novel ends with their marriage.

This plot and character type are the paradigm for the belle figure in American fiction; it differs significantly from that in a great deal of women's fiction in the 1800s because of the plantation setting. Nina Baym in *Women's Fiction: A Guide to Novels by and about Women in America, 1820–1870* (1978) surveys the domestic and sentimental novel in which a young woman is cut off from her family, must earn her own living, fend off seducers, and marry Mr. Right, all because she rejects emotion as her only lodestar and prefers to view life sensibly. The southern belle, however, is usually not orphaned (although she often has lost her mother), remains in the plantation setting, may be temporarily attracted to the unsuitable seducers and sometimes rejects the sensible in favor of the easy, the vain, the rich. Placing the domestic heroine on the plantation leads absolutely to plots, characters, and feelings that were unacceptable in novels set elsewhere. Then as now, in southern literature, the influence of place is astonishing yet inevitable.

The literary portraits of the southern belle in antebellum novels emphasize aspects of the belle that reflect several concerns and ideals of the social and literary milieu in which these novels were written. The milieu that produced the first literary southern belles such as Bel Tracy blended a number of social and literary factors. Southerners' notions of the superiority of their way of life and the actualities of plantation life are among the social factors. In addition, the already established literary conventions of sentimental novels influenced a new subgenre, the plantation novel.

Southerners were, in their moral ideals, Victorians who reacted strongly against the corruption of their society. To them, the Industrial Revolution appeared to have brought more harm than good: materialism, greed, poverty, and prostitution seemed to be undermining human morality. The Victorian counter to the corruption of the materialistic, industrialized world was the home. During the first half of the nineteenth century, both in England and in the United States, the home was elevated to the status of a sacred refuge from the corrupt world; the home became the temple of civilization's most cherished values and virtues.[5] As Walter E. Houghton contends in *The Victorian Frame of Mind*, woman's place was as a guardian of this sanctuary; her influence was meant to correct the sins of "revolution, prostitution and atheism."[6] The horror of the fallen woman—whether the prostitute or the unfaithful wife of Victorian fiction and nonfiction—resulted in part from a horror of the corruption in society that the fallen woman represented. As Houghton points out, pure, spiritual love was consequently "exalted as a corrective for two of the marriage evils of the time: prostitution and a marriage system dominated by the commercial spirit."[7]

The Victorian tendency to idealize home and its guardian, woman, was abetted in the southern United States by southerners' belief that their civilization was superior to that of the North. Upper-class southern landowners believed themselves to be descendants of English aristocracy, particularly the cavaliers of the seventeenth century.[8] The plantation owner and his family ruled legitimately because of their "noble blood." His sons and daughters were by analogy princes and princesses in their dominions.[9]

The psychological frame of mind of southern men also contributed to the portrait of the belle in this period. After the exhilaration of the revolutionary period, a feeling of social decline seemed to pervade the South. Jeffersonian democracy flourished, as opposed to Hamilton's more aristocratic notions, which southerners would have preferred. Southerners became a bit uneasy about their undemocratic, hence un-American social order. As William R. Taylor explains in *Cavalier and Yankee*, "They grasped for symbols of stability in order to stem their feelings of drift and uncertainty and to quiet their uneasiness about the inequities within southern society."[10] One such symbol was medieval feudalism, which provided the metaphor of southern men not simply as country squires but as gallant knights. The immense popularity in the South of the novels of Sir Walter Scott is logical in this context. The other symbol of order was the home, which southerners, as Victorians, understood must be guarded against the chaotic and immoral forces of industrialization and of democratic change. Thus the anxiety of the southern gentleman was parallel to that of the Victorian in England, with the added incentive of aristocracy impelling him to worship the home.

The southern belle as an ideal woman would be sanctioned by Victorian morality and by southerners' image of the home as a persistent standard of order and decency. Southerners' notions of their aristocratic origins assured that the belle would be protected from reality, championed, and wooed as befits a princess in her realm. In addition, the realities of plantation life were well-suited to the idealization of woman, since women were kept isolated from the "world" by the nature of their life on a plantation. A young girl had few tasks other than to be obedient, to ride, to sew, and perhaps to learn reading and writing. Unlike her brothers, who attended preparatory schools and college, a girl was to stay home until such time as a suitable—that is, lucrative—marriage was arranged for her. If she was pretty and charming and thus could participate in the process of husband-getting, so much the better. However, the career of a belle was not long-lived. After marriage, a girl was expected to become a hard-working matron who was supervisor of the plantation, nurse, and mother.

Plantation life in the South engendered a subgenre of the novel which embodies many of the values of southern life and in which the first literary southern belles appear. These novels, written from the 1820s to the 1850s, resemble the popular sentimental domestic novels of the day in that they concern the activities of young women whose goal is marriage and of wives whose interests are the home and children. But the plantation novel is more complex than the sentimental novel. As William R. Taylor and Francis P. Gaines contend, these novels are not literal reflections of the actual plantation economy. They were written because of a "defensive attitude" among southerners whose social and economic order was perpetually under attack by the democratic and industrial North.[11] The planter wished "to appear aloof from money-making, and the plantation was to be represented as something other than a setting for human and economic exploitation."[12] In fact, the plantation was often represented as an ideal oasis of civilization in a corrupt world. The enclosed nature of the plantation—its seclusion and isolation from other people, hence other influences—made it potentially the ideal Victorian home, untouched by the evils of industrialism and urbanization. If the maiden-belle in these novels seems to us a bit too sweet, it is because she is represented as the ideal, uncorrupted daughter of this way of life. Plantation novels also depict the matron-wife she becomes as retiring and self-sacrificing, more noticed in the abstract than in reality (after what was often a flamboyant career as a belle). The fact that the southern belle is often motherless in the novels suggests that authors were inadvertently showing the insignificance of the married woman in terms of her status on the plantation even though she was probably among the most overworked people on the plantation, as the accounts of Harriet Martineau, Fanny Kemble, and Charlotte Gilman report.

Anne Firor Scott's insightful history, *The Southern Lady* (1970), makes clear that life was difficult at best for southern women. The image of the southern lady, with her cluster of attributes of appearance and purity, belied the reality of her situation; while "the mythology assured every young woman that she was a belle, endowed with magic powers to attract men and bend them to her will," her real-life experience, as revealed in diaries, letters, and magazine articles, was the contrary.[13] Often disappointed by the gentleman who turned out not to be the cavalier, who married her because her "magic" attraction was her dowry, often distressed by her change in status from a pampered, sought-after belle to a hardworking but anonymous wife, the belle-turned-matron was herself a laborer on the plantation. Catherine Clinton writes in *The Plantation Mistress* (1982) of the constant threat of disease, the dangers of childbirth, and the unrelenting loneliness of plantation women who at best developed a stoic tolerance of the situation.

The plantation novel embraces the heroines from sentimental, domestic novels in that the belle is presented as a maiden with many threats to her purity that she must successfully overcome. But plantation novels also assert that the girl's own nature should be carefully controlled, since feminine assertiveness and vanity could be dangerous. In the novels of the 1830s through the 1850s, the seducer is no longer the kind of man depicted in novels such as *Clarissa* and *Pamela* but is implicitly a materialistic father, or an indolent brother. Without the presence of a mother, the heroine is entirely dependent on her male relatives, particularly her father, who is often austere and authoritative. Bel Tracy, for example, has a stern father and a philandering brother, Ralph, whose influence on Bel is considered dangerous to her character. Her father's influence demands repression of her liveliness and obedience to his authority. Thus Bel is meek and lively at once, her purity threatened more by her loose-living brother than an outsider. Mild as these incestuous themes are, they are covertly present in southern fiction of this period.

The position of woman as an ideal in the plantation novel was also a response to the infant movement for women's rights, much in evidence in the journals of the time. The "new woman" of the move-

ment was altogether condemned by most of the authors of plantation
novels; women were offered the compensation or, rather, the "higher
offices" of home and hearth. The domestic pedestal was supposed to
offer the highest possible achievement and satisfaction, preferable
certainly to jobs, votes, and other alternatives championed by the
women's rights movement.

Plantation novels are only indirectly concerned with what moti-
vates the characters, correct behavior being the higher concern. Yet
the psychology of a Bel Tracy, her drives, needs, and instincts, can be
deduced. In fact, novelists often presented heroines whose personalities contradicted conventional notions of what women should be
like. Women authors in particular rebelled against the conventional
wisdom found in a good deal of the nonfiction of the day. The psychology of the feminine ideal of the time is found in the remarks of
Thomas R. Dew in four issues of the *Southern Literary Messenger*. "On
the Characteristic Differences between the Sexes and on the Position
and Influence of Woman in Society" (1835) explains that woman and
man are physically different, such that woman's "inferior strength
and sedentary habits confine her within the domestic circle."[14] She is
therefore forced to rely upon man as her "shield." Her means of winning this protection is not by changing property laws, by logic, or by
education; it is by "those qualities which delight and fascinate—
which are calculated to win over to her side the proud lord of creation, and to make him a humble supplicant at her shrine. Grace, modesty, and loveliness are the charms which constitute her power." Dew
is suggesting that woman is a mysterious flirt, a benign temptress.
Her power "to delight and fascinate" arises from her physical appeal,
which contrasts curiously with her personality, which is meek, modest, and chaste.

Dew then calls for woman, whom he acknowledges to have "passions" and "desires" like any man's, to repress her sexuality except to
use it deceptively to snare men into marriage. He continues: "she
cannot give utterance to her passions and emotions like a man. . . .
She is thus frequently required to suppress the most violent feelings;
to put a curb on her most ardent desires, and at the same time to wear
the face of contentment and ease."[15] Dew uses the vocabulary the
modern reader has come to associate with the defense mechanisms of
the ego described by Sigmund Freud; in particular, Dew recognizes
the belle's suppression and repression—she must deny her sexual
feelings, yet present the facade of passion without feeling it. If the

Victorian male is a hypocrite, as Houghton argues, so is the Victorian woman. Dew presents the coquette as the epitome of this system, citing the "wonderful control which the coquette ultimately acquires over her feelings. The general opinion is, that coquettes are cold and feelingless . . . that all their demonstrations of emotion, are the result of hypocrisy. This may sometimes be the case, but not always. Persons of this description, may even have intense feelings; but from constantly restraining and curbing them . . . they acquire perfect mastery over them."[16] Dew does not explain, however, *how* a woman is to avoid repressing positive feelings such as warmth and affection. He acknowledges that vanity and hypocrisy frequently characterize coquettes, but he does not explain *how* one can avoid these vices.

Dew contends that a woman who possesses these personality traits before marriage is the glory of hearth and home after marriage. His imagery describing marriage suggests an Edenic scene created by a married Eve who before marriage seemed more a Lilith: "Such a companion makes the home of her husband a paradise on earth, and the thought of him and his happiness, soon interweaves and intertwines itself with all her little schemes and projects, with all her desires and ambition, and her house becomes the true scene of domestic happiness and of the domestic virtues."[17] Woman cannot expect to excel in any walk of life but the domestic. Her inferior intellect, as shown by her lack of achievement in the arts, will ever prevent her from leaving the home.

From a contemporary perspective, the personality Dew endorses is childlike, docile, passive, and powerless—a convenient personality in a society that was based on a rigid caste system. The woman who possessed it had to overlook her brother's or husband's black children and to deny the anxiety her cloistered existence engendered. As Irving H. Bartlett and C. Glenn Cambor point out in their essay "The History and Psychodynamics of Southern Womanhood," women were offered the "overcompensation" of the idealized stereotype of the angel of the home "in order to make up for a series of devaluations. The early basic devaluation was that of abandonment by her nonsexual, childish white mother to a devalued, but sexual and maternal black mother; the later devaluation was through her cultural role which deprived her of her sexual identity and her maternal identity."[18]

From the perspective of Dew's contemporaries, Sarah J. Hale, Caroline Lee Hentz, and Harriet Beecher Stowe, popular women writers after 1835 (the date of Dew's remarks), Dew's assertions were

entirely unacceptable. The fiction of these women writers shows that
they agreed that vanity was a terrible flaw in women and that women
best served in the home; but they insisted that women were not intel-
lectually inferior, and they were challenged by the prescriptions
against "warmth" in women. As Nina Baym shows in *Women's Fiction*,
women writers before the Civil War continually presented plots in
which a young girl with a slight ego or sense of self matures into a
responsible, even self-supporting young woman. But these writers
did so against the weight of commentaries such as Dew's.

During this period the most influential writer on the image of the
literary belle was Sarah Josepha Hale, essayist, novelist, and editor
for forty years of *Godey's Lady's Book*, the magazine that became the
arbiter of decorum for three generations of Americans from 1828 to
1877. Throughout her magazine articles and fictional works, Hale
continuously champions a more abundant and better education for
women, countering the tendency of male writers like Dew to encourage woman, as her sole purpose in life, "to heighten and set off her
personal attractions by dress and accomplishments, that she may thus
secure the constant devotion of some gallant knight."[19] Because Hale
agrees with Dew that vanity is woman's worst fault, she proposes
education as a corrective to the shallow emphasis on feminine beauty:
"It is the bane of beautiful women to trust in their beauty; yet while
they are continually receiving homage for their charms, how difficult
it is to convince them it will not always be thus! Nothing . . . except
the most watchful discretion and . . . education . . . can prevent such
a female from becoming vain."[20] She also believes that it is woman's
duty to correct male obsession with wealth. In her novel *Northwood*
(1827), the narrator states: "This inordinate thirst for riches is the be-
setting sin of Americans; situations, institutions, education, all combine to foster it."[21] To save men from this obsession by providing corrective moral and cultural influences on husbands and children, Hale
argues, women would have to be educated.

Hale's fiction is devoted to the sad consequences awaiting a woman
of faulty education. In particular, she often treats the topic of the belle
whose feeble education has developed only her narcissistic opinion of
herself as a lovely bauble, whose attempts to fill up her empty head
are comprised of fantasies of gallant and mysterious gentlemen.
Beautiful though these girls are, their characters are lacking; they do
not prefer "good health, good habits, and good morals" in a husband.
Lydia Romelee in *Northwood* rejects a worthy suitor to wed a rich but

dissolute plantation owner whom she has known for only three weeks. Her fickleness is attributed more to "an injudicious education than to her heart."[22] The marriage is an unhappy one. Lydia is ostracized as a foreigner by Charlestonian society, whose women think her nose is too long, her forehead too low, her complexion painted, and her manners "rustic if not dowdyish." The men, however, think she is an "angel," but the narrator makes it clear that Lydia needs the comfort of women friends more than the admiration of men. Her husband is a tyrant who allows her no life of her own: "He thought . . . his wife's happiness must consist in studying and contributing to his. . . . Her wishes had, beneath the paternal roof, been laws to all who approached her; and the transition from a goddess receiving adoration to an obedient wife, was a falling off . . . she had never anticipated."[23] Hale is careful to show that the fault is not one of southern or northern temperament, but of a wife whose vanity has blurred her judgment and whose education has not prepared her to reform the intemperance of her husband.

Caroline Lee Hentz's heroines combine the virtues Hale extols with the beauty and liveliness of the belle that John Pendleton Kennedy prefers. Hentz, a northerner by birth, moved to Chapel Hill, North Carolina, where her husband held the chair of *belles lettres* at the university. The author of eighteen novels, three plays, and miscellaneous poems, she was one of the three most popular American authors as late as 1892. The heroine of *Linda; or, The Young Pilot of the Belle Creole: A Tale of Southern Life* (1850) is "the most spoiled, petted, warm-hearted, impulsive, generous little tyrant that ever ruled over a Southern plantation."[24] Like many southern belles, she is motherless and has a close relationship with her father. When he remarries, the stepmother's cruel treatment of Linda resembles that of the evil stepmothers in fairy tales such as "Cinderella" and "Snow White" (see chapter 7 for further discussion of fairy-tale motifs). Linda's consolation is education, so that when she matures into a lovely, ringleted belle, she has been sobered by suffering and learning, unlike the sheltered Bel Tracy in Kennedy's *Swallow Barn*. Bel is educated at home and Kennedy, unlike female authors of the time, is quick to discourage parents who would even consider educating their daughters in schools located in the impure world.

Linda's troubles begin in earnest when her stepmother asks her to marry her stepbrother, Robert. Linda is horrified by what she considers to be a "wicked," incestuous match with a man she has always regarded as a brother. Hentz makes it clear that the stepmother's evil stems from materialism: "Robert is rich, and you have a large fortune. We wish to unite them. An all-sufficient reason, and one which . . . outweigh[s] every other."[25] It is this attitude that Hale and Hentz denounce vehemently—that women are chattels, bought and sold by parents in the guise of marriage. Linda's unswerving morality eventually reforms Robert, and the novel ends with the death of Linda's father, an event that releases Linda from her close ties with him, so she can marry the man she loves.

The influence of seduction-novel motifs is strong in this novel. Robert is a typical swarthy, black-eyed villain, who wants to commit incest with his sister (at least this is the pious Linda's interpretation). The incest taboo is often a theme of seduction novels such as *Lucy Temple* (1828), Susanna Rowson's popular sequel to *Charlotte Temple* (1791); authors usually defused the volatility of the subject by making the man a stepbrother. Leslie Fiedler has written about the Freudian implications of the recurring use of the incest theme in the American novel (a brother can be a substitute for the father)—that it demonstrates the failure of the authors to deal with adult heterosexuality.[26] Certainly female authors were not so timid. Hentz confronts this theme directly, recognizing that Linda must defend her virtue and reject her stepbrother, assert the value of love over money, reform her would-be seducers, overcome her attachment to her father, and overcome her fear of adult love to marry the good man she loves. This is quite a task Hentz has given her heroine, but, ideal woman that she is, Linda triumphs.

The hero of Hentz's *Eoline; or Magnolia Vale* (1852) is Eoline Glenmore, a motherless girl who longs to remain with her father on his plantation and desires no activity other than to sing with her lovely voice, like the eolian lyre whose name is like her own. She has no "wish to be a belle"[27] but could be if she wanted, since her modesty and self-reliance are matched by her beauty: "Her complexion had the fairness of the magnolia blended with the blush of the rose. Her hair, of a pale golden brown, reminded one of the ripples of a sunlit lake by its soft waves. . . . Her eyes, blue, soft, and intense as the noonday sun in June, had a kind of beseeching loving expression—an expression that appealed for sympathy, protection, love."[28] Considering this saccharine description, it is remarkable that Eoline also has the courage to refuse her father's wish that she marry the neighbor's son to join their estates. To avoid this materialistic marriage, she breaks with her father completely, is disinherited, and accepts a life of poverty as a music teacher.

Unlike Victorian male writers, Hentz takes a unique and courageous stand against the notion of Thomas Dew and others that an ideal woman must also be repressed. Eoline reveals that she is as passionate as she is courageous. She prefers a man who is Byronesque: "I am wicked, because I feel as if I could really admire a man more, who is capable of some great crime nobly repented of, if he have correspondingly greatness of character, than one amicably weak and constitutionally timid."[29] Hentz makes it clear that Eoline will not marry a timid man, but one for whom Eoline feels what Hentz calls "animal magnetism," a nineteenth-century euphemism for sexual attraction. When Eoline finally marries, she chooses on the basis of an attraction of this type that has matured into love. The man who fulfills her requirements is fortunately none other than the neighbor's son whom she had earlier rejected. She marries for love and, thank heaven (the reader of 1852 must have thought), she got the money in the bargain; on her wedding day she appears "fair as the magnolia of the South, and blushing as its rose."[30]

So far, the image of the belle in these novels is one of a beautiful, intelligent, yet modest woman with impeccable morality, who has no mother and hence is quite close to her father (although the closeness can be in a relationship of rebellion), and who seeks a gallant but gentle authoritarian (like her father) to marry for love, not money. That he and she both usually have money is meant to appear incidental, since money, the Victorians believed, led invariably to evil. In only one novel published before the Civil War does one find a portrait of a belle who is not admirable, but who defines and reinforces the image of the belle as ideal by being its opposite. This novel is Harriet Beecher Stowe's *Uncle Tom's Cabin or, Life Among the Lowly* (1852).

The novel itself is an inverted plantation novel; instead of the usual pattern of life among the aristocracy, Stowe presents the reader with life among the lowly, as the subtitle asserts. The novel's portraits of blacks had great popular appeal and are no less powerful than its unique portraits of whites. Instead of the benevolent white plantation owner, the reader meets three who are progressively worse: Mr. Shelby, whose financial difficulties force him to sell his black friends; Augustine St. Clare, whose artistic, careless, and indolent temperament produces a man of all thought and no action; and Simon Legree, a *nouveau riche* Snopes from the North, whose cruel and licentious treatment of the female slaves represents the nadir of the southern plantation owner.

Two women characters in this novel reveal Stowe's attitudes toward both the ideal woman and the belle. Evangeline St. Clare—Little Eva, as the dramatic versions of the story call her—is the pure young virgin who, as her name implies, is the inspirer of two of the men in the novel: her father and Uncle Tom himself. Stowe describes her as everything a belle should be: "The shape of her head and the turn of neck and bust was peculiarly noble, and the long golden-brown hair that floated like a cloud about it, the deep spiritual gravity of her violet blue eyes, shaded by heavy fringes of golden brown." [31] She is so lovely, in fact, that her father fears she may grow up to become a coquette like her mother was. But Stowe avoids this pitfall by not allowing Eva to grow up at all. Eva is quite attached to her father: they hold hands and play games of "pelting each other with roses." Eva plays the role of moral guide that Victorians believed was woman's duty; she tries to convince her father that slavery is wicked and to correct his tendency toward dissipation. She argues that owning slaves has caused a weakening of his character. Eva, as a child, is irreproachable in her love of a black man, Uncle Tom, and in her closeness to her father. Stowe spares her the complications of adolescence, the turmoil of courtship, the danger of mercantilistic marriage. She dies the pure virgin, an embodiment of antislavery sentiments and Christian virtue.

If Simon Legree is the villain of the novel, then Marie St. Clare is his female counterpart. Marie, though a belle, represents the antithesis of the Victorian ideal woman; her attitudes are deliberately assigned to contrast with the virtues of Eva, her daughter. Like so many of the belles before her, Marie is a motherless only child who is spoiled by father and servants alike. That she has slaves to wait on her, Stowe implies, is responsible for the failure of her marriage. She expects others to give her love and attention without receiving anything from her in return. Thus she cannot be her husband's moral guide, a role Eva assumes; instead, her vanity and selfishness leave her barren of love, morality, and inspiration. St. Clare marries her because she is "the reigning belle of the season. . . . he became the husband of a fine figure, a pair of bright eyes, and a hundred thousand dollars . . . and none of these items were precisely the ones to minister to a mind diseased." [32]

The failure of a southern belle to be the moral ideal that Hale, Stowe, and Hentz espouse is a direct result of an indulged and narcissistic childhood, Stowe asserts. Never developing anything other than her beautiful facade, Marie cares only for attention and for her wardrobe; she goes to church not to be reverent but to show off her clothes. Marie cannot adjust to marriage; when St. Clare discontinues the "gallantries" of courtship, she pouts and cries. Later, when Eva is born, Marie regards her daughter with suspicion and jealousy, as a rival who now claims her husband's attention. Bored, with no inner resources to provide her with strength, in a few years "the blooming young belle changes into a faded, sickly woman, whose time was divided among a variety of fanciful diseases."[33] Hypochondria and hysterical demands for attention replace coquetry as her characteristic behavior.

Marie is a case study in defense mechanisms. To preserve her image of herself as a misunderstood and sickly woman, she denies she is selfish and projects her worst qualities onto the black slaves about her, calling them selfish ingrates. Believing that blacks are "selfish" and "over-indulged" allows Marie to rationalize her cruel behavior toward them. Stowe is intent on showing that Marie's ideas of humane treatment of her slaves are parallel to the rationalizations of many southerners for retaining the institution: Marie explains that a certain slave was "never whipped more than once or twice." Marie tells the northern visitor, a common character in plantation novels (here Cousin Ophelia): "you don't know what a provoking, stupid, careless, unreasonable, childish, ungrateful set of wretches they are."[34] Yet Stowe carefully shows that it is Marie who is all these things: even as a housekeeper she is "indolent, childish, unsystematic."[35] Such domestic failure would horrify Hentz and Hale, for whom the orderly home is a second Eden. As her ultimate villainy, Marie orders the pretty young quadroon, Rose, to be taken to the local whipping house, where, Marie knows, Rose will be sexually abused as well as tortured. Marie's jealousy of Rose's youth and beauty is the spiteful envy of a fading belle; it is also parallel to her envy of her daughter, whose sweetness and beauty are capturing the hearts of the men on the plantation, white and black. Her paranoid outburst when the northerner, Ophelia, opposes her ("Everybody goes against me") reminds one of southern defensiveness under northern criticism.

Thus, while Eva is an inspiration for women, Marie St. Clare embodies the worst offenses of the South. Stowe is careful to appeal to her female audience's preference for the sentimental novel by countering Marie's failure as a mother with the poignant story of Eliza, a mother who attempts to protect her child and stay with her husband. This audience might be shocked by Simon Legree's sadistic licentiousness; but they would be even more appalled to see families, even black families, split apart. Finally, to see a white upper-class matron order one slave sold and another to be sexually abused was to the reader an abomination of the ideal that white women were supposed to represent. Thus the intense adverse reaction to *Uncle Tom's Cabin* resulted as much from the portrait of a depraved southern woman as from that of southern male slaveholders.

The outcry came from citizens, clergy, politicians, essayists, and writers of fiction. One irate reader sent Harriet Beecher Stowe a severed ear of an unfortunate black slave. Writers published books in retaliation. Several of these responses appeared in 1852, the same year *Uncle Tom's Cabin* was published in book form; it had appeared in serial form the previous year. Caroline Lee Hentz's *Marcus Warland* asserts the benevolence of the plantation system and the virtues of southerners. Hentz was writing with a new purpose—to vindicate: northerners "may believe that we have thrown too fair a colouring over our picture of Southern life, and that we have attempted to palliate traits in themselves harsh and repulsive." Hentz wanted to let the "domestic manner of the South be more generally known, and to avoid the separation of North and South."[36] Another of her novels, *The Planter's Northern Bride* (1854), didactically combines a rationale for retaining slavery with a pleasant story. Sarah Hale's *Northwood* was reissued, revised to extol marriage between northerners and southerners as a solution to the political rift between the two sections, a pattern that became typical in post–Civil War novels. William Gilmore Simms, whose earlier books, *The Partisan* (1835) and *Katharine Walton* (1851), had presented southern life and women as ideals, continued to do so in *The Golden Christmas: Chronicle of St. John's Berkeley* (1852).

Perhaps more understandable in the context of *Uncle Tom's Cabin* is Almira Lincoln Phelps's "Southern Housekeepers" in *Women of the South* (1861), in which young ladies are exhorted "to know what labor is, that you can feel sympathy for the slaves."[37] The highest office of woman is "to arrange and control in the little empire of the home . . . to minister to your parents . . . even though it call for the sacrifice of your own enjoyments. This picture may be far different from the one of your own fancy, where gay parties with all the excitements of a life of pleasure occupy the foreground."[38] Phelps acknowledges the detrimental effects of belledom in her essay "Belles," in which she asks the young girl to observe that "those who, like the butterfly, flit from flower to flower, selfishly seeking pleasure and amusement, are wholly indifferent as to the effects of their heartless attention upon the future happiness of those whom they may choose to flatter."[39] Caroline Hentz herself writes in "The Beauty Transformed" of the deleterious effects of the beauty ethic, which encouraged fragile health: "From a child, every instruction she had received seemed to have for the ultimate object external attraction. She was excluded from the sun and air . . . lest they should add a deeper shade to the roses and lilies of nature—her hands were kept imprisoned in gloves, to preserve their snowy tints . . . 'Katy, my dear, don't run,' said her mother, 'it will make your complexion red—Katy, my love, don't eat too much, it will make your complexion coarse'."[40]

These comments are a sample of the remarks of many writers whose essays and novels reiterated the value of education, the dangers of vanity to the belle, and the rewards of home life after the publication of *Uncle Tom's Cabin*. Essayists asserted that southern women should strive to be an ideal, and novelists depicted her as such. But the one nineteenth-century literary belle who did not follow this advice, Marie St. Clare, became the prototype of a character who has dominated southern fiction in the twentieth century.

2

The Belle as the Fallen South

The preeminence of place in all of southern literature is by now such a cliché that one may be tempted to look instead for other influences. Yet it is astonishing how multifaceted this influence is, for in the southern novel (and some think in southern life as well) place—or setting, a fine word that encompasses both time and place—determines character. After the Civil War, novels set during the period of the war and Reconstruction tended to allegorize the belle as a representative of the South. As Reconstruction progressed, however, the belle resumed her metaphorical and mythic significances. A central metaphor evolved in fiction: The Edenic Garden has been devastated by war and Reconstruction; the pure flower of that Garden, the belle, suffers from the harsh, chaotic forces set loose; increasingly, the belle's suffering is likened to that of the South. Because the topic of the southern Garden is so important to southern literature, I discuss it fully in part 3 of this book. Moreover, the association of the belle with the South emerges rather slowly in the postwar literature.

At first, the belle was portrayed as a spokeswoman for the South after the war. In *Miss Ravenel's Conversion from Secession to Loyalty* (1867), by John William De Forest, Lilly Ravenel appears to be the stereotypical belle from antebellum plantation novels. She is eighteen, blonde, motherless, beautiful, modest, and demure. When Lilly speaks, however, she speaks for the South. Although she lives in the North with her father, she is proslavery, pro-South, and believes a dissolute rake, Colonel Carter, to be a superior man simply because he is a southerner. She is talkative and opinionated, but uneducated, "delightfully innocent of all the ologies."[1] Her patriotism consists of "declaring that Louisiana was her country, and that to it she owes her allegiance" (p. 68). Unlike his contemporaries, however, De Forest

resists the usual sanction of a young girl's inexperience and innocence. He indicates that these conventional personality traits are detrimental to Lilly, for she is easy prey to the smooth charms of Colonel Carter and marries him. Like Emily in Thackeray's *Vanity Fair*,
Lilly has a faithful Dobbins (here Colonel Colburne), who waits for
her.

Unlike antebellum authors, De Forest confronts some of the South's
most disturbing issues. Antebellum authors wrote on the hot issues
of their day, which were the education, the "place," and the "nature"
of women; slavery became such a topic only after the publication of
Uncle Tom's Cabin in 1852. De Forest embodies the miscegenation taboo in Lilly, a racist who "loves aristocracies." She rejects the ad-
vances of the worthy Colburne because he has visited the home of a
métis, or mulatto, Creole family in New Orleans. Lilly is shocked
when Colburne says he admires their manners and education and
"did not see much difference" between the white people of New Orleans and the brown. Lilly cannot even remain in the room with one
who has been in the parlors of "a bastard race" (p. 186).

De Forest also expands the plantation novel's capacity to incorpo-
rate the novel of seduction. He gives Lilly a foil—Madame Larue, a
temptress with eyes like "beautiful spiders, weaving quite visibly
webs of entanglement, the threads of which were rays of dazzling
light and subtle sentiment" (p. 221). De Forest shrewdly depicts her
as a female Satan: "Milton should . . . have represented Satan as a
female of French extraction and New Orleans education" (p. 221).
Her name—a pun on *la rue*, which denotes a commonly frequented
street—indicates that she is like a streetwalker; it is also a pun on *la
rouée*, the female Don Juan, the Dark Lady who is the foil to the
White Virgin. That Larue is a French name was probably sufficient to
evoke in the audience of 1867 the notion of licentiousness. That she
is from New Orleans is worse, for she may possess a drop or two of
dark blood; the loose morality of black women, always a prejudice in
the minds of the readers, could account for her behavior. De Forest
means Madame Larue to be the temptress in the Garden, the woman
who wishes to ruin the pure Lilly's happiness by seducing her husband. He has given her almost the same name as Mlle. Le Rue, the
seductress in America's first seduction novel, *Charlotte Temple* (1791).
In Madame Larue, De Forest defines the belle by presenting what a
belle should not be. The reader realizes that while Lilly is in one
sense seduced by her southern prejudices, the real threat to bliss is

the sensual, dark-skinned siren who admits she wants not marriage, only sex. That Carter, a "typical" southern gentleman, succumbs to her spell illustrates one of De Forest's themes: an innate southern sin was the inability of its men to resist temptation.

Lilly's southern chauvinism, which has been nurtured by ignorance and avoidance of the realities of the southern system, is cured by her experience on a plantation, where she accompanies her father, a northern professor, when he moves to the plantation to reorganize its labor system. Lilly learns to appreciate the northern work ethic. Her father, an abolitionist, corrects her naive misconceptions about slavery; under a system of slavery, no such men as Uncle Tom can exist: "Uncle Tom is a pure fiction," he says (p. 269). Lilly is convinced that slavery is a dehumanizing institution only when she sees the situation of blacks at first hand. Her blindness to reality, which De Forest carefully parallels to southern blindness, is cured only through experience.

Lilly believes that "A woman is only happy when she is the slave, body and soul, of some man. She is happy, just in proportion to her obedience and self-sacrifice" (p. 280). This attitude causes her "papa-worship," as De Forest calls it: "with her the sentiment of filial affection was almost a passion" (p. 229). De Forest clearly implies that she transfers this passion to her husband, refusing to acknowledge his drinking and gambling when he returns from the war. She discovers too late the results of avoiding reality when her husband strays to a more passionate woman. A shrewd psychologist, De Forest picks up a detail of the stereotyped image of the belle—that she is motherless—and expands its consequences, foreshadowing the observations of Freud on the Oedipal situation. After Carter conveniently dies, she marries the earnest Colburne, a northerner who equals her in restraint but is more rational and authoritarian than she. Thus, De Forest establishes himself as a realist who contends, through the character of Lilly, that the South's nemesis is a rosy romanticism which must be tempered with northern rationalism and hard work.

In 1881, De Forest's *The Bloody Chasm* appeared; its heroine, Virginia Beaufort, no longer is simply a spokeswoman for the South: she *is* the South. De Forest has by now clearly identified the clichés of the southerner and the belle, and he proceeds methodically to show the deficiencies of the stereotypes. Virginia used to be "the flower of the low country" at her family's plantation before the war, a belle surrounded by her father and four brothers; now she is alone, impoverished, and malnourished in their dilapidated city home in Charleston (compared to a Babylon gutted by "a whirlwind of death"). Virginia is the last of a great family; of such families, one character exclaims: "how crushed and defiled we are. Trampled into the dust and dishonored! This [the Beaufort family] is only *one*. There are hundreds more—the flower of South Carolina—reduced to this, or worse!"[2] The despair of the speaker, a former general, exemplifies the feelings of loss and impotence of southern men who can no longer hold up the banner of the Lost Cause and who are powerless to assist the women they are honor-bound to protect.

Virginia must support her mammy, Chloe; her aunt; and a young black servant girl. When a northern visitor offers Virginia the opportunity to save all of them from starvation by marrying a distant northern relative, Harry Underhill, an ex-colonel in the Union Army, she is outraged and tempted simultaneously. She realizes that the marriage would be veiled prostitution; however, it is more the fact that Harry is a northerner that horrifies Virginia: "The Yankees always had money on their minds—the busy, eager vultures! . . . I never can accept a favor from a Northerner" (pp. 141–42). Like many southerners, Virginia sees the North as a rapacious predator whose interests are purely materialistic and against whom she must forever take her stand. One of the central notions on which southerners prided themselves was that they were uninterested in commercial success. Page, Bagby, and the idealizers of the postbellum period were adamant about the South's superior system of values. De Forest carefully presents Virginia's patron, Silas Mather of New England, as a representative of the Puritan North—benevolent, saddened, and himself a widower as a result of the war. Virginia, like the South, is poor, beautiful, but still proud and rebellious in her hatred of the northern "race" of Yankees. More than a literary stereotype of a frivolous belle, Virginia represents the South itself, and De Forest makes the association consciously. Says Mather: "The girl is behaving just as the whole South behaved." General Hilton responds, "And suffering as the whole South suffers" (p. 70).

In this novel, we also witness an early appearance of the mammy, a companion to the belle in many subsequent novels. The mammy's role is that of a mother substitute to the usually motherless belle. She is a loving character who has common sense and is often the only assertive female model in the belle's life; but ultimately she has no real power because she is not the belle's mother and because she belongs to a disenfranchised race. Virginia's mammy, for example, ad-

vises her to make the marriage deal: "Womenfolks is like niggers—
can't get deir way much in dis yer world; gits along easier ef day *can*
change deir minds" (p. 96). While this homely assertion indicts an
entire social order, it was inconsequential coming from a black, and it
would not have offended most readers in 1881.

Virginia asserts that she would rather die than take the money, and
she is perceived as being singularly proud ("no other girl in the
South is scorning such a fortune for the sake of Southern principles"
[p. 96]). The food supply exhausted, however, she becomes defiant,
vowing never again to keep Lent, never to be hungry again.[3] Her
hunger and concern for her friends finally drive her to capitulate; she
consents to marry Harry but not to sleep with him. The marriage
completed, she faces the truth: "I have been bought." Her husband
resolves to win her ("I will win her as surely as the North won the
South") and when told, "You are the North incarnate," he responds,
"And my wife is the South" (p. 145). Their marriage union is *the*
Union.

This is the turning point in the novel. The first half is a melodrama
of disease, poverty, and the evils of mercantile marriage. The second
half is a light, witty drawing-room farce, in which Virginia travels to
Paris, realizes that "Charleston is only a hamlet," and begins to see
that her own views of North and South are narrow and ignorant. This
section of the novel extends the allegory of Virginia as the South.
After the first ten years of Reconstruction, the South entered a new
phase in which many of its citizens who were educated or who traveled outside the South recognized the provincialism of their antebellum ideals. Southerners were also eager to rehabilitate the reputation of their country in the North and in Europe;[4] travel was often
extolled as the best method of encouraging mutual trust. Virginia
reads, educates herself, and becomes disillusioned with southern
ideals. When her aunt rhapsodizes on the glories of the lost South,
she responds, "Oh, the dreadful subject! I used to want to talk about
it. Now I don't" (pp. 158–59). Virginia now embodies the position of
the advocates of the "New South," one that is based on cooperation
with rather than rejection of the North.

De Forest also continues his interest in the psychology of the belle
figure by presenting her foil, Lotharinga Fitz James of Baltimore,
who, as her name implies, is a sensuous, amoral seductress, like a
serpent; she attempts to interfere in the relationship between Virginia
and Harry. As in *Miss Ravenel's Conversion*, De Forest is not willing to

relinquish the conventional passionlessness of the belle figure; he equates feminine passion with depravity. Masks removed at last, with one and all realizing that Virginia's refusing to live with her husband is like the South's "refusing to recognize an accomplished fact" (p. 276), the novel ends with the reconciliation of lady and gentleman, South and North, the bloody chasm healed.

Healed, but what was the nature of the wound? The words *bloody chasm* refer, of course, to the separation of North and South by the Civil War. But the associations of these words also bring to mind the injured genitalia of the ravaged female; since the South in this period is so often represented as female, "her" violation, painful and bloody, occurs in the Civil War and Reconstruction. The suggestion of rape, oblique in the plot of the novel, occurs overtly in the imagery. De Forest thus joins the historical novelists of the late Reconstruction and early twentieth century who make rape the central plot element. Because this motif is so important in novels on the belle, I discuss it at length in chapter 11.

Cary Eggleston's historical novels glamorize the antebellum plantation using the postbellum belle-as-South motif. In *Dorothy South: A Love Story of Virginia Just Before the War* (1902), Dorothy is an unabashedly allegorical character, named for that which she represents; her vigor and her naiveté parallel Eggleston's ideas of the antebellum South. However, Eggleston's attitudes about women, embodied by Dorothy, reflect the views of a man of 1902, not the antebellum period. As is common in historical novels, the novel reflects the author's view of the present as well as the past.

Our first sight of Dorothy, when she puts her fingers in her mouth and lets out a shrill whistle, reveals that she is vigorous and lively. These are the conventional attitudes of a Bel Tracy, but, unlike Kennedy, Eggleston inadvertently parallels the heroine's innocence, beauty, and deficient education with the virtues and defects of the antebellum South.

The southern way of life is presented as the paragon of human civilization. Dorothy vigorously and passionately champions the institution of slavery and the virtues of unselfishness and generosity that slavery inspires in whites:

One woman—very intellectual, but a cat—asked me yesterday how I could bear to hold negroes in slavery, and buy fine gowns with the proceeds of their toil. I told her frankly that I didn't like

it, but that I couldn't help it. . . . I told her how hard you were
working to discharge the debts of your estate in order that you
might send your negroes to the west to be free. . . . In Virginia I
always visit every sick person on the plantation everyday. We
send for a doctor in every case, and we women sit up night after
night to nurse every one that needs it. We provide proper food
for the sick and the convalescent from our own tables. We take
care of the old and decrepit, and of all the children. From birth to
death they know that they will be abundantly provided for.
What poor family around the Five Points [New York] has any
such assurance? Who provides doctors and medicine and dain-
ties for them when they are ill? Who cares for their children? . . . I
go every morning to see every sick or afflicted negro on my own
plantation and on that of my guardian. How often have you
gone to the region of the Five Points to minister to those who
are ill and suffering and perhaps starving there?[5]

These zealous opinions are only reinforced by her travel to the North,
which she finds cruel and materialistic in its exploitation of workers.
Eggleston was apparently unimpressed by the opinions of those sa-
vants of the New South who advocated travel for southerners as a
way of ending the provincial isolationism that was thought to engender southern attitudes of superiority.

Eggleston uses De Forest's genre of choice, the *bildungsroman*, and
weds it to the plantation novel, for his main topic is truly Dorothy's
education—in fact, what female education should be, a topic as current in 1902 as in the 1850s when the action of the novel takes place.
Eggleston attempts to write a realistic historical novel and is scru-
pulous in his choice of historical detail, unlike his contemporary,
Thomas Nelson Page, whose hazy settings result from his avowed
intention to be a myth-maker, as I discuss in part 3.

Eggleston's choice of suitable readings for female education, for instance, includes "Childe Harold" and the novels of Sir Walter Scott.
Dorothy also reads the *Southern Literary Messenger* (as a "matter of
Patriotic Duty") as well as *Blackwood's*, all standard fare of the reader
in the 1850s. But she also reads Fielding, Richardson, and Sterne;
Eggleston does not seem to notice that he allows his heroine to complete these novels, even though she finds them "disgusting."

Eggleston tries to present Dorothy as meek and submissive, but
because he attempts to be a realist, he creates a vital, assertive charac-

ter who seems to get away from him in an otherwise conventional
plantation novel. To Eggleston, Dorothy's courage, vigor, outspokenness, and reading matter point to one conclusion: Dorothy is affectionate and passionate, thus potentially a dangerous woman. Like
Eve in the Garden, she seems headed for a fall. While Dorothy
warns, "I will never consent to be disposed of in marriage by the orders of others, as princesses and other chattel women are" (p. 423),
she surrenders her independence because of a worse evil than the
mercantile marriage: becoming an unruly woman. Dorothy believes
that "dogs and women need strict control. A mistress will do well for
dogs, but every woman needs a master" (p. 53). This fear that women
possess a latent animal-like nature pervades the novel. In *The Dangerous Sex: The Myth of Feminine Evil*, H. R. Hays points out that men
who fear female sexuality prefer docile, unthreatening women. Dorothy tries hard to be meek because she fears her own nature; her
runaway mother left because her husband did not rule with an iron
hand. Thus at the novel's end, when Dorothy's aunt selects a husband
for her, Dorothy has successfully restrained her vigor; she does not
even ask who he is, but simply says that she will obey. A northern
visitor asserts that Dorothy should be allowed to live her own life,
but the novel asserts that he is mistaken. Women without restraints
become wantons, Eggleston states; like horses, they must be tamed
or they will stray.

Eggleston's anxiety about Dorothy as an outspoken, vigorous
woman and his association of her with the female archetype of the
seductress reveal his unconscious association of inappropriate attitudes in women with those he would expect in a prostitute. To Eggleston, a woman is either a Victorian angel or a whore. Hence, in his
portrait of Dorothy, he alludes to his society's profound anxiety
about women and the necessity to restrain them.

3

The Southern Renaissance: Demythologizing the Belle

By the 1920s, writers were accustomed to the belle as a symbol for the South but had begun to use the character not to praise the South but to criticize and, at times, condemn. Writers focused on one or two aspects of the belle's traditional upbringing that shaped her personality and prevented her from adjusting to modern life. Because these authors emphasized depth, not breadth, each of them featured the belle as a character only in one or two novels. Yet all of them perceived that the belle plays a crucial role in the mythology of the South; by placing her not in a nineteenth-century setting but in their own time, they could examine the forces of change released by World War I—the new morality of the Jazz Age, the disillusionment with southern myths, and the materialism of the postwar years. They were quite aware of their role as demythologizers; even the titles of their novels indicate their self-consciousness: *Not Magnolia; Narcissus; The Hard-Boiled Virgin; Southern Charm.* Sarah Haardt, Evelyn Scott, Ruth Cross, Edith Everett Taylor Pope, Isa Glenn, and Frances Newman joined the two great writers of the age, William Faulkner and Ellen Glasgow, in grim recognition of the belle's narcissism, which is a consequence of the beauty ethic of the South; her sexuality, which some authors suppress but others celebrate; and her penchant for self-sacrifice, which can only be associated with masochistic self-abnegation. Glasgow and Faulkner presented a comprehensive portrait of the belle—her psychology, culture, and life history; the rest of these authors made one or two traits the motif of an entire novel, so that a trait could be examined minutely. Overall, during this period—known as the Southern Renaissance—the portrait of the belle increasingly darkens.

The Southern Renaissance merits clarification as a central part of the milieu that produced the "new" southern belle. As with most literary periods, there is disagreement over the dates of the period. John M. Bradbury in *Renaissance in the South* says that the Southern Renaissance began as early as 1917 with H. L. Mencken's challenging "Sahara of the Bozart," in which he taunts the South for its cultural and literary retardation,[1] but John L. Stewart dates the onset of this era as late as 1925.[2] An early date is more appropriate, however, in order to include writers such as Ellen Glasgow and James Branch Cabell, as well as scores of minor figures.

In fact, 1914, the beginning of World War I, is the most suitable date, since the causes of the Southern Renaissance were actually the effects of this war upon the United States, the southern states in particular. These effects can be identified as extrinsic (those which affected the economy and the social order) and intrinsic (those which influenced the psychological and philosophical orientations of the southerner). The war machine brought industrialization to the South, which, even after the Civil War, remained an agrarian economy. The southern economic market required workers to produce cotton goods for the war, but because much of the white male labor force was in Europe, a labor shortage developed. Many owners of vast tracts of land, having fewer laborers to work their farms, moved into town; small farmers came to town to fill the more lucrative positions at the mills. As money became tighter, land was sold or rented in smaller and smaller chunks to lower-class whites who had heretofore owned no land.[3] Southern mills were often owned by absentee northerners who, caring little for southern taboos, hired blacks to work in the mills or lured them away from the South altogether to jobs in the North. Women began to enter the labor force in factories, offices, and traditionally white male semiprofessional and professional positions.[4] The labor force thus included more blacks, poor whites, and women than ever before, and these groups became part of a growing middle class that challenged the aristocracy for "elite" status in the community. Caste, class, and sex roles, the foundation of the southern "squirearchy," were upset.

As the South became more industrialized, efficient means were needed to transport goods rapidly; new railroads and highways encroached upon the traditional isolation of the South. Radio, movies, and the telephone (which had really defeated the South, as Allen Tate and others asserted in *I'll Take My Stand* [1931]) presented the southerner with a new, northern perspective. Yet these sociological changes were only the beginning. The intrinsic effects of the war upon the psychology and values of southerners were even more disruptive to the old order.

Bradbury identifies as the first of five causes of the Southern Renaissance the malaise of young men returning home to old-fashioned values and provincial prejudices. Men who had seen violent death were no longer willing to accept the status quo, down home on the farm. (Wilbur J. Cash vehemently contends that these men were shocked and frightened by the changes in their world and in themselves—by the fact that supposedly civilized southerners had returned to "savagery" in the fields of war.[5]) Second, Bradbury continues, southern intellectuals rankled under Mencken's criticisms and sought to defend themselves. Third, the literary atmosphere was stimulated by the "new poetry" of poets such as Ezra Pound, T. S. Eliot, and William Butler Yeats. Fourth, the midwestern school of realism, led by Sinclair Lewis's *Main Street* (1920) and Sherwood Anderson's *Winesburg, Ohio* (1919), challenged southerners to examine their own region for literary material. Finally, the little-magazine movement throughout the South signaled an act of rebellion against literary conventions.[6]

A crucial factor in this discussion of milieu, and one not included in most discussions of the Southern Renaissance, is the emergence of women in the economic and political arenas. In 1919, women gained the right to vote after ninety years of lobbying. Although it is possible that President Wilson at last endorsed women's suffrage only to appease critics of his handling of the war,[7] the First World War itself changed the economic situation of women. While many of the women in the movement were among the leisure class, even more were working-class women who were now at work in the places of men and who comprised a powerful labor lobby. The southern woman, traditionally at odds with the suffrage movement and with the working woman, was daily confronted with entirely new concepts of women's roles. Historian Anne Firor Scott points out that southerners considered the vote a threat to the primary functions of woman as wife and mother and to her secondary function as an upholder of Christian piety.[8] In an 1877 speech Senator Joseph Brown of Georgia reasoned that women should not get the vote because woman is "alone fitted for the discharge of the sacred trust of wife and the endearing relation of mother. While the man is contending with the sterner duties of life, the *whole time* of the noble, affectionate and true woman is required in the discharge of the delicate and difficult duties assigned her in the family circle, in her church relations and in the society where her lot is cast."[9] Nevertheless, southern women, like their northern counterparts, continued to read articles on women's problems that urged not simply suffrage, but also better education for women, reformed divorce laws, and improved working conditions. Scott points out that the southern opponents of suffrage were often in sympathy with other types of women's issues.[10]

Women were also affected by the postwar morality of the Jazz Age, which presented the flapper and the career woman as radical alternatives to the traditional roles of wife, mother, spinster, and belle. The number of women in secondary schools and colleges increased as coeducation and colleges for women were established. Education lessened the traditional isolation of the southern woman; no longer was she sheltered from society until her debut. Education exposed to her what the rest of the world was doing and thinking and presented her with alternatives to the traditions of the community. Furthermore, a young woman at a college or university had a new freedom almost unheard of; she was often unchaperoned and permitted to be with "dates" of her own choosing—quite a change from the old order, in which her parents arranged her social life.

Thus, both men and women were caught up in a set of forces that culminated in the final and most profound cause of the Southern Renaissance. Allen Tate's insightful remarks in 1942 summarize the attitude of the young southerner during this time: "After the war the South again knew the world, but it had a memory of another war; with us, entering the world once more meant not the obliteration of the past but a heightened consciousness of it; so that we had . . . a double focus, a looking two ways, which gave a special dimension to the writings of our school—not necessarily a superior quality— which American writing as a whole seemed to lack."[11]

Louis D. Rubin, Jr., C. Hugh Holman, and John M. Bradbury, who have all comprehensively examined the "double focus" of southerners after World War I, provide illustrations of Tate's generalization.[12] Rubin's imaginative re-creation of the childhoods of the great southern writers of the twenties and thirties (who were born just prior to the turn of the century) in his essay "Southern Literature: The Historical Image" (1961) illustrates Tate's argument. Rubin asserts that Faulkner, Glasgow, Porter, Davidson, and Gordon were all young enough to see and speak with the veterans of that other great war, for many southerners the only war. The older generation told stories and created legends about the Civil War and the South as it was before that war. Yet these same writers were old enough to see this southern

past juxtaposed with the new post–World War I milieu with its attendant cultural and philosophical changes.[13] The writers saw the old order assaulted by the "dazzling materialism"[14] of the twenties and
were compelled to adopt at least a "double focus" and "a looking two
ways," in Tate's phrases; but the tension was not simply between past
and present. The panorama of their vision in the literature of the
Southern Renaissance has the complexity and ambiguity of the vision
of Janus. To some southerners it seemed that the past deserved to be
resurrected, while to others it needed to be buried. Those writers
who condemned the past of the South were often even more repelled
by the present, and both groups contemplated a gloomy future.

The enormous upheavals of the twenties and thirties reminded the
southerner of the South's unique sense of itself and its history, a self-
consciousness borne out of its being the only region in the United
States to know failure and defeat. Far from turning its back on the
past, the South after the Civil War had mythologized the past and
then had yearned nostalgically for this fantasy. Feelings of failure and
defeat were assuaged by praising the old order, its gentility, honor,
and chivalry—the qualities that made it spiritually superior to the
crass materialism of the northern conquerors. The Civil War, in purg-
ing the evil of slavery, also destroyed an entire social order that was
good and noble; from the southern point of view, this was a tragedy
in the classic sense of the term. Thus, the southerner's view of the
past aroused the bittersweet feelings of nostalgia for a past of military
glory, of secure values, of a rich and harmonious social order; on the
other hand, it also evoked feelings of failure, inadequacy, weakness,
and unconscious guilt for the unjust treatment of blacks.[15] These all
contribute to a sense of tragedy indigenous to the South alone; the
southerner's experience has been unique among Americans until the
defeat in Vietnam.

For the southerner, the tension between nostalgia on the one hand
and a guilty sense of failure on the other provoked recognition that
the southern past was composed both of actual events and of legends.
This moment of recognition, parallel as it was to the shock of recognition that sparked the American Renaissance of the 1800s, is cogently
analyzed in John Stewart's remarks:

> Recognition of the two kinds [of the past], the legendary and the
> actual, and of the great diversity of the latter was one of the un-
> avoidable and definitive moments in the artistic maturity of these

writers. For some such as Faulkner and Miss Porter this recognition provided the ultimate source of many of their most intensely moving and meaningful fictions: untangling the threads of the actual from the glamorous fabrics of the legendary furnished them with story after story, while refurbishing the legend to serve as a means of binding up and giving shape and meaning to the pile of lint which was "what really happened" was the most difficult, profound problem confronting them.[16]

Thus, the Southern Renaissance was a birth, not a rebirth, of self-awareness in southern culture, beliefs, ceremonies and rituals, legends—in fact, the myths at the core of southern consciousness, the assumptions by which the southerner lived.

The belles presented in literature during this period are not allegorical representations of the various factors in the complex milieu that produced them. Here and there, one sees that the change in a belle's portrait is a logical result of changes in the environment, but none of the authors discussed in this chapter attempts a comprehensive portrait. For example, these writers are generally unconcerned with the new symbol of the age, the flapper, whose brash conversation and brazen behavior are entirely antithetical to the image of the sheltered and repressed southern woman. Only occasionally does the other female figure of the age, the career woman, appear in fiction about the southern belle, although both she and the flapper appear in many other works of fiction.[17]

To these authors the new morality is not necessarily preferable to the old, but it does place the old order in a new perspective; thus, the inadequacy of traditional southern ethics for the southern woman is the theme of these novels. Ironically, they show that the virtues southern tradition has reserved for the belle are actually destructive to her and to others. In particular, the belle is no longer a paragon of purity; in fact, Francis P. Gaines says in *The Southern Plantation* that in the novels of the 1920s "the Magdalen has eclipsed the Madonna."[18] Authors who present the belle in candid sexual scenes, however, are not merely being sensational, as Gaines's comment might imply. Rather, they carefully show that society's attitudes motivate the belle's behavior.

These writers criticize southern society's traditional emphasis upon the beauty of the belle, its insistence that she be innocent, its denial of her sexual desire, and its forbidding her to have sexual experience.

They contend that society's emphasis on the beauty of the belle can produce a selfishness and narcissism that cause her to ignore the development of positive aspects of her personality. Taught to see herself as a beautiful object, the belle accentuates only her appearance and is not concerned with any talents that do not contribute to the goal her society has chosen for her: winning a man. These authors also show that the sheltering of the belle leads to a harmful innocence: she cannot adequately interpret the behavior of men who do not believe in the code of southern chivalry that respects the purity of women. Moreover, they condemn the repression required by the "ethic of purity" which leads to a variety of physical and mental disorders, including frigidity and exaggerated subservience. Authors of the period also began to be aware that the new morality of the twenties lessened taboos on women's sexual activity; some belles were suddenly without rigid guidelines. As this repressed aspect of their personalities was released, they became hypersexual. In his writings at the end of the decade, William Faulkner especially emphasizes this theme.

Reacting to the prescribed myths of the old order, writers of the 1920s also rebelled against its predominant styles of fiction. Rather than present sentimental domestic romances or historical plantation novels (though these returned in the 1930s), they followed the school of realism as exemplified in Sinclair Lewis's *Main Street*. Rarely in these books are belles set like jewels on a plantation background as they are in nineteenth-century novels. They now live in towns, where their interactions with the society that has formed them can be minutely observed. This fictional situation parallels the actual situation in the South after the Civil War; many plantation families lost their land and moved to town, there to maintain the memory of their former wealth. Many of these families became the aristocrats of the town— the judges, the lawyers, or perhaps families living in genteel poverty. A March 1921 editorial in *The Double Dealer*, a literary journal published in New Orleans, declares: "We are sick to death of the treacly sentimentalities with which our lady fictioneers regale us. The old traditions are no more. New people, new customs prevail. The Confederacy has long since dissolved. A storied realm of dreams, lassitude, pleasure, chivalry, and the Nigger no longer exists. We have our Main Streets here, as elsewhere."[19]

The little magazines of the early 1920s, which helped to create the atmosphere in which writers could comfortably chip away at the South's gilded images, contain pieces by Ellen Glasgow, James Branch

Cabell, Julia Peterkin, Frances Newman, Sarah Haardt, and H. L. Mencken, Sarah Haardt's husband. Some of the most piercing satires of the traditional belle appear in several numbers of *The Reviewer*, all of them written by Sarah Haardt. In "Paradox" (1925) Haardt shows that the beautiful, blonde, flirtatious Eileen is capable only of loving her fiancé's flattery. When he announces he is leaving for India to work with the poor, Eileen realizes that she cannot face a life amid dirt and disease. She entreats her plain, dark-haired friend, Mary, to invent any excuse for her. For her selfishness Eileen is rewarded with a broken engagement; the more courageous Mary returns to tell Eileen that she herself will accompany the young man to India.

In an essay on the southern lady, written in 1925, Haardt openly describes the negative aspects of a typical belle. She is a "slave to conventions," a person characterized by conformity and demureness, a combination that is "the most subtle and sinister of her charms. She shrinks from the shrillness, the vulgarity, above all, the pettiness of 'taking her own stand'. It is easier and more convenient to follow the old order; it saves her from thinking; and she has witnessed the utter impossibility of thinking intently and looking pretty at the same time."[20] The southern woman of the twenties was afraid of innovation, of smoking cigarettes, and of the "new freedom," as it was called; she was no flapper, according to Haardt. As it always had been, the home was her sphere. She might consequently be bored and live vicariously in her fantasies or in the fiction of a Thomas Dixon. She joined clubs. She took stands for noble causes and tried to appear self-sacrificing, reticent, and demure. She preferred the old regime because it allowed her to "pose" against a lovely background of romance, and she wanted to retain "the divinely appointed role that the Southern gentleman has always held up to her: the painted halo, the remarkable virtues, the painful modesty, the piety, the irresistible tenderness, frailty, helplessness. It is the last, glamourous touch of chivalry in a harsh, unromantic age. What if it is preposterous, insincere, untrue—a mere gesture signifying nothing? It is often graceful, and that is enough" (p. 61).

Narcissistic Mothers

Evelyn Scott, remembered as the editor who "discovered" *The Sound and the Fury*, was in her own right an innovative stylist who sought to bring to her fiction the perspective of her own "dual vision." A native of Tennessee, Scott was the daughter of a southern mother and a Bostonian father. Scott reports that she thus acquired a detachment from the antebellum tradition of her upbringing because of the austerity of her "Puritan" half. Educated in New Orleans, she ran away from home: "I rejected the idea of being a Southern Belle like everybody else."[21]

Scott's fiction asserts that not only are the traditional virtues of a southern woman inadequate, they are actually dangerous to herself and to others. What happens if a girl—having had a successful season as a belle and married as she ought—refuses to relinquish the personality of a belle in order to become a sober matron? The transition from belle to matron requires an entire shift of personality traits, from coquette to helpmate, from flirt to nurse, from child to mother, from indulged and self-concerned to selfless and self-sacrificing. In *Narcissus* (1922) Scott studies a belle who clings to her vanity even after twenty years of marriage. Like Narcissus of the myth, Julia loves to gaze at herself in mirrors: "Her dressing table with its triple mirror stood in an alcove. It was a very fine severe little table. It was Julia's vanity to be very fine and dainty in her toilet. When she was before the glass she enjoyed the defiant delicacy which she saw in the lines of her lifted head, and there was a thrill she could not analyze in the sight of her long white hands lying useless in her lap. They made her in love with herself."[22]

As she ages, her vanity needs constant reinforcement; she takes a lover, even though her husband is attentive, and she flirts with her daughter's boyfriend, who is twenty years her junior. While she craves the admiration of others, she has no love to give any of them in return, including her daughter. Julia is beautiful but vacuous; in a rare moment of insight, she realizes that "these men were strangers to her, that she loved and wanted only herself" (p. 58).

Unlike Narcissus of the myth, Julia is not destroyed by self-love, but her narcissism has a sinister effect on her daughter, May. Julia flirts with May's boyfriend, Paul, but (true to the code) will not ultimately have sex with him. He retaliates by seducing May; the act is a nonviolent but actual rape, for May is too ignorant and passive to prevent the action. In fact, May is so entirely lacking in self-esteem that she attempts to satisfy her need for love with an exaggerated helplessness. She reacts to her first sex act by wishing "She was dead. She wanted to think she was dead" (p. 122). Her wish for self-annihilation is the result of her upbringing by a selfish mother who has taught her daughter nothing but submission to the wills of those about her; this strategy prevents May from being a rival for male attention. May loves her persecutor, Paul, and fantasizes that she deserved to be raped, an act she associates with dying: "She tried to imagine that, because she was ugly and impure, Paul had already killed her. The strangeness and exaltation she felt came to her because she was dead. She loved him for destroying her" (p. 133). This masochistic pleasure is like Temple Drake's in Faulkner's *Sanctuary*; psychoanalyst Karen Horney explains that such suffering is pleasurable in that it reinforces a feeling of contempt for oneself, and one thus becomes the willing victim of others.[23] Because May has always felt insignificant compared with her mother, she accepts attention in any form and gains satisfaction in the loss of the self she despises.

Repression

Edith Everett Taylor Pope's fiction harshly indicts the traditional belle's tendency to become self-sacrificing in order to serve and help men. Pope's psychological novels explore the minds of southern woman, and she draws an analogy between the setting of her novels, her native Florida, and the psyche of the heroine. The heroine of her first, *Not Magnolia* (1928), published in the same year as her own graduation from Bryn Mawr, is Leigh Pomeroy, who attends college but otherwise is a traditional daughter of the aristocracy. Leigh rejects the handsome and ambitious northerner, Oliver, preferring Stephen, the conventional weak southern aristocrat, who is in this novel both physically and mentally ill. Oliver's ambition and energy seem exhausting to Leigh, who prefers the somnambulistic calm that she associates with the proper behavior for a southern lady and which the Florida climate favors. Oliver accuses Leigh of "neglecting your talent of being a woman for the lesser one of being a lady. There aren't many women, Leigh. There are flappers, and ladies and peasant girls and destructive feminine forces, but you'll do nothing with any of them. You're unstirred. And smug about it. Escaped you have . . . from the annoyance of feeling anything. You want death on earth—none of the annoyance of living."[24] He calls her a "frozen slut" who prefers to recede from life as her chosen Stephen has done. While Oliver seems to be describing a death wish, Leigh in fact is motivated by a fear of feeling in general and a fear of sexuality in particular; the sickly Stephen poses no physical threat to her. The more vigorous Oliver demands emotion and sexuality, both of which Leigh has repressed in order to be a "lady."

Leigh's Aunts Belle and Beulah represent the two varieties of adult womanhood to which Leigh could aspire. Belle is the narcissistic, selfish woman that her name suggests, and Leigh rejects her coquetry outright. On the other hand, Beulah is the genteel lady who has lived the sheltered, repressed life of a spinster lady but feels that such a life has cheated her. Beulah does not want to see Leigh similarly disappointed: "I wanted only one thing for you, that you get into the main current of life, that you realize your possibilities" (p. 29). Beulah has realized that repression does not make a woman happy; she appeals to Leigh: "Love is no lace paper Valentine. . . . Nor life a flower to be prettily worn. Will you choose to stagnate here, Leigh? No, and no duty excuses a woman marrying a man who is not her peer in strength, and in vitality. Will you live like Belle . . . like the other women of Goodwind, pretty and passionless, flowering like a magnolia, with beauty, but without color, against a dying background? Choose to be anything, but not a magnolia" (pp. 212–13). Pope deftly used the magnolia, the standard emblem of the purity and beauty of the southern belle in nineteenth-century fiction, as a symbol of decay and sterility. Beulah's appeal reaches Leigh, who in marrying Oliver leaves the South; her journey expresses her release from the illusion of what a southern lady should be.

The bizarre connection between the traits of the vain narcissist and the self-sacrificing masochist is shown in Southern Renaissance fiction about the southern belle. The self-sacrificing behavior endorsed for the southern matron is consistent with the ego-denying personality development of the girl destined for her brief day as a belle. The narcissist, who is trained to seek the attention of men and who thereby develops only traits with which to do so and ignores and suppresses any others (such as assertiveness, intelligence, logic, confidence), is a person whose sense of worth is achieved only through the attention of others. If that attention is removed, the person is left feeling worthless, a failure, perhaps deserving of punishment for her inadequacies. Since punishment brings attention, negative though it is, such attention is preferable to no attention at all. This situation, a logical development of narcissism, is present in several novels of the 1920s and '30s, discussed in depth in part 2.

Among the most compelling and straightforward of these books is Zelda Fitzgerald's semiautobiographical novel, *Save Me the Waltz*

(1932). Fitzgerald, herself a belle whose father was a judge in Mobile, Alabama, provides a uniquely self-conscious perspective on the belle figure. Fitzgerald's protagonist, Alabama Beggs (whose name reveals both her regional affiliation and her relationship to others), believes that her beauty is her most important attribute and that winning the attention of others is her chief purpose in life, and her family nurtures her narcissism. Trying to win the attention of her father, an austere judge, provides Alabama with plenty of opportunity to practice the skill of attracting men.

The experience of being in love with David Knight, the character certainly based on F. Scott Fitzgerald, confirms Alabama's narcissistic dependence not simply upon her father but upon other men who seem to her to replace her father. Using his name to suggest a knight in shining armor whose task is to rescue fair damsels, the author reminds the reader of the code of chivalry in the South, which enjoins men to be like knights and encourages girls to look for gallant protectors. Alabama's love for David is an extension of her self-love: "So much she loved the man. . . . That he became distorted in her vision, like pressing her nose upon a mirror and gazing into her own eyes."[25] Lacking a sense of self-esteem based on attributes other than her beauty and charm, Alabama fantasizes in one surrealistic passage that she crawls into "the friendly cave of his ear," losing her identity altogether by becoming part of her lover's brain. Such images betray Alabama's anxious need for the continual presence of another as a reinforcer of her self-image or as an opportunity to lose herself entirely. Her desire to lose her identity to David, to regard herself as weak and helpless without him, is the first sign of her using masochism as a new way to attract the attention of men.[26] David contributes to this trend by wishing that she were his "princess" whom he could "keep . . . shut forever in an ivory tower."[27] This echo of the Rapunzel fairy tale reveals a typical female fantasy about the pleasures of slavery, of being will-less, of belonging to a man. To be possessed as an object, not a person, becomes Alabama's goal. Karen Horney points out that the child who is treated as a "princess" develops "the feeling that she is loved for imaginary qualities rather than for her true self. . . . Her own will, her own wishes, her own feelings, her own grievances become paralyzed."[28] Thus, Alabama's early relationship with David harms her self-esteem.

Alabama's subsequent worsening mental state is inevitable. Already a person for whom appearance is of paramount concern, she becomes a celebrity in a world that worships appearances. The flapper's propensity for outrageous antics at first suits Alabama's sharp sense of humor and fulfills her desire for attention. Her frivolous life in the public eye leaves her with a terrible longing for something more meaningful to "do" in life. At first, David willingly keeps her entertained, but as his work requires more and more time, he tells her "she couldn't always be a child and have things provided for her" (p. 80). Alabama misses David's exclusive attention and tries to obtain from motherhood and friendship the satisfaction her relationship with David had temporarily afforded; but her world has always centered either on her father or David. She begins to blame David for her boredom and failures and simultaneously begins to be envious of more attractive women. She seeks some fulfilling activity but lacks the inner resources to discover her own talents.

A narcissist needing attention, a person without a sense of worth, she settles on an impossible goal to provide her life with meaning: she chooses to become a ballet dancer in her late twenties, too late to achieve such a goal. She relentlessly exercises until she is covered with bruises, as if she were punishing herself for being worthless. She believes that if she achieves her goal, she will "drive the devils that had driven her—that, in proving herself, she would achieve that peace which she imagined went only in surety of one's self—that she would be able, through the medium of the dance, to command her emotions, to summon love or pity or happiness at will, having provided a channel through which they might flow" (p. 124). Her narcissism betrays her, for the "constant whip of her work" can never make her younger or provide her with self-esteem. When she becomes ill from blood poisoning, ironically caused by the glue in a ballet slipper, she is once again entirely dependent on David.

Alabama's physical illness metaphorically suggests her mental illness, and perhaps, the dawning mental illness of the author. She chooses an unrealistic and self-defeating goal because her anxiety about her own worthlessness can be deadened only by obsessive pursuit of work as a narcotic. Her masochistic injuries to her body achieve her original purpose as a narcissist: to receive the attention of others. She selects this goal, uses her physical weakness to receive attention from David, and places responsibility for her life on him— all of which characterize the masochist, who, like the narcissist, exists as a self only in relation to others.[29]

4

Frances Newman: Experimentation as Convention

Growing up at a time when she could hear eyewitness stories of the Old South and was herself a witness to the birth of the Jazz Age, Frances Newman (1888–1928) was not only one of the most brilliant, eccentric, and important literary innovators of the Southern Renaissance, she was also the first to identify it. Her essay in the *New York Herald-Tribune* of August 16, 1925, "The State of Literature in the Late Confederacy," maintained that James Branch Cabell's *Jurgen* (1919) and H. L. Mencken's slam at southern literature, "The Sahara of the Bozart," were spurs to a new surge of literary activity in the South. She asserted that 1917 was the beginning of "modern" literature because of the work of Cabell, Sherwood Anderson, and Willa Cather. Considering this sort of insight, together with her tight, perceptive book reviews, her two startling novels *The Hard-Boiled Virgin* (1926) and *Dead Lovers Are Faithful Lovers* (1928), her study *The Short Story's Mutations from Petronius to Paul Morand* (1924), her translation of *Six Moral Tales* by Jules Laforgue (1928), and her prize-winning short story "Rachel and Her Children," not to mention her highly original life-style as recorded in her *Letters* (1929, ed. Hansell Baugh), one wonders, why have few people heard of Frances Newman?

Although she had all the credentials of a southern belle, Newman chose a life of movement, achievement, and eccentricity. The daughter of an Atlanta judge, Newman at age ten wrote a novel but abandoned it when her elder sister and a suitor laughed at the manuscript. Her education at Agnes Scott College and the Sorbonne and employment as a librarian in Florida and at the Carnegie Library in Atlanta occupied her early life. When her library notes for the *Atlanta Sunday Constitution* attracted the attention of Cabell and Mencken, a rich and productive period in Newman's life commenced during which she was appreciated and even revered critically and personally.

Her network of literary friends was enormous. Emily Clark, editor of the Richmond-based little magazine *The Reviewer*, thought Newman among the most vital, energetic women of her time; Clark recalled in *Innocence Abroad* (1931) that Newman, dressed all in purple, the only color she wore, was as startling and controversial in person as her books. Through Clark, Mencken, and Cabell, Newman met Edmund Wilson, Sherwood Anderson, Thornton Wilder, and Henry Seidel Canby, for whom she wrote the lead article, "A Literary Declaration of Independence," in the first issue of *The Saturday Review of Literature* (1925). At first Newman was quite dazzled by the glitterati, but she became more discriminating; soon Mencken was commenting that she had succeeded in her book reviews in offending most living writers, including F. Scott Fitzgerald, at one time or another.

After her mother's death in 1922, Newman lived with her nephew, whom she adored, and her mammy, Susan Long, who had attended her birth. This entourage traveled with Newman whenever she could afford it, but, she wrote to Emily Clark, money was a constant problem and coming to New York to see friends, publishers, and later doctors was a strain because she had no job there. Not a declared feminist, Newman lived a life of freedom with responsibility, a rare combination for women in the 1920s. She had at least three lovers, all of them younger than herself; she was uninterested in marrying, but she supported a household, and she pursued her work with utter seriousness and passion.

Her work is brilliant, witty, satiric, abrasive, and wise. Content and form challenge and enrich the reader. Her novels have intricate syntax (called "vague" by Mencken), are full of exotic allusions, and often contain no dialogue whatsoever—critically unacceptable to many of her contemporaries. Donald Davidson said her style "exploited all the worst faults of freshman themes."[1] Her content was even more shocking. Sex is her subject, the sexuality of the heroine and how society's taboos repress and warp this most natural of urges. But Davidson called her fiction "mere autobiographical documents, slightly disguised but barely concealing the vitriolic social criticism which animates them."[2] He compared her work to the "ugly whisperings of a repressed and naughty child," and Newman herself to the "defeated European" Joyce and the "jabbering expatriate" Gertrude Stein.[3]

Rebecca West recognized Newman's stylistic repetitions as a technique of driving home the "discomforts and humiliations" of women trapped in a sheltered society.[4] But she ultimately dismissed *The*

Hard-Boiled Virgin as "too simple" and as possessing "that dreadful tabloid quality."[5]

In fact, her frank treatment of menstruation, of sexual desire, of fear of pregnancy is not prurient, as West and Davidson contended, but is representative of female experience. *The Hard-Boiled Virgin* is her semiautobiographical *bildungsroman* of a southern belle's initiation into sexuality and a literary career. *Dead Lovers Are Faithful Lovers* (1928) counterpoints the views of a man's wife and his mistress, and particularly illuminates the psychological realities of adultery: the insensitivity of the egocentric husband, the inadequacy of the vain but cool wife, the anguish and depression of the other woman (a librarian, like Newman). These novels condemn society for extolling only innocence, sublimation, and intellectual stupidity in women. Intelligent, curious women could not contend with this ethic. Thus Newman's themes challenged the basic assumptions of her milieu, and her stylistic innovations paralleled the work of Virginia Woolf and James Joyce.

Why, then, has she been forgotten until fairly recently? Her critical reputation suffered when she died from an overdose of Veronal™ at age forty, an event that apparently aroused not pity in her friends but embarrassment. Her mentor Cabell and her literary friends quickly disavowed her. Cabell took her act as a personal affront to his sponsorship (as he reports in a letter to Mencken). In fact, the suicide probably resulted from Newman's continuing ill health. For years she had struggled with an eye condition that had led to almost total blindness and had caused a constant painful pressure behind her eyes (possibly the result of high blood pressure); she had also suffered repeated bouts of pneumonia.

Recent critics have treated Newman more kindly. A new edition of *Dead Lovers* (Arno Press, 1977) has an insightful introduction by Elizabeth Hardwick. Anne Firor Scott's *The Southern Lady* (1970) comments appreciatively on Newman's work, and Scott's introduction to a new edition of *The Hard-Boiled Virgin* (University of Georgia Press, 1980) compares the novel to the works of Virginia Woolf. Anne Goodwyn Jones's *Tomorrow is Another Day* (1981) devotes a solid chapter to the relationship between Newman's life and her art. Newman's work reveals a first-rate wit, bold assessments of the place of women in the South and shrewd probings into feminine psychology, and a willingness to violate taboos against a list of topics rarely mentioned previously in American literature: puberty, pubic hair, birth control, venereal disease, abortion, and, not least by any means, the use of the word *virgin*.

The Hard-Boiled Virgin (1926) enjoyed the distinction of being one of the first novels banned in Boston. It is a fine example of the *bildungsroman*, a genre typical of the 1920s. Its main character, Katharine Faraday, is a belle from Atlanta whose natural instincts are almost entirely suppressed in her childhood by society's prescribed code for appropriate behavior. According to this code, proof of aristocratic breeding is innocence, so Katharine is sheltered from knowledge of her own body, and is completely shocked by her first menstrual period. As a girl Katharine is full of unorthodox desires—she wants to write great novels, she wants to learn about her body. But from her mother she learns that her goal must be to arouse "ardent but honorable" passions in a man so that she can capture the prize of a belle's career, a husband. Marriage is the only method society endorses by which a woman can obtain security and satisfaction.[6]

Katharine learns the coquetry and charm appropriate to a belle, and, as men respond favorably, a narcissistic need for flattery begins to override her desire to become a writer. Mysteriously, however, she finds she is growing older and is still unmarried. A pattern has developed in her relationships: as soon as her current beau takes her hand and kisses her, she finds that his touch disturbs and repulses her and she loses all desire to marry him and breaks off the relationship. She begins to understand that her culture's emphasis on the purity of a belle at marriage has created in her an anxiety about the sex act. She recalls: "in Georgia no lady was supposed to know she was a virgin until she had ceased to be one."[7]

Realizing that she has no future as a writer in the South, Katharine takes her partially written play to New York and joins the literary circle. She falls in love, now with a novelist, now a playwright, but is still unable to marry or have sexual relations. She prefers famous men, for she fears that she will never herself be important, and that only a famous husband could substitute for her deficiencies. She also prefers married men, who are unavailable and less threatening to her. Her desires for such men may result from the fact that her father and brother died early in her life, so that—having also had a sheltered upbringing—she was essentially unfamiliar with men as a girl.[8]

Katharine's dilemma increasingly disturbs her. She wishes to fulfill society's dictate that her chief goal be marriage, yet she finds, paradoxically, that society's emphasis on female virginity prevents her from being able to yield her virginity, even to a loved partner. She begins to compose imaginary letters and to write letters she never sends to her lovers, actions that suggest a repressed need to communicate with men. She begins to have dreams "which she thought were giving her insight into a nature very unlike the nature a Southern lady should have had" (p. 247). Her lovers are challenged by her virginity; one of them tells her she can never write a good play as long as she is a virgin and offers to relieve her of this "impediment." Yet she feels the "weight of her virtue . . . she began to fear that she was really a Southern lady and that she would never be swept off her feet" (p. 253).

When she decides to have sex, the sex act seems to her "much more remote than a kiss," and her lover is unable to melt "the hard little core of consciousness she had instead of a soul" (p. 273). It is too late for her to experience pleasure, passion, even warmth. Like the hard-boiled egg to which the title of the novel refers, she has toughened and is no longer capable of growth or change. Paradoxically, in her professional life Katharine feels a new freedom; perhaps sublimating her sexual urges, she is able to complete her play. When it is produced, she finds she is bored by celebrities, for she has herself achieved fame and no longer needs to cling to the famous. By the end of the novel Katharine has rejected marriage as her goal, a rejection of the ultimate goal of the belle, for she has achieved her earlier dream of becoming a writer. That a career may be consistent with marriage, however, is not an alternative Newman considers, either in this novel or in her own life.

In *Dead Lovers Are Faithful Lovers* (1928), Newman even more pointedly criticizes society for the narrowness of the roles it offers women. The patriarchal society she describes fosters neurotic helplessness and submissiveness in women, and their sexuality is not allowed expression even in marriage. Men like Charlton Cunningham, the protagonist, are permitted a wife and a mistress, neither of whom enjoys the sex act. Charlton's wife and mistress both regard themselves as entirely dependent on men; Evelyn Cunningham is economically and emotionally dependent first on her father, then on Charlton, and Isabel Ramsey, the mistress, needs Charlton to fulfill society's dictum that she must be associated with a man. While Isabel is not restricted to the home as her sphere (like Newman, she is a librarian in Atlanta), she nevertheless longs for it. She considers her career a feeble substitute for marriage, which she believes offers the principal opportunity for happiness.

Evelyn's marriage is cold and barren, but because she has a gift for self-deception, Evelyn believes it to be the best of all possible marriages. She is "the last of the Virginia Belles," as her father says, whose only goal in life is to love and serve a man. She marries Charlton to fulfill her dream, but the reader soon observes portents of an unhappy marriage. On her honeymoon, Evelyn arises early as Charlton sleeps to redo her hair and remake her face so that her husband can awaken to a "perfect" woman. Her desire never to appear mussed suggests that she may not desire the sexual activity that causes the mussiness. Evelyn remains a "perfect" wife, her perfection based on her beauty; however, because she never bears a child, the reader suspects that she and her husband do not have sexual relations. Thus, Newman implies, Evelyn's lack of passion drives her husband into the arms of an imperfect but more affectionate woman. Evelyn cannot understand why "love should be the emotion which leads to such strange results as babies."[9] She is thus depicted as a perfect product of southern culture, which had long enjoined upper-class women to be unconcerned with fleshly matters; inadvertently, this attitude encourages her husband's infidelity. Her life is spent choosing pretty gowns to suit her vanity and to please her husband; she never suspects that she is forcing him away from her.

Isabel Ramsey's condition as the mistress of Charlton is no more to be preferred than Evelyn's role as his wife. As a librarian with a dull, cloistered existence, Isabel feels alive only in Charlton's presence. Newman's portrait of Isabel is a superlative depiction of obsessive love. When he is absent, she feels incomplete. Her life revolves around him as surely as does Evelyn's life. When Charlton becomes ill while visiting her, Isabel must endure the torment of having to conceal their relationship. When he dies, she must sneak into the funeral.

Ironically, Charlton's death does not free Evelyn or Isabel. They remain trapped in their preoccupations. Isabel returns to her career even more dissatisfied with her life, and Evelyn returns to her self-concern and delusions as she prepares to memorialize her "perfect" marriage. Evelyn salvages the illusion of serenity from Charlton's death; as she gazes in her mirror, she looks forward to a life in which she will cherish Charlton's memory. She feels she is at last at peace since she can now walk upon a "green oasis of a memory over which she was dropping the victorious curtain of her very long black crepe veil" (p. 295).

As an example of a twenties writer who is virtually unknown,

Newman is a good candidate for critical reassessment. Her work was largely unappreciated in her time because of critical assumptions that (1) valued—in the extreme—rationalism, logic, analysis, and classification, (2) celebrated the male experience, (3) denigrated the female experience, even the female body, as subordinate, secondary, and inferior, and (4) thereby gave little credence to values such as those revealed by intuition and emotion. Thus ideas about both woman's self and woman's other have been at the heart of the problems women face, a dualism described eloquently by Adrienne Rich in *Of Woman Born*. The origin of this dualism is encapsulated in Descartes' dictum, *cogito, ergo sum*, which implies that only the processes of "mind" and "thought" can make one human. Feeling, intuition, even the body itself are "not-being," unhuman, subordinate, "other." It follows that woman—so controlled, it would seem, by her body (its menses, gestation, lactation)—is the incarnation of otherness, of the subhuman that must be avoided (or even annihilated).

A holistic critical approach, one which rejects dualism, with which we can "think through the body,"[10] to use Rich's phrase, allows the virtues of Newman's work to shine. When evaluating Newman's work, we might ask:

(1) Does it offer a holistic point of view? Does it value intuitive, spiritual, psychological reality as much as the rational and analytic? Donaldson and other critics took *Dead Lovers* to task because it is not "logically" developed; but the book discusses the psychological reality of adultery—the insensitivity of the egocentric husband, the inadequacy of the vain but cool wife, the torment of waiting experienced by the other woman—all irrational states that often do not develop logically.

(2) Does the work present the realities of the body as being equal to or even part of those of the mind? The realities of the body are not separate from those of the mind—a modern medical fact that is consistently expressed in Newman's works, written in the twenties. Katharine Faraday is innocent of sexuality, of culture, of the intellectual life, and her initiation into these aspects of reality is not prurient but rather is the logical result of the sheltering of women in southern society.

(3) What is the nature of women characters' encounters with the values denigrated by patriarchal society? Newman's work deals entirely with the effect of such an environment on individual personality. This theme was not valued by critics like Donald Davidson; a

member of the Fugitive and Agrarian groups, he would be expected
to praise the order and stability of the male hierarchy endorsed by
this milieu, rather than censure it. When Newman's characters try to
explore their sexual desires, they are condemned for doing so, for female sexual desire is devalued in this society.

(4) How do women authors define their milieu and the position of
women in it (do they differ from male authors in their definition)? For
Newman, society extols innocence, sublimation, and intellectual va-
cuity in women; Katharine Faraday, for example, is too intelligent and
too curious to be content with this ethic. Newman defines her milieu
quite differently than do Davidson, Allen Tate, and even Caroline
Gordon, for Newman sees southern society as ideal only for white
males, an observation in which she is joined by William Faulkner and
Ellen Glasgow.

Thus Newman's themes challenge several of the assumptions of
her milieu. If we use traditional literary criticism to further our evaluation, we can appreciate her stylistic innovativeness and clarity,
qualities she has in common with Joyce, Virginia Woolf, and Cabell
in *Jurgen*. Moreover, Newman understands the genre of the *bildungsroman* as the genre of choice for presenting a belle, but she extends its
narrative boundaries by using the stream-of-consciousness technique. Like Ellen Glasgow, she is a satirist of her culture, with the
addition of an acerbic, crackling sense of humor. Her influence on
future writers and readers will doubtless increase since her works are
available again.

Newman and all the authors of the twenties mentioned in this
chapter portray the destruction of the belle by emphasizing at least
one of the following: her ignorance of sex, her repression of her natural desires, her inability to assert her right to be happy, her self-
concern, or her self-sacrificing attitude. They contend that her beauty
and coquetry, so admired in the Old South, can lead to a narcissism
so strong that she can love no one except herself. Her inhibitions,
learned from a society that teaches that inhibitions are proper for a
"good" woman, may prevent her from being able to marry or may
cause sexual frigidity. The self-sacrifice expected from a belle after
she marries can grow into masochism. All the portraits of the belle in
this decade harshly indict several aspects of southern tradition. The
belle is branded as "diseased" by the very traits that are supposed to
allow her to flourish.

5

Historical Novels of the Depression

The image of the southern belle of the 1920s as destroyer and destroyed persists in novels set in the 1930s, such as Ward Greene's *Death in the Deep South*, Hamilton Basso's *Cinnamon Seed*, and John Peale Bishop's *Act of Darkness*. These novels criticize southern life, especially restrictive codes of behavior for both men and women, fear of outsiders, and hatred of blacks. And in these novels (discussed in chapters 11 and 12) the experiences of the belle figure clearly represent those of the South itself.

But a great many other novels of the 1930s reaffirmed the life of order, quality, and harmony associated with the antebellum South. Reacting both to harsh appraisals of southern traditions by the demythologizers of the 1920s and to the sterile materialism of the modern "wasteland" of the Depression, the Agrarians wrote historical novels that are thematically similar, such as Caroline Gordon's *Penhally*, Stark Young's *So Red the Rose*, William Faulkner's *The Unvanquished*, and Margaret Mitchell's *Gone with the Wind*.[1] In these novels, set during the antebellum period, the Civil War, and Reconstruction, the southern belle to some extent recovers the traditional attributes of purity and beauty that she had lost in the novels of the twenties. There is no return to the days of Thomas Nelson Page, however; motifs of violence, disorder, insanity, sexuality, and miscegenation, all of which frequently culminate in the rape of the belle, dominate both sets of novels. The belle herself is presented as the repository of southern values; the rapist is typically an outsider who represents the antithesis of these values. The rape of these belles is a symbolic action that represents the violent disordering of a harmonious society. Authors use this metaphor because it is suitable for the situation of the South both during Reconstruction and during the moral and economic upheavals of the post–World War I period. A discussion of the rape motif appears in part 3 of this book.

In reaction both to fiction criticizing the South and to the dehumanizing influences of "progress" and materialism, twelve writers
of the Southern Renaissance who came to be known as the Agrarians
contributed essays to the collection *I'll Take My Stand* (1930). Looking back to the antebellum South as the model for a life based upon
harmony and stability, they wrote in the introductory essay: "genu-
ine humanism, was rooted in the agrarian life of the old South . . . it
was deeply founded in the way of life itself—in its tables, chairs, portraits, festivals, laws, marriage customs."[2] They believed that the industrial way of life, associated both with the North and with the
twentieth century, only repressed creativity and resulted in "increasing disadjustment and instability" (p. xxviii). Lewis A. Lawson summarizes their ideas by identifying "two opposing clusters of images.
One cluster pictures a chaotic, frenzied acquisitive life fruitlessly performed by impotent automatons. The opposing cluster contains a
conception of rural or semi-rural life enriched by tradition, religion,
stable and predictable social behavior, and feelings of individual
worth."[3]

As might be expected, the genre of choice for the Agrarians was
the historical novel, usually set in the antebellum South. Their novels
are not as blithely complimentary of southern life, however, as the
essays in *I'll Take My Stand*; the one exception is *So Red the Rose*. In
their fiction, most Agrarians acknowledge the violence and exploitation existing side by side with genteel refinement in the South; their
apparent purpose is to show that the southern ethos disintegrated because of the inadequacy of southern ideals, the failure of individuals
to pursue their ideals, and the inability of southerners to resist con-
tamination by materialists who do not believe in the southern code of
behavior.

Caroline Gordon's *Penhally* (1931) resembles the plantation novels
of the nineteenth century, in particular in its presentation of Alice
Blair, a blonde, gray-eyed belle. But there are some significant differences. For example, Alice flirts with many gentlemen even though
she is engaged. And she is courageous and vivacious; when she and
John Llewellan are swept away by a river, she controls her frightened
horse, swims the stream, and laughs at the danger rather than suc-
cumbing to it. Like Betty in Glasgow's *The Battle-Ground*, she is figur-
atively being "swept away" by her budding passion for John; later she
presses against him and says, "You know I love you." Thus she lacks

the belle's traditional repression; and John, solid southern gentleman that he is, is too intimidated by a woman of passion to pursue her.

After the Civil War, John once again has the opportunity to marry her, but Alice has been painfully disappointed by his seeming rejection of her love. When she sees him again, she feels alienated and frightened because "she had been living so long on the edge of nothing . . . she had never really endured any suffering, except in anticipation."[4] The deprivation caused by the war is less painful to her than the denial of warmth from the man she loves. Eventually she marries a merchant and leaves the plantation to grow old in a loveless marriage. Her tragedy is thus not of her own making but has been brought about by the effects of repression on southern men who are unable to respond openly to affectionate women of their class.

A far more benign treatment of the Old South is found in the work of Stark Young, who writes in *I'll Take My Stand* of the important attributes of the Old South that had been lost: "Your family lived in a big house, not without elegance, hospitality, and affection; and what made your position was not power necessarily or any eminence in the country's history, but rather your settled connection with the land; it was the fact that your family had nurtured a certain quality of living and manner throughout a certain period of time."[5]

In his popular novel *So Red the Rose*, third on the 1934 best-seller list,[6] the antebellum society of Natchez, Mississippi, embodies this ideal. John M. Bradbury asserts that this novel "reestablished in critical grace the Civil War genre which had for so long been bogged in . . . crinolines and . . . magnolias and darky banjos."[7] In fact, however, Young's belle, Julia Valette Somerville, is conventionally crinolined; she is pale, beautiful, constantly compared with a rose, and coquettish as a "butterfly." Although as chaste "as Diana," she flirts coyly with her many beaux. Young sentimentalizes the master-slave relationship as well, relating that "Valette had a way of ordering the servants like a young tyrant, and the Negroes at Portobello adored her" for it.[8] Strolling in the moonlit garden of her plantation home, Valette wishes that she were a frozen statue like the Greek imitations in the garden: "if I too were a marble goddess, I could go on forever" (p. 65). She wants to be the quintessential work of art of southern society, a static object rather than a person. This metaphor anticipates the work of Gilbert and Gubar, who write in *The Madwoman in the Attic* that historically women have been enjoined to fashion themselves as objects of art: beautiful, malleable, and still. One of Julia's suitors associates her statuelike perfection with the grace and beauty of the South itself: "He wanted his country to be perfect just as one thinks of a beloved girl as perfect . . . the Southern cause passed through his mind like a face that was still vague but would be beautiful yet, and a voice whose sweetness he felt but had not heard" (p. 85). The novel might as well have been written in the postbellum period, so reminiscent is it of Thomas Nelson Page's hyperbole about the perfection of the belle as symbolic of the South.

Young directly associates the southern belle with the South. When Duncan, the hero, returns from the war, he thinks "how wonderful and beautiful and open-hearted and good" Valette is, for "in his mind he was identifying her with his country . . . and with the resolution and spirit he felt in him for taking up this new life ahead in the South" (p. 294). Thus, the romantic fantasies of men make Valette into an allegorical figure; in this allegory her selfishness and repression become positive attributes. Young seems to be entirely unaware that he is presenting an unfavorable portrait of Valette. She is a sexless goddess whom he sincerely represents as the respository of all the South's best attributes; he does not perceive her shallow personality, narcissism, and repression.

Moreover, Valette has nothing to do in the novel; along with the other characters, she is given no actions to perform that relate to the plot. Historical figures such as Lee and Sherman are carted into the story for brief history lessons, but neither Valette nor even Duncan are affected directly by their visits to the plantation. Even the battles occur offstage; the reader hears reports from returning messengers. Thus, Young's portrait of the belle results in part from his falling into all the worst traps of the historical novelist, although it is most consistent with his ideas about the antebellum South as expressed in his essay in *I'll Take My Stand*.

William Faulkner handled the historical-novel genre well and was writing very much as an Agrarian by the end of the 1930s. In *The Unvanquished* (1938), Faulkner takes on the stereotype of the pure, fragile belle, but in a Civil War setting in which she is very much an actor. He uses the war not as a glorious cause led by heroic Lees and Shermans but a time when chaos destroyed traditional mores and released new sources of strength. In this novel women and blacks reach their fullest potential only during the war; after it, they must again conform to social expectations. Ringo, a black child, can use his considerable intelligence to participate in a wide range of experiences during the war, but afterward he must return to his role as subordinate. Rosa Millard and Drusilla Hawks both exhibit personality traits entirely opposed to the prescriptions of genteel behavior for southern ladies and belles.

Rosa must defend her grandson and the whole plantation while the men are away at war. When she thinks her grandson and Ringo may have killed a Yankee, she shields them by lying to a Yankee officer. A strong southern woman who transcends the stereotype of the southern lady who ran the plantation during the war, Rosa forges orders, lies, and steals, but also retains her sense of moral order and confesses to God that she has sinned: "I did not sin for gain nor for greed . . . I sinned for justice . . . I sinned for the sake of food and clothes for Your own creatures who could not help themselves," for those who had lost fathers, husbands, and sons to a "holy cause, even though You have seen fit to make it a lost cause."[9] Rosa is ironically defeated not by the war but by her own belief that bargaining for horses with "Southern men . . . would not be a risk . . . because Southern men would not harm a woman" (p. 171). Her belief that the chivalric code will protect her proves to be her downfall; a gang leader who is rumored to have served in the Confederate army kills her.

Drusilla Hawks is a spirited young belle who thrives in the atmosphere of the social upheaval caused by the war. If Rosa is reluctantly "unladylike" when she lies and steals, Drusilla exults because she is freed from the restrictive set of expectations for a southern girl. As she explains:

> Living used to be dull. . . . Stupid. You live in the same house your father was born in, and your father's sons and daughters had the sons and daughters of the same Negro slaves to nurse and coddle you, and then you grew up and you fell in love with your acceptable young man, and in time you would marry him in your mother's wedding gown perhaps and with the same silver for presents she had received; and then you settled down forever more while you got children to feed . . . until they grew up too; and then you and your husband died quietly and were buried together maybe on a summer afternoon just before suppertime. [pp. 114–15]

To Drusilla, life now is "fine," because the house is burned, the silver stolen, the Negroes gone, the young men she might have had to marry killed. She is free to rule her own life rather than be governed by her society; she chooses to wear pants, to carry a gun, and to ride next to men in Colonel John Sartoris's regiment, like a southern Joan of Arc. Her hands lose their "ladylike" softness, and she crops her hair to ride against the Yankees.

Like Joan of Arc, Drusilla remains chaste and pure throughout her campaigns, but when the war is over, she must reenter southern society, which will not tolerate her behavior. The "decent" women of the town believe that she must have indulged in sexual relations with the colonel, for any unchaperoned young girl in the midst of rough military men surely could not herself guard her honor, which, as Wyatt-Brown points out in *Southern Honor*, for a woman meant her virginity. Drusilla is appalled by their false accusations but finds that while she could easily contend with Yankees, she cannot disagree with her community if she wishes to remain in it. She wants to prove to them that she has retained her honor; her self-esteem demands it. She puts on a dress, washes her dirty hands, and marries John Sartoris. As John says to her, "They have beat you Drusilla" (p. 234).

In the last chapter of the novel, "The Odor of Verbena," the reader meets Drusilla eight years later. Her marriage is childless, a fact that suggests either John's impotence or a lack of love and sexual desire in the marriage, for the reader learns that Drusilla still is not a repressed southern lady. She wears a sprig of pungent verbena in her hair, because, as she tells Bayard (John's son by another marriage, now a man of twenty-three), "it is the only scent that is stronger than the smell of horses and courage" (p. 253). When Drusilla urges Bayard to avenge John's murder, she offers him two dueling pistols as "slender and invincible and fatal as the physical shape of love" (p. 273) and kisses him passionately. Although the scene suggests that Drusilla has become a priestess of violence, in fact she has become a devotee of the cult of honor in which women urged their men to redress grievances themselves rather than by law.[10] In spite of her youthful rebellion against social codes, her offering the pistols to Bayard is quite conventional. Women were never expected to exhibit physical aggression; their role was to remind southern men of their responsibilities to their clan and its "good name." What is unconventional in this scene is her passionate association of violence and sex. She can be united to Bayard by an act of violence. Her marriage to an impotent man has transformed her courage into reckless aggression. Passionate both in her love of Bayard and in her adherence to the code of honor, Drusilla is an unconventional belle whose society eventually inhibits both her strength and her passion so that it emerges in bizarre exaggeration. Only in a violent setting can she be a vital woman.

The most compelling of all the novels of the 1930s in its depiction of the southern belle is Margaret Mitchell's *Gone with the Wind*. The number one best-seller in 1936 and in 1937, the novel sold one million copies in its first six months and has never been out of print since.[11] The novel continues to exert a tremendous influence on women for whom reading it remains a formative passage in adolescence. A deft and accurate historical novel, *Gone with the Wind* has characters who are full of energy and whose actions create the plot of the novel. Convention and irreverence stand in dynamic tension— the historical novel and *bildungsroman* blend as we witness the growth and education of an antebellum belle whose upbringing goes awry because of the events of her time. But the novel is also "about" the 1930s; the wasteland of Tara, Scarlett's blistered hands working in the red clay, and the slow economic recovery represented by the lumberyard tell us much about the workings of capitalism in the Depression South.

The main character, Scarlett O'Hara, is both conventional and unique. In her famous first-line description ("Scarlett O'Hara was not beautiful, but men seldom realized it when caught by her charm"[12]) Mitchell captures the essentials of the belle's attractiveness; since Bel Tracy in *Swallow Barn* (1832), the belle has not always been a great beauty, but rather seems to be considered one because of her charm. The imperfect beauty of the belle reflects authors' acknowledgment of female readers who certainly are not all beauties and can better identify with a heroine who is more like themselves. Such a description reassures the reader that being alluring, finding a husband, and establishing a happy life are possible even for those who are not born beautiful. Scarlett's "magnolia-white skin" is conventional enough, but her inner vivacity and passion are betrayed by her "turbulent, willful" green eyes, "distinctly at variance with her decorous demeanor" (p. 3). Of all the belles I have studied, she is the only one with green eyes. By assigning Scarlett this eye color, Mitchell both acknowledges and overturns this small detail of the belle stereotype. It is a technique Mitchell uses masterfully throughout the novel; with it, she compliments her audience's knowledge of and affection for the stereotype, but uses it for her own purposes.

Like other novelists of the Southern Renaissance, Mitchell indicts the code of correct female behavior. Scarlett is essentially incapable of conforming to the ethic of self-sacrifice and demureness that southern society demands of its young women. She is not only a narcissist who "could never long endure any conversation of which she was not the chief subject" (p. 5) but also has a self-centered, willful personality that demands the attention of others. Surrounded by beaux, she makes her suitors beg for her as a dancing partner; she dangles them merrily in order to extract from them every ounce of attentiveness. Mitchell carefully shows that, as a narcissist, Scarlett cannot return love and caring except in her fantasies. Her attraction to Ashley Wilkes is not so much love as it is an instinct, inexplicable and compelling: "She had wanted him . . . as simply and unreasonably as she wanted food to eat, horses to ride and a soft bed to sleep in" (p. 25). Her narcissism denies introspection, and she cannot understand Ashley's complex ennui. Pampered by her indulgent and boisterous father, whom she resembles, Scarlett longs to be like her repressed, martyrlike mother, whom she compares to the Virgin Mary. Scarlett is torn between her impulsive, passionate nature and her desire to conform to the role of submissive woman. The former usually predominates, although she is able to convince herself in her fantasies that she will someday be the genteel lady whom Ashley will love.

To her, Ashley represents a spiritual man, unconcerned with the physical passion that she fears in herself. Scarlett believes she loves Ashley beyond passion, with a "sacred" love. Several incidents should convince her that Ashley is both weak and strong, spiritual and passionate, but she persists in rejecting all the evidence. She is surprised when she learns Melanie is pregnant, a fact that confirms Ashley's "baser" nature. She is shocked when Ashley kisses her passionately. Yet she responds, "There's no reason why things won't come out the way I want them—if he loves me. And I know he does!" (p. 73). Rationalization and fantasy are Scarlett's ways of avoiding the unpleasant reality that she cannot win the spiritual love of this man.

Scarlett is so attractive a character precisely because part of her does try to rebel against the restraints of a code of behavior that relentlessly attempts to mold her into a form to which she is not naturally suited. She complains, "I'm tired of everlastingly being unnatural and never doing anything I want to do. I'm tired of acting like

I don't eat more than a bird, and walking when I want to run and saying I feel faint after a walk, when I could dance for two days and never get tired. I'm tired of saying, 'How wonderful you are!' to fool men who haven't got one-half the sense I've got" (p. 79).

Scarlett is attracted to Rhett Butler's rebelliousness and sexual appeal, but their relationship is always thwarted by the part of her that wishes to be a "lady"; thus Scarlett fears Rhett's intensity and passion, which ironically are so like her own. Interestingly, Rhett's muscular body with his "animal-like teeth," swarthy skin, and black hair remind one of the men forbidden to her in her society, the blacks, who are assumed to be "darkly" passionate. Scarlett's initial indignant reaction to Rhett results from the fact that he inadvertently sees her without her mask of demure coquetry; Scarlett realizes then that she can never control him with her charm as she does the other men in her sphere. She wishes to bring Rhett under the spell of the illusions she creates, but Rhett (unlike most southern gentlemen, Mitchell implies) is singularly unimpressed by illusions. With his statement to the indignant southern gentlemen that the North has the money and the South has only "cotton and slaves and arrogance. They'd lick us in a month" (p. 111), Rhett rejects their illusions about the South as surely as he rejects Scarlett's illusions about herself.

The section of the novel set in Atlanta resembles in its characters and theme John W. De Forest's *The Bloody Chasm* (1881), in which Virginia Beaufort lives with her aunt (a predecessor of Aunt Pittypat) and a silly servant (surely Prissy's ancestor). The theme of a southern belle's being "bought" permeates De Forest's novel and is crucial in this one also. Scarlett's reunion with Rhett occasions several acts of rebellion against southern codes. In her widow's weeds she dances with Rhett, who has purchased the dance at a charity ball for the scandalous sum of $150. She despises the seclusion and bleak clothes of mourning and is delighted to be enjoying the attentions that a belle craves. The sale of her favors is Scarlett's first act of discarding the pretense of being a lady. She then accepts a bonnet from Rhett, "a gift no lady can accept and still remain a lady" (p. 246). Eventually Scarlett begins to run a business and finally marries Rhett, which means that she then has the money to restore Tara. Like Virginia Beaufort of *The Bloody Chasm*, she sells the right to her body for money.

Unlike Virginia, she never learns to care for the man who really loves her until it is too late. Rhett's kisses send "something vital, electric," through her body, but she is afraid of this feeling, suppresses it, and remains frigid after her marriage to Rhett. Scarlett imitates her mother's purity, a victim of what Karen Horney has called "the cult of saintliness in women"; she conforms to "the conviction that the decent, respectable woman is asexual."[13] Her coldness drives Rhett to another belle, Belle Watling, the town madam. Mitchell clearly implies that the repression endorsed by southern society leads to an overt fear of sexuality.

In the ambiguous climactic scene of the novel, Rhett carries a screaming Scarlett to their bedroom, where she is raped by her own husband. This event is significant for several reasons. First, Scarlett experiences an orgasm for the first time: "she had a wild thrill such as she had never known; joy, fear, madness, excitement, surrender" (p. 940). She tries to hate Rhett, but while "He had humbled her, hurt her, used her brutally through a wild night, . . . she loved it" (p. 940). Her masochistic surrender in the scene suggests that women secretly desire to be taken by force. Second, when Scarlett awakens the next morning, she feels refreshed, happy, and very much in love with Rhett. The violence of this sex act was essential for Scarlett, because only when coerced can she stifle the feelings of guilt and revulsion she usually associates with the sex act. She realizes that a "real lady" would be ashamed, but Scarlett is thrilled that for the first time in her life she has felt the rapture of passion. Third, Scarlett has been raped within the bounds of marriage: it is a rape but it is not. Rhett, her attacker, is a devoted husband and father, but he is also a controversial figure in the community, a dark, mysterious, passionate man who has taken an unwilling woman. The tensions of this paradox at once titillate the reader with the black male/white female pattern of rape that has been standard in novels about the belle (discussed in part 3) and yet reassure the reader that this sex act is entirely sanctioned by marriage. The scene allows the reader of the 1930s to associate Rhett with the swashbuckler of romance and the hard-boiled hero of thirties fiction who takes what he wants. But Rhett is no stereotyped gothic hero, for Mitchell is too adept at overturning these stereotypes. Unlike most seducers, Rhett is moved to act because he wants the woman to love him, and afterward he is ashamed of his behavior.

Scarlett's return to Tara suggests a regression to her adolescence. She reverts to her fantasies for solace, as she did in the days when she longed for Ashley: "She could get Rhett back. She knew she could. There had never been a man she couldn't get, once she set her mind on him. 'I'll think of it all tomorrow'" (p. 1037). Fantasizing that the future will resolve her problems allows her to avoid direct confrontation with her own self. She avoids introspection because her selfishness prevents her from wanting to understand her own drives and feelings. Preserving her narcissistic personality is of paramount importance to her. Her love for Rhett, aside from her parents the only person she ever really loves, dissipates as she returns to the self-centered optimism that shields her from self-knowledge. Scarlett is trapped by a code that has created her narcissism and prevented her from accepting her own sexual passion. As a result, she cannot love either Ashley or Rhett. Torn between her passion and repression, she is fated to follow a pattern of rationalization and denial of reality to handle the anxiety such a pattern causes. This pattern forces Scarlett to believe in unrealistic fantasies located in some unspecific future.

The account of Scarlett's rape, which lingers with the reader long after the novel has been read, is the dominant event in fiction of the 1930s in which the belle appears. Depicted as narcissistic yet sexually inhibited, the pure white belle at last meets her mythic nemesis, the dark-skinned assailant who wishes to violate her purity. Writers of the 1930s, however, are not satisfied, as was Thomas Dixon, Jr., with the mere repetition of this myth; many of them show how the southern code of behavior for men and women paradoxically contributes to the conditions that might bring about such events. With the exception of *So Red the Rose* and the complicated portrait of Melanie in *Gone with the Wind*, novels in the 1930s reveal the inadequacy of the old order to rear a southern woman who has sufficient self-esteem to allow her to love other people in any way other than as mere reflections of her own self-image. In the rare situation in which a belle can love, as is the case with Alice in *Penhally*, she is usually unrepressed and passionate, qualities to which southern gentlemen react with anxiety. Placed either in the ruined Garden of the reconstructed South or in the bleak cities of the Depression, the belle is represented as the lonely victim of a code that fosters violence and hatred rather than harmony and love.

2 / The Psychology of the Belle

6

Memory and Illusion

The heyday of the belle is short-lived; from a debut at sixteen or seventeen to the threat of spinsterhood by nineteen, her career lasts for the few short years in between. The excitement of those years is intense: a belle is the center of male and female attention; all her actions are designed to attain the end for which her childhood has prepared her and on which her future depends. Indeed, the courtship phase of her life is the only phase over which she has at least some control, when her decisions might be based on preference. A belle may well remember these days, as her life progresses into a more staid matronhood, as even more glamorous than they were.

The former belle and the aging belle nurture illusions about their youthful allure. This remnant of their youthful narcissism leads them to regale their family with stories of the numerous gentlemen callers who desired them. Amanda Wingfield in Tennessee Williams's *The Glass Menagerie* sees the world through a veil of fantasy and illusion. The faulty perception of such women clarifies the rigorous upbringing that endorsed such perception. Indeed, narcissism enjoins one to consider only the self as an object to be perceived, so that clear perception of the world at large is not something in which a belle has much practice.

Ellen Glasgow develops the motif fully in her portrait of Mrs. Blake in *The Deliverance*, the number two best-seller of 1904 and Glasgow's first popular success.[1] Glasgow parallels Mrs. Blake's flaws with those of the South, in particular the South's preference for illusions over reality. Not only is Mrs. Blake actually blind, a literal allegory of her emotional blindness, but she also believes that the South won the war. Considered too delicate and pathetic to face the truth, Mrs. Blake spends her days tirelessly repeating stories of lavish balls, devoted beaux, and famous flirtations in which she was the center of attention. She is, as Louis Auchincloss points out, "the symbol of the Old South that rejected reality."[2] She is a burden on her children, not so much because of her actual blindness but because of the efforts they must make to prevent her from knowing the truth—not an easy task, since their plantation is now owned by its former overseer. Her deathbed scene is written with the grim humor that Glasgow uses so effectively: Mrs. Blake enjoins her son, "Promise me that you will always use an ashtray," reaffirming one last time her lifelong devotion to form over substance. Her final words indicate her complete regression into the past: "I am engaged for this set, sir . . . but if it pleases you, you may put your name down for the next." She dies with "her arch smile frozen upon her face."[3] Glasgow thus inaugurated a convention in southern literature: the death scene of the belle that includes a senile regression to her youth, the moment of her most triumphant narcissism.

Edith Everett Taylor Pope's *Old Lady Esteroy* (1934) strips away the tyrannical behavior of the protagonist Valeria Esteroy to reveal the rage of a disappointed narcissist. Valeria deludes herself about her youth in order to forget the central incident in it: a painful attachment to a married judge, whose strict morality prevents his eloping with Valeria. To mask her disappointment, Valeria creates the story that she was a typical belle, who danced all night and slept all day but was nonetheless pure and interested only in the most suitable gentlemen, not forbidden married men. However, since her one true passion led only to pain, Valeria becomes cold and intolerant of tenderness in others. When we first meet her in the novel, she has become an aggressive old lady who spends her life breaking up the romances of others because she cannot bear to see them happy. Her intolerance leads to her daughter-in-law's suicide and to her granddaughter's eventual elopement with an "unsuitable" young man.[4] Valeria is left alone with her illusions. Like Mrs. Blake in Glasgow's *The Deliverance*, Valeria regresses into the past, when she was loved and desired; her monologues are interrupted only by the visits of her physician.

Dissociation from reality, often a feature of the deathbed scene of a former belle, dominates the entire life of Eppy Spurlock in Ward Greene's satire of southern mores, *Weep No More* (1932). Greene, a North Carolinian, worked as a reporter for *The Atlanta Journal* and later was an executive for King Features Syndicate. His training as a journalist made him a shrewd observer of the South in the 1930s; in particular his portrait of Eppy allows him to satirize the failure of southern culture to provide women with a set of values that would engender the development of a healthy personality.

Eppy's father, a severe Calvinist, rears her alone with a sternness rivaling that of Mr. McEachern toward the young Joe Christmas in *Light in August*. Spurlock, imbued with a peculiar ferocity against the sins of the flesh, is certain that women are basically fallen and thus susceptible to sin; this belief guides his prayers over the six-year-old Eppy, who he fears will become a tramp. Eppy grows up to believe not only that sex is wicked but that not being "pure in heart" is just as heinous. Her child's mind believes that her father, whom she worships in the manner of little girls in the midst of Oedipal attachment, must be praying for some reason, so she assumes that she has already sinned. Indeed, according to strictest Calvinist doctrine, a child is born sinful. Eppy feels she received her "scarlet letter" when she was six.

Her fear of sexuality generalizes during her adolescence so that eventually she cannot read a book in which the heroine chastely kisses her fiancé, without trembling and blushing. Parties, the proving ground of the belle, become impossible because she fears men in general. Unable to overcome her inhibitions, she decides that she can never marry, so she embarks on a career. At thirty, she is firmly accepted in her social niche as the town's old maid.

Eppy's repression of her natural desires, though extreme, is standard enough. But as she proceeds to adulthood, she begins to develop an entire fantasy world that mimicks the courtship she never had as a girl, a world that parodies her society's ideas of what her life ought to be. Too repressed to love a real man, she invents one. Her fantasy love is the son of an old Virginia family, attends Harvard, is rich, and plays polo at his home on Long Island. Eppy even produces a photograph, really that of a radio singer. The townspeople, whose approval she constantly seeks, are impressed.

What begins as an amusing white lie for Eppy becomes a desperate masquerade. She travels to New York for her marriage with a man who does not exist; when he fails to meet her at the train, she is bewildered. She has lost contact with reality altogether. She finds no listing for him in the telephone book. Realizing she cannot face being humiliated by her friends back home, she goes to the city morgue and claims the corpse of a derelict as that of her fiancé. The police remark, "She's a real little Southern Lady. . . . By God, I almost ast her to come again."[5] Eppy returns to her town in triumph, urn of ashes in hand, and receives the sympathy and admiration of the townspeople, who arrange an elaborate funeral. Eppy becomes a widow before she is a bride; since widowhood is a far more desirable state than spinsterhood, Eppy's life is now a "success."

The town functions very like Faulkner's town in "A Rose for Emily" in that it is the chorus that comments on the action and is also a source of action itself, like a character in the novel. The town is one in which girls must be belles, must marry, or else their lives are considered to be failures. At the same time, the town also decrees that sexuality is a powerful evil. Eppy, desiring to please her society by being a belle, but incapable of overcoming that society's rigid upbringing, resolves this conflict by entering a fantasy world.

Repression and Distortion of Reality

Ellen Glasgow identifies the tendency to distort reality, to impose a false coherence on reality, as a trait common to individuals in the South but also to southern society as a whole. She indicts the postbellum enshrining of southern history and personality as a complex, pathetic mechanism for coping with the severe realities of life in those times. The importance of seeing the world as society demanded required a strenuous attempt to alter one's perception of reality, quite literally to see selectively; the effort expended to repress any perceptions or feelings not sanctioned by code or legend was enormous.

The epitome of a woman devastated by the dictates of the old order is Virginia Pendleton in Glasgow's *Virginia* (1913). Only Eva Birdsong in Glasgow's late novel *The Sheltered Life* (1932) rivals Virginia in virtual self-destruction under the guise of womanly virtue. In the preface to the 1929 Old Dominion edition of *Virginia*, Glasgow reports that a friend, a war widow who could have been the model for Virginia, remarked to her in 1913:

> Do you really think, my dear . . . that a young girl could be inspired to do her duty in life by reading *Virginia?* I do not deny that there is truth in your book, but don't you feel that it is always a mistake when Southern writers stop writing about the war? . . . If only I had the gifts, I should devote them to proving to the world that the Confederacy was right. Of course, I know that even the best novelists are not so improving as they used to be; but I have always hoped in my heart that either you or Annie

Cabell's son would write another *Surrey of Eagle's Nest*. . . . Her type has vanished now as completely as the wasp waist, the sense of duty, or the code of beautiful behavior. And yet no social history of Virginia could be authentic unless it enshrined her.[6]

Glasgow did not wish, as her friend suggested, to condemn the traditional values of the South in the person of Virginia. Indeed the tone of the novel gently eulogizes the loss of women as intelligent and selfless as Virginia; yet Glasgow nonetheless relentlessly reveals that Virginia has little chance to be anything other than a victim. Her education and her mother conspire to convince her that repression is a woman's cardinal virtue.

Glasgow carefully models Virginia on the nineteenth-century stereotypes of the belle's appearance, behavior, and personality, but shows that instead of prospering by such attributes, Virginia is doomed by them. Virginia is a blonde, peaches-and-cream belle whose education has been correctly limited, effectively preventing her from perceiving reality as it is. Her teacher, Miss Priscilla Batte of the Dinwiddie Academy for Young Ladies, has taught her that in a well-bred young lady, "a curiosity about the universe was the beginning of infidelity . . . [that she must] paralyze her reasoning faculties . . . solidify the forces of mind into the inherited mold of fixed beliefs."[7] A "maiden lady" left alone and destitute by the Civil War, Miss Batte teaches the "evasive idealism" of the Old South which encourages Virginia to avoid trying to see her world clearly and to direct all her energies into finding a suitable husband. Virginia is "a woman whose energy of soul had been deflected by tradition and education into a single emotional sphere . . . she was an exquisite, if slightly fantastic creation" (p. viii).

The sphere into which Virginia directs her life is love. As an unmarried belle, Virginia's only thoughts are about perfecting her clothes and appearance as a way to entice the attentions of the man around whom her romantic hopes revolve, the would-be playwright Oliver. Like nineteenth-century belles such as Lydia Romelee in Sarah Hale's *Northwood* (1829), Virginia rejects the sane and solid John Henry because, as a seller of bathtubs, he is not her romantic ideal. Having selected Oliver as the object of her love, she is completely obsessed with him; her entire life is consumed by her love.

When she becomes a mother, however, she abandons the role of belle so completely that she sacrifices her appearance, her health, and the order of her home to do her "duty" to her children. Neither her husband nor children can bear her subservience, and they take advantage of her devotion, the husband straying to more attractive and more independent women, the children treating her more as a servant than a parent.

All of Virginia's circumstances have conspired to blind her to reality; she refuses to understand, much less to acknowledge, any deficiency in the life she is leading. Her anguish over her husband's increasingly distant behavior is soothed and sublimated by the love she imagines her children give her. Though intelligent, she cannot be her husband's intellectual companion because Miss Batte's educational precepts failed to develop Virginia's intellect: when Oliver asks for her opinion of his latest play, she replies that it is splendid; unfortunately, she had said the same about his previous fiasco.

An even more insidious influence upon Virginia is her mother. Mrs. Pendleton was a belle who "remained one when the props and the background of a great lady had crumbled around her; and though the part she filled was a narrow part, a mere niche in the world's history, she filled it superbly" (p. 39). Now poor, Mrs. Pendleton hands down to Virginia "sacred heirlooms" such as the belief that the antebellum period was "attained perfection." All the flaws of modern society—unhappy marriages, faithless husbands, divorces, irresponsible servants—she attributes "mainly to the decay of antebellum institutions" (p. 35). In one splendid passage, Glasgow describes the Pendleton view of a city street versus the actual street:

> The three stood in silence, gazing dreamily, with three pairs of Pendleton eyes, down toward the site of the old slave market. Directly in their line of vision, an overladen mule with a sore shoulder was straining painfully under the lash, but none of them saw it, because each of them was morally incapable of looking an unpleasant fact in the face if there was any honourable manner of avoiding it. What they beheld, indeed, was the most interesting street in the world, filled with the most interesting people, who drove happy animals that enjoyed their servitude and needed the sound of the lash to add cheer and liveliness to their labours. Never had the Pendleton idealism achieved a more absolute triumph over the actuality. [p. 65]

The passage is more than an illustration of the way southerners ratio-nalized slavery; it explains the working of the "evasive idealism" of the old order, which Virginia uses as a veil through which to view life. Mrs. Pendleton's advice to her before she marries is: "Whenever your ideas cross, it is your duty to give up, darling. It is the woman's part to sacrifice herself" (p. 199). As the narrator comments, "It was characteristic of her—and indeed most of the women in her genera-tion, that she would have endured martyrdom in support of the con-secrated doctrine of her inferiority to man" (p. 200).

Virginia becomes the martyr that her mother was before her. After seven years of marriage, Virginia is hysterically fearful about her children's health, frugal to the point of deprivation, servile to her fam-ily, and completely uninterested in sex. She dresses now like Miss Priscilla Batte; ironically, spinster and mother merge under this ethic. Even when another woman threatens her marriage, Virginia represses her anger: "Passion could not banish for long that exquisite forbear-ance which generations had developed from a necessity to an art" (p. 314). Tradition has taught women to submit to humiliation. Virginia's repression of all feeling is the eventual result of her silent suffering. When she and Oliver finally separate, she feels nothing. Her repres-sion of self—of the instincts and feelings that could have saved her marriage, gained the love of her children, and made her happy—is complete.

Repression, Male Fantasies, and Misogyny

Repression is the requisite personality trait for the girl who wishes to be the madonna-angel of male fantasy. Repression is also the most convenient female trait from the male point of view because it safely ensures that a woman will not reprimand a man when he dallies, that she will not dally herself, that she will find sex an imposition at best, thus providing him with a rationalization for seeking out those fallen women on the other side of the archetype. Repression, encouraged by men who want to control women, is repeatedly indicted by female and male authors alike as a crippling trait in women, one that helps them become successful belles and capture suitable husbands, but then ruins the rest of their lives.

Julia de Graffenried in Isa Glenn's *A Short History of Julia* (1930) is trapped by repression without insight, self-reliance, or the chance for a better future. In her youth, Julia has all the beauty and charm of a belle but is even more "reserved" than her society deems appropriate. Her sudden passion for the handsome but austere Carey Gordon is immediately condemned by her mother, who believes white women should be passionless. Nonetheless, Julia does feel lust and love, as the imagery throughout the first section suggests: "Within her breast there was this strange new feeling of something swelling, something opening, something akin to the garden and to the things that grew because the sun made them grow."[8] Glenn effectively uses the garden metaphor to describe Julia; the lovely, sheltered garden in the novel, though sometimes bright with blossoms, is patterned too precisely and geometrically, like Julia's life.

Julia's reserve is further reinforced by Carey himself; Julia's quietness and modesty elicit Carey's loquacious admiration for what he calls Julia's serenity. For a partner in marriage, however, Carey prefers and marries Julia's younger sister, Marietta. Thus, Julia is not rewarded for her maidenly reserve, but rather suffers for it.

Julia spends the rest of her life suffering silently. Her inability to express her wishes, to assert her right to happiness, is part of the ethic of self-sacrifice that Glasgow criticizes. Julia's inhibitions not only prevent her from expressing her feelings to Carey but also from admitting even to her mother or sister that she cares for Carey. Only her black servant, Cynthia, knows about her desire; Julia is more open with Cynthia, who is not bound by the white southern ethic, than she can be with her family. Mrs. de Graffenried eventually realizes Julia's terrible disappointment in losing Carey and uncharacteristically advises her daughter, "The next time, Julia, let go of yourself" (p. 165). It is too late, however; Julia can never let go. Eventually she even develops a dislike of being touched.

Julia's inhibitions are condoned by Carey. Even Mrs. de Graffenried can see that Carey is a "cold fish" who believes that women should have a "cold purity" and who flinches when his wife touches him. When Julia remarks that Carey reminds her of her father, Mrs. de Graffenried agrees, remembering the cold, unfeeling man who preferred prostitutes to her. Carey, like Julia's father, believes that a decent woman is asexual, an "angel," and that enjoyment of sex is appropriate only with prostitutes. To the embarrassment of his wife, he visits prostitutes, rationalizing his behavior by expressing a profound contempt of women:

"I think the feel of bare backs, or merely partly veiled backs, under women's flimsy pretenses of clothing in the evening is disgusting." He meant that he did not like the sensation of alien flesh so close to his own body. He wished that it was possible to speak frankly to nice women. . . . He growled to his conscience that when he needed women he went out in the coldest of moods and took a professional at a stipulated price. . . . What was wrong with this procedure? It had always been done. Passion was a commodity. When he was hungry he paid for, and ate, a good meal. . . . A gentleman did not brood over the meal just eaten. . . . So should it be when it was a question of the daughters of joy. He told himself that his eccentricities were the result of his sense of decency. But they were the result of his annoyance at living . . . with other human beings. [pp. 247–48]

Carey prefers his women to be objects, either the type that can be bought or the type that can be worshipped. He admires Julia but only when she resembles a work of art—beautiful, sexless, inert. "Always fix yourself up that way," he advises her, "and be very quiet; and you'll be a picture." Julia is the perfect product of this attitude. When she falls in love with another man at age forty, Carey belittles her ability to love; he cannot believe that this "work of art" has any desires. He ridicules her because the man she has chosen "has muscles," and tells her that she has "reverted to the cave woman point of view. Quantity, not quality" (p. 260). Julia is frightened into silence once more, and again loses her beau to another woman.

Only the blacks in the novel are spared the hypocritical separation of sex and love. As Julia grows old and lonely in her empty house and her garden loses its original splendor, her maid, Cynthia, receives callers in her hut at the back of the house. Julia increasingly envies Cynthia. Unlike Julia, Cynthia would never pretend to condone her sister's marriage or pretend to be pleased if her sister bore the baby of the man she loved. "To be a lady was to be a hypocrite," Julia bitterly reflects (p. 184). Cynthia may not be a "lady," but she is happy. Trapped by her code, Julia does not have the happier alternatives that are available to Cynthia.

Hiding both her love and her disappointment, Julia remains a "lady" to the end. In the final scene, Carey cruelly taunts Julia about her lost beau, and Julia turns to him with a smile, her face frozen to conceal all the pain and loneliness she feels. Carey persists: "You're

the only woman I know who could sit there—in your admirably designed simplicity of costume, and nothing in your head! . . . I've all
my life wondered how the Mona Lisa got that way. The smile I
mean" (pp. 312–13). As Julia continues to smile, he ponders what
the Mona Lisa might have experienced or learned in order to smile as
she does, concluding, from what he knows of Julia: "Nothing! Absolutely nothing!" Too resigned to be angry, too inhibited to assert her
own right to happiness, Julia can nonetheless be praised for recognizing the futility of trying to penetrate the selfish illusions of men like
Carey. She uses her smile as a defense, but it is a pathetic and feeble
mask that conceals despair and loneliness.

The fear that even an angelic, repressed woman has at her core a
nature as flawed as Eve's reveals not mere anxiety about women but
often a fundamental misogyny. While some female authors express
this misogyny as male anxiety, as does Isa Glenn in *A Short History of
Julia*, male authors often unconsciously embody misogynist attitudes
in male characters and in the narrative point of view. An example is
George Cary Eggleston's *Dorothy South: A Love Story of Virginia Just
Before the War* (1902). As was typical in postbellum novels, Eggleston
allegorically presents Dorothy as a representative of his fantasy of
the antebellum South. Eggleston's novel is interesting, however, not
because of this conventional association, but because he created in
Dorothy a girl of zest and liveliness, not a sweetly simpering belle. At
this early date such a character was not a suitable model on whom to
base an allegory of the South; Eggleston had stumbled into an uncharted zone. When we first meet Dorothy, she puts her finger into
her mouth and lets out a shrill whistle. This tomboyish gesture suggests some role misunderstanding on Dorothy's part, because she
feels comfortable having a few of the aggressive traits traditionally
reserved for men. With this image in mind, the reader is hard pressed
to believe the narrator's subsequent assurances that Dorothy is meek
and submissive. Indeed the narrator so zealously describes her courage, vigor, and outspokenness that he must then conclude that she is
also affectionate and passionate. Dorothy warns, "I will never consent to be disposed of in marriage by the orders of others, as princesses and other chattel women are."[9] Obviously, Dorothy is potentially dangerous.

Having set her up as independent and autonomous, Eggleston then
must control her and do so quickly. We soon learn from the narrator
that women possess a latent but powerful animal-like nature. Dorothy

tries to be meek because she fears that she may be like her runaway mother, who left, we are told, because her husband did not rule with an iron hand. She left, of course, because her passionate self was not permitted expression. Eggleston allows Dorothy to triumph over her nature, so that by the novel's end, Dorothy permits her aunt to select her husband. Dorothy must work at repression, but she manages to become the docile, unthreatening woman whose essential sexuality and all its components are eliminated. As H. R. Hays points out in *The Dangerous Sex: The Myth of Feminine Evil*, this sort of fear of female sexuality masks, and in Eggleston's book rather flimsily, a fear of women. Eggleston, as discussed earlier, believes that women must be tamed or they will stray.

Education as Antidote

Is it possible for the belle to become a healthier, more complete person, or is she trapped within the conventions of her culture? As far as I know, no author has yet had the belle embark on a five-year course of psychotherapy, but several have presented solutions.

An early and persistent recommendation in the literature is the saving grace of education. Nineteenth-century writers such as Hale and Hentz and contemporary writers such as Gail Godwin have endorsed both education and travel as ways of shedding the isolationist provincialism of the South. Christopher Lasch asserts in *The Culture of Narcissism* that to reclaim the past, to feel a part of one's history and traditions—to learn to recognize the problems of the human condition as being more grave than whether one has an eighteen-inch waist or a blemish on the face—are essential qualities in a healthy person. But the belle, for all that she represents her culture and its past, is singularly unaware of history, culture, or the past. Twentieth-century authors also present answers to the narcissist problem, from the simpler solutions of Evelyn Scott in *Migrations* to the more cosmic and comprehensive meditations of William Faulkner, which are discussed in chapter 8.

Evelyn Scott's *Migrations* (1927) begins as a historical novel set on a Tennessee plantation, where Melinda has married for money: "cold-bloodedly" she went after "a mansion with snow-white pillars . . . a lineage of Virginia aristocracy."[10] Melinda is entirely artificial and self-concerned: "She rested her elbow on the window ledge. Melinda was always uncomfortably self-conscious. She could not make any gesture without wondering if the posture she assumed was a becomingly modest one" (p. 82). She believes her chief duty is to live up to her reputation as a beauty, but also to be the modest and spiritual woman she has been taught that men prefer: "As a rule she tried to conceal her delight in food. Someone had told her that men could not bear to see women eat. She had resented this story but it had impressed her against her will. Certainly, the physical life had its repulsive aspects, but men . . . did not make much ado about indulging themselves in some line at least" (p. 91). Thus Melinda at the opening of the novel is presented as a typical belle, beautiful, selfish, and sexually repressed.

By removing Melinda from the shelter of her southern home, Scott shows the reader how the belle can be educated. Melinda's husband takes her on a sea voyage to the gold fields of California. At first, Melinda filters her new experiences through a veil of romantic fantasies; suppose, she muses, her husband abandoned her and she became prey to the "indelicate lusts" of the ship's sailors. But when she coquettishly flirts with the sailors and male passengers, she is shocked when one of them suggests she might actually have an affair with him. Because this would-be lover is not a southern gentleman, he mistakes her intent; what to her is a game is very real to him. Melinda only wishes to entice men and to fantasize in the vaguest terms about sex; the actual gratification of her or their desires is unthinkable.

Her education continues as she observes that life for most people is not a romance; when the ship docks in an impoverished Mexican town, she is appalled by the suffering of its people. Her fellow passengers, pilgrims seeking gold, are reduced to poverty in their quest. Besides Melinda and her husband, the party consists of a Creole gambler, a foppish and sadistic Englishman, a "white trash" couple, and an actress, people whom a belle would seldom meet on the plantation. The women become sick and skinny, the men drop all pretense of gentility, and Melinda is astonished that among so many men, she is not noticed. The heat and damp melt her prettiness, and she finally denounces "the wretched lot of women," which demands far too much clothing and ladylike behavior in conditions of such heat and discomfort.

When she gets to know a woman of the lower class, it becomes clear that Melinda is experiencing a metaphorical migration from self-centered belledom to a more sympathetic womanhood. Miss Slater is an actress whose name allegorically reveals her true profession, prostitution. Melinda begins to wonder who is "respectable," a wife like herself or Miss Slater, for both can be bought with money. She recalls that she married her husband for his money as surely as Miss Slater might be purchased for an evening. Melinda's illusion of her own purity crumbles as she sees that a "bad" woman and a "good" woman can be so similar. As her knowledge of the world increases, Melinda finds herself looking at the world as it is, understanding and caring for other people, regardless of their class, and finally appreciating her husband as a person rather than a means of support. Thus, Scott endorses the experience of new people and new places as the antidote to the belle's vanity and the means by which she can learn tolerance and love.

7

Culture and Personality: Ellen Glasgow's Belles

In Ellen Glasgow's *The Miller of Old Church* (1911), a minister reminds his congregation of the attributes of the "womanly woman":

> [she was] an Incentive, an Ideal, an Inspiration. If the womanly woman possessed a talent, she did not use it—for this would unsex her—she sacrificed it in herself in order that she might return it to the race through her sons. Self-sacrifice . . . was the breath of the nostrils of the womanly woman. It was for her power of self-sacrifice that men loved her and made an Ideal of her. Whatever else woman gave up, she must always retain her power of self-sacrifice if she expected the heart of her husband to rejoice in her. The home was founded on sacrifice, and woman was the pillar and the ornament of the home. There was her sphere, her purpose, her mission. All things outside of that sphere belonged to man, except the privilege of ministering to the sick and afflicted in other households.[1]

Stunning insights, such as this one about women's place in southern society, abound in Glasgow's work, and it is tempting to present one passage after another of her aphoristic indictments of the effect of the old order on women. Role, Glasgow observes, was not merely a set of polite mannerisms but a complex of personality traits and behaviors that were imperative because religion sanctioned them as a moral responsibility.

   Her belle characters show that her novels are not simply a "necessary bridge" between the literature of Thomas Nelson Page's generation and that of William Faulkner,[2] but rather are a terminal where she describes, mixes, and evaluates the cultural values of the Old South and the New. In particular, Glasgow's early novels identify a belle figure who clearly is a victim of the traditional mores of southern society.[3] While the later novels continue to present the traditional belle-victim, they also present the belle of the twentieth century, who is victimized still—not by external forces but by her own internal desires, especially her sexuality. This relationship between society and self is Glasgow's fundamental preoccupation. The characters she chooses to embody the old and the new are mothers and their daughters, for mothers are the culture-bearers in this society.

Julius Raper's books on Glasgow's early and later work, *Without Shelter: The Early Career of Ellen Glasgow* and *From the Sunken Garden: The Fiction of Ellen Glasgow, 1916–1945*, make a strong case for considering Glasgow's works in two parts. My observations support and expand his hypothesis. At first Glasgow looked at the world as an observer who believed society to be the cause of earthly suffering; but as she matured as a novelist, she decided that character is indeed fate, that internal decisions, albeit influenced by society, determine one's life. More miserable, then, are the victims who choose to suffer than are those who have suffering thrust upon them.

At first glance, Glasgow's women in her first novel on the social history of the state of Virginia, *The Battle-Ground* (1902), seem no different from characters in plantation novels such as George Cary Eggleston's *Dorothy South*, published in the same year. The time of *The Battle-Ground* is the antebellum and Civil War period; the place a stately plantation. The characters are members of two neighboring aristocratic families. The heroine-belles are Virginia, a dovelike blonde, and middle-class Betty, a redhead. The subplot concerns the war, and the plot concerns love.

Glasgow was familiar with the nineteenth-century models: she relates in *A Certain Measure*, her interpretation of her own fiction, that the usual pattern of the plot required that "a gallant Northern invader . . . must rescue the person and protect the virtue of a spirited yet clinging Southern Belle and beauty."[4] She did not, in 1902, disturb the pattern. Her explanation is that she wished to commence her social history by re-creating the legend: "In *The Battle-Ground*, I have tried to portray the last stand in Virginia of the aristocratic tradition."[5] She admits that this novel is tinged with what she terms "romantic idealism" and with "ancestor worship,"[6] rather than the irony characteristic of her later novels. But she denies that this is an apprentice novel (which imitates rather than creates), stating that her intention had been to objectively re-create the legend. One cannot be certain, despite her later assurances, that in 1902 she did not believe the legend. Hindsight tends to assume orderly patterns.

But a figure like Mrs. Brooke, the wife in a decaying aristocratic family, had never appeared in a previous novel. She is not ennobled by the domestic arts, a stance typical of the nineteenth-century domestic novel. Housekeeping gives Mrs. Brooke a life of drudgery and pain: "Fate had whipped her into submission, but there was that in her aspect which never permitted one for an instant to forget the whipping."[7] Her obsessive desire to do housework from morning to night causes imaginary headaches and pains. She has embraced housework, the narrator tells the reader, because she has no other outlet for her talents, and because her disappointments are numbed by hard work. Moreover, her motives for self-sacrifice are not refined and generous; Mrs. Brooke feels morally superior to her weak husband by working in contrast to his idleness. She prefers "a domestic rather than religious martyrdom. The rack would have been to her morally a bed of roses" (p. 105).

Glasgow also deromanticizes housework because, in fact, domestic work in the nineteenth century was enormously difficult and time-consuming; Catherine Clinton in her fine history, *The Plantation Mistress*, describes the daily chores of even the most privileged matron, chores including the preparation of pickle brine, which destroyed a woman's lily-white hands. Just the task of knitting one sock took six days; multiplying this by the number of slaves and family members, we see that a woman could knit her life away.[8]

Glasgow's rejection of the domestic novel as her genre of choice, and of its theme of the saving graces of the home, led in her next novel to an even more piercing observation of her society. *The Deliverance* (1904) shows the antebellum belle as a victim of her culture. In this novel, as we saw earlier, Glasgow presents a southern woman who represents the South's preference for fanciful idealizations about itself, its clinging to class vanity in a postwar milieu that no longer honors class lines, and its tendency to prefer the beautiful to the useful in women. Mrs. Blake, an ex-belle now in old age, is Glasgow's humorous exaggeration of the South's postwar tendency to glamorize itself. Still beautiful, she is a useless, selfish anachronism living in a time that demands self-reliance and hard work. When she learns who won the war, she collapses from a stroke, lacking the strength to face this reality because she has always relied on her beauty and her social class to solve problems.

Mrs. Blake's opinions on love and marriage are especially significant because they represent Glasgow's earliest evaluations of southern attitudes on these topics. Mrs. Blake clings to aristocratic notions that prevent her from accepting her daughter's middle-class fiancé: "one should never do anything so indelicate as to fall in love with someone who isn't a desirable match."[9] Believing that marriage is more a duty than a pleasure and that marriages are made in the marketplace, Mrs. Blake advises her son to choose a wife with the coolness of making "the selection of a brand of flour" (p. 201). She encourages her two daughters to seek out husbands by considering their family connections, not their behavior. As an illustration of correct marital attitudes, she relates a tale of a belle of her day who eloped with a man who gambled, debauched, and drank. When the fellow at last died, the Bishop of the town reminded the wife of the husband's behavior; the wife replied that she was thankful that at least her husband had never chewed tobacco. Mrs. Blake's idea of suitable behavior endorses a double standard of morality for the male maintained through delusion and blind self-sacrifice in the woman.

Heiress to this tradition is Mrs. Blake's daughter, Cynthia, the first of several Glasgow characters whose lives are characterized by neurotic self-sacrifice. Cynthia makes herself into a martyr, a drudge, and a champion of a tradition she barely remembers. So that her prettier sister, Lila, can keep her hands white and ladylike, Cynthia cooks, cleans, and takes in laundry to earn money. But Glasgow again rejects the domestic ethic by revealing that Cynthia's self-sacrifice for her sister and family is actually a form of selfishness, a way of gaining attention and esteem by preventing others from doing good deeds. The key to Cynthia's love of suffering is the fact that she is not beautiful, nearly a crime in a society that idealizes feminine beauty. She has, consequently, never had a lover, or even a kiss. The martyr, writes psychoanalyst Karen Horney in her essay "The Problem of Feminine Masochism," is often the woman who attempts to win her family's love out of fear of not being loved.[10] Cynthia fears that because she is plain she will not be loved and becomes her family's servant to win their love. She must reject the role of belle altogether since she was not born "beautiful."

Lila, who would have been a traditional belle before the war, is not bound to the southern traditions of aristocratic grandeur, since they do not exist any longer and she is too young to remember them. She has no illusions about the past and seeks to live a normal life with the man who loves her. Until she is thirty, however, Lila submits to her mother's and sister's wills, finally summoning the strength to defy tradition by marrying middle-class Jim. Lila, unlike so many of Glasgow's blonde belles, asserts her right to happiness because the deprivations of the Reconstruction era have made her strong. But because she is a minor character, the reader does not learn much about her assertiveness.[11]

The Deliverance identifies the pattern of self-victimization and indicts it. Glasgow observes that in this postbellum society, the ideal woman was one whose only longing was to love and be loved by a man; thus women were urged to overvalue romantic love, to develop what Horney calls a neurotic need for love. If a narcissistic emphasis on external beauty could not draw masculine attention (often confused with love), then a submissive, helpless attitude would both arouse masculine pity and reinforce men's notions of themselves as protectors of fragile womanhood.

Glasgow's fiction bitterly criticizes this ethic of self-sacrifice, with its attendant emphasis on illusion, external beauty, and helplessness, because of its devastating effects on generations of southern women. In *The Woman Within* she asserts, "I revolted from sentimentality less because it was false than because it was cruel."[12] She saw woman as the victim of "evasive idealism,"[13] ready to sacrifice everything for the attentions and the comfort of men. James Branch Cabell points out that Glasgow's southern woman is "the predestined victim of male chivalry."[14] In fact, she is worse than that; the southern code of behavior for women, as it is depicted in Glasgow's fiction, strikingly resembles Karen Horney's assessment of the five traits that most often characterize feminine masochism.

Horney writes perceptively about personality disorders in women who live in patriarchal societies. In particular, she emphasizes the interplay of cultural roles and expectations with an individual's personality. Her comments on masochism and on "the neurotic need for love" provide useful metaphors with which one can concisely describe the behavior of Glasgow's belles. Horney points out that patriarchies block women's opportunities for expression of talents, intellect, and sexuality; confine women to the home as the only sphere in which they can obtain emotional satisfaction, security, and social recognition; and enjoin women to be economically dependent on men.[15] The theory that cultural beliefs and practices can encourage personality disorders is one of Horney's major contributions to psychology and is certainly relevant to the study of Glasgow's southern belles. Horney's traits of feminine masochism are: (1) inhibiting direct demands and aggressions; (2) regarding oneself as weak, helpless, or inferior, and implicitly or explicitly demanding considerations and advantages on this basis; (3) becoming emotionally dependent on the other sex; (4) being self-sacrificing, submissive, used or exploited, or putting responsibilities on the other sex; (5) using weakness as a means of wooing and subduing the other sex.[16] As one reads Glasgow's fiction, one sees each of these traits embodied in the belles who cling to the old order. And because Glasgow is concerned with the interplay of personality and culture, various characters and institutions in her fiction carry the banner of the Lost Cause, urge conformity to the old ways, and personify cultural expectations. Glasgow's novels are never set in antebellum times, because she is concerned with the myths about southern men and women that had grown *after* the war. In particular she uses the mothers of the belle figures, men of all ages, and various teachers to embody the old order and urge the belle to accept it.

One of the most striking differences between Glasgow's fiction and nineteenth-century fiction is that Glasgow's belles have mothers. Because nineteenth-century belles in fiction were often motherless, they were closely attached to their fathers, a pattern that reflected the fact that illness and childbirth might very well bring early death to a young woman. But more important, as I discussed in part 1, the South's social structure placed the girl in the position of being property—her father's most valuable property, to be sure. With the mother absent, that relationship could become even more close. Nineteenth-century authors realized the insignificance of the married woman in their society; the ethic of self-sacrifice encouraged a flattening of personality in the married woman, who was trained from birth to defer to her husband.

In contrast, Glasgow is preoccupied with the old-fashioned belles who become mothers and as culture-bearers affect generations of modern belles. Mrs. Blake in *The Deliverance*, for example, influences her daughter Cynthia to cling to the traditions of feminine self-sacrifice, and her extreme preoccupation with class barriers nearly prevents the marriage of her daughter Lila. In *The Ancient Law*, written four years later in 1908, Glasgow examines the personality of a mother who retains the traits of the belle and has also passed them on to her daughter. Lydia Ordway's daughter, Alice, is as vain as her mother, but she so overwhelmingly craves masculine attention to re-inforce her vanity that she elopes with a dissolute fellow. Having been taught nothing but the importance of her beauty, Alice has no moral judgment. She eventually forges a check and acknowledges no responsibility for her crime. Her mother, who has always shielded her, convinces her father to take the blame for the crime and serve Alice's jail sentence.

This rather astonishing plot grows out of the character of Lydia, who believes that having her husband go to jail will "keep up appear-ances." She is a cold, detached southern beauty whose lack of passion at first attracts but then repels her husband. Ordway asks himself, "Were all pure women as passionless—as utterly detached—as she had shown herself to him from the beginning? And was the coldness, as he had always believed, but the outward body of that spiritual grace for which he had loved her? . . . had she ever belonged to him . . . even in the supreme hours of their deepest union? Had her very innocence shut him out from her soul forever?"[17]

Lydia is concerned only with her personal appearance and the ap-pearance her family makes in public. The imagery Glasgow uses clarifies her character. She is always shown in her perfumed bed-chamber, where she is sheltered from the world as a precious jewel in a box or a rare bird in a cage, where her only activity is gazing in the mirror.[18] Lydia's desire to keep up appearances and her coldness to-ward her husband are, the narrator explains, "spiritual infirmities which were not less to be pitied than an infirmity of the body" (p. 357). Far from condemning Lydia, Glasgow asks for the reader's understanding, for she and her daughter are full of fear; their cold beauty is an illusion beneath which is "the skeleton which her radiant flesh clothed with life, and beneath Lydia's mask of conventionality her naked little soul, too delicate and shivering to stand alone" (p. 433).

In *The Romance of a Plain Man* (1909), the selfish and haughty Mitty Bland, who has been the only mother her niece Sally has known, advises Sally not to marry the Horatio Alger protagonist of the novel: "What are six feet, two inches without a grandfather?"[19] Intrinsic attractiveness is nothing, she urges, next to breeding: "He is a magnificent animal, but he has no social manner" (p. 153). Sally is a belle with the small hands and feet that her aunt swears are the badge of aristocracy, but also with dark hair and a full mouth that indicate an untraditional warmth. The reader first sees her, not in a stuffy room, Glasgow's usual setting for the belle of the old order, but in a garden. She is snipping geraniums, a rather bourgeois flower unlike the roses and magnolias associated with a belle in the nineteenth-century novel. She is a democratic, unrepressed Eve; she has the courage and intelligence to defy tradition, to favor women's rights, and to marry Ben. She is not content to live in the "stained-glass seclusion" of Aunt Mitty. Sally believes in hard work and wants to escape the narrow rooms of her sheltered ancestors. However, the reasons why Sally can spurn tradition in this manner are not well defined in the novel.

Glasgow most often embodies the voice of tradition in a mother or close female relative, but she points out that older men also encourage young men to marry only the beautiful but submissive women of the stereotype. A veteran general of the Civil War advises Ben to "find a good sensible woman who hasn't any opinions of her own, and you will be happy. A woman who stops believing in gentleness and self-sacrifice . . . ceases to be a woman" (p. 180). The General believes that suffragettes like Sally have "unsexed themselves. Every man knows there's got to be a lot of sacrifice in marriage, and he likes to feel he's marrying a woman who is fully capable of making it" (p. 180). The General's comments call to mind several of Horney's cultural conditions under which feminine masochism most often occurs, especially the subordination of women to men and the restriction of women to the sphere of the home.

Even the reading habits encouraged by the traditional South for its young women fostered the preoccupation with beauty and fantasy that typify the belle's attitudes. In *The Ancient Law*, Milly Trend possesses the traditional belle's attributes and is compared to "peach blossoms and spring sunshine"; but she is also a selfish, narcissistic girl, whose fantasies, based on romantic novels, nearly destroy her life. Like Dorinda Oakley in *Barren Ground*, Milly is able to "bear" her humdrum life in a small town by fantasizing about a gallant man who will whisk her away to a glamorous but vague future: "Being plain she would probably have made currant jelly for her pastor, and have taught sedately in the infant class in Sunday School; being pretty she read romances and dreamed strange adventures of fascinating highwaymen on lonely roads. But many a woman who has dreamed of a highwayman at eighteen has compromised with a bank-clerk at twenty-two" (p. 53). Glasgow continues a convention used as early as 1832 by John P. Kennedy in *Swallow Barn*, in which Bel

Tracy's longings for a gallant knight blind her to the virtues of Ned
Random, so much so that he must play the courtly lover to woo and
win her. Girls were to wait patiently in their homes for a handsome
knight; little wonder that the Cinderella tale has persisted as a favorite female fantasy, as Colette Dowling shows in *The Cinderella Complex*. Such a fantasy comforts and consoles girls whose adolescence
may be lonely or tedious, who await the beginning of womanhood,
symbolized by the phallic slipper that is the right "fit."

Glasgow attempts to create a character who resists. In *Virginia*,
Glasgow's eulogy to the victims of the old order, Susan Treadwell,
whose name reveals her character, is a self-reliant woman, like Betty
in *The Battle-Ground* and Sally in *The Romance of a Plain Man*. Susan is
Virginia's foil—tall, "sensible," attractive, but not a beauty. She has
mysteriously resisted the teachings of Miss Batte, although the reader
is never told how she has done so. How she escapes Virginia's fate is
not clearly explained either, since her parents are much like Virginia's.
For example, Susan abhors coquetry, though her mother urges her to
seek masculine attention and to be a belle. In this book Glasgow has
not yet fully realized the woman character who chooses not to be a
victim, who will "not accept destiny but command it" (p. 256); Susan
says this of herself, but the source of her courage is unexplained.

Glasgow spent the first two decades of her career analyzing and
satirizing the old order that had created such stern conditions for
women. Yet just as she sees the old order crumble, and the new
woman emerge, unencumbered by tradition, Glasgow discovers that
the flaw that renders women victims is not external but within. She
calls it "life," but by this she means the sexual drive, which she sees
as a predetermined force that robs women of their wills and makes
them slaves to their desires. That sex is a more insidious enslaver
than the traditions of southern society is a major theme of Glasgow's
later fiction. In her early fiction she sporadically refers to the sexual
drives of her women characters: Betty's orgasmic dream in *The Battle-
Ground*, Maria Fletcher's yearning for the muscular Christopher in
The Deliverance, and Sally's preference for the "animal-like" Ben in
The Romance of a Plain Man. Even in *Virginia* the belle has a brief moment of sexual passion; when she and Oliver first speak to each other
and their hands touch, "Little thrills of joy, like tiny flames, ran over
her . . . so subtly did life use her for its end that the illusion of choice
in first love remained unimpaired" (pp. 70–71).

Beginning with *Life and Gabriella* (1916) and proceeding to *Barren*

Ground and the three novels of the Queenborough trilogy, Glasgow is preoccupied with the theme of free will versus determinism. Her own particular twist on this theme is that yielding to sexual drives will cause one's destruction. For a Glasgow heroine, the only way to avoid suffering, to exert one's will against a force that drags one into oblivion, is to reject sexuality altogether.

Life and Gabriella was meant to be the second of three books, Glasgow reported in a 1916 interview: "When I began *Virginia* I had in mind three books dealing with the adjustment of human living conditions. . . . Virginia was the passive and helpless victim of the ideal self-sacrifice. . . . Gabriella was the product of the same school, but instead of being used by circumstances she used them to create her own destiny."[20] This novel differs even more dramatically from *Virginia* than Glasgow's comment indicates; it marks the beginning of the second part of Glasgow's *oeuvre*. Gabriella is the tall, slender, sallow-complexioned, dark-haired heroine whom Glasgow generally prefers to the stereotypical fragile blondes such as Virginia, from nineteenth-century fiction. Gabriella's sister, "poor" Jane Grace, as she is always called, is the pink and blonde belle whose beauty droops early like a dying flower. Like Virginia, Jane is a martyr with a husband who is unfaithful and beats her. Jane will never leave Charlie, for separation is a worse alternative to her than the painful keeping up of appearances. Jane believes, as did the nineteenth-century belles discussed earlier, that it is the woman's responsibility to inspire and reform her husband; in a perverse way, the worse her husband behaves, the more satisfaction Jane experiences in trying to reform him. Charlie chafes under her righteous nagging; his story—the trials of living with a saint—is not fully told until *The Sheltered Life*, in which George Birdsong is another Charlie.

Repulsed by Jane's submissiveness, Gabriella offers to break her own engagement and work as a shop girl to support Jane, if only Jane will consent to leave Charlie. Her mother and sister are horrified that she should consider such an "unladylike" profession; they urge her to teach or to sew lampshades, the only acceptable options available to a well-born girl of a destitute family. Glasgow tells the reader, with the words that will be a constant refrain in this and future novels, that a "vein of iron . . . held her, in spite of her tempting youth, to the resolution she had made."[21] The temptation of youth Gabriella has resisted is the lure of Arthur, the last of a family of Virginia aristocrats. His feelings about her are based on his fantasy that she is "sacred . . .

starlike and remote." He projects upon her all the qualities of the ideal woman (as Ordway does for Lydia in *The Ancient Law*): "By the simple act of falling in love with her he had endowed her with every virtue except the ones that she actually possessed" (p. 34). Like her mother and sister, he is shocked at her choice of employment.

Gabriella is fatherless, an unusual trait for a southern belle and one that might account for her willingness to assume the traditionally masculine role of breadwinner. Her mother is incapable of earning a living; like Jane, she is of "the snow and roses sort" (p. 176), a hypochondriac with attacks of neuralgia. She believes that as a result of being sheltered, women's natures are more "spiritual" than those of men, and that women are thereby spared the "temptations" to which men are exposed. Like many of the mothers in Glasgow's novels, Gabriella's mother is a pathetic and not very admirable woman; thus Gabriella's rebellion becomes more plausible to readers who would expect a mother to be a source of strength. As Linda Wagner points out, "By slanting her readers against the very women characters who should be beloved . . . Glasgow in effect, justifies the rebellious daughters."[22]

Gabriella, however, is not spared temptation, for she cannot resist George, a philanderer whose physical appeal so overwhelms her that she ignores his selfishness, carelessness, meager intelligence, and frivolous nature. George has learned these traits from his mother, a spoiled Virginia belle—sons also suffer from such mothers, Glasgow observes. Even an independent woman like Gabriella can love a man like George by projecting onto him all sorts of qualities he lacks. She believes, for example, that George's inarticulateness is evidence of an inner profundity that renders him speechless. As with a child, time means nothing to George, but everything to Gabriella; she is full of hopes for the future, and her hopes are based on the fact that she can work. In contrast, Virginia, Mrs. Blake, and other traditional belles in Glasgow's early works are consumed by the past, hopeful of an undefined future, or inarticulate and lost in the trivia of the domestic present.

Gabriella hopes marriage will change George, but in four months his desire for her fades, and he turns to other women. In a moment of self-assertion, Gabriella decides that she must renounce not only George but love forever: "It's life I'm living, not a fairy tale. . . . After all, you can't be a victim unless you give in . . . and I'll die rather than become a victim" (pp. 200–201). Realizing she is now in the same position as her sister, her "vein of iron" causes her to reject sex, which becomes "sordid and ugly" and fills her with "profound disgust" and "revulsion" (p. 247). George, sex, love will not, she vows, crush her and ruin her life. Thus the "life" in the title of the novel becomes a malevolent force that seeks to crush its victims by creating in them a desire for sex and for love. Life is the adversary.

When George finally deserts her for a blonde belle, Gabriella must rear her two children alone and does so by becoming a successful career woman. But her courage is purchased at the price of suppression of her need for love. Her anxiety and fear of men cause her withdrawal into the safety of her work, a common mode of sublimation. But Glasgow shows that this kind of escape does not bring peace. Gabriella is troubled by headaches, a psychogenic illness that often characterizes the repressed woman in Glasgow's fiction. When she meets O'Hara, a virile, self-made railroad millionaire, she is at first frightened, thinking of him as a "force," not a man. She begins to fantasize, after seventeen years, about Arthur, who is a refined gentleman, unlike the lowbred O'Hara. Arthur represents all the southern traditions that she has cast aside but still desires, while O'Hara elicits the sexual drive within her which she fears will make her a victim again. Her dilemma is resolved when she returns to Virginia, a metaphorical journey to be sure, and sees that Arthur lacks the faith in the future and the willingness to work toward goals that characterize Gabriella and her Horatio Alger hero, O'Hara. She at last sees the past as it is, and lets it go.

Gabriella is permitted the ultimate satisfaction Glasgow occasionally allows her heroines. The dissolute George returns to her, ill, destitute, friendless, and dies in her arms. Glasgow often rewards her heroines by killing off the men who have victimized them. One emotion Glasgow never overtly assigns to her women is anger; fate comes to their rescue instead. Her heroines most often are stoics who learn to accept suffering as a part of life and try to make the best of their lives in spite of the blows dealt them by the weak, dissipated men they invariably select. Glasgow's women, in particular Gabriella and Dorinda Oakley of *Barren Ground*, have good reason to be angry with men. Both have been deceived and disappointed by men as a result of their own sexual longings. Both must fight a male-oriented society to eke out a living for themselves. Both have seen the suffering that men cause other women they love—their mothers, for example, and Gabriella's sister. Thus their unconscious wish is to take vengeance against men, in particular the men who hurt them. They can do so by entering the male working world and proving they are more competent than their men. And, like Jane Eyre, they have the final victory by seeing their deepest revenge fantasies fulfilled; George and Jason in *Barren Ground*, for example, come to ignominious ends.[23]

Life and Gabriella was Glasgow's pivotal novel in her portrayal of the southern belle, because in it she discovered the theme of her later novels: the victimization of the protagonist by the sexual impulse. Between that novel and her next important novel, *Barren Ground* (1925), a period of nine years intervened, years of drastic change. The Old South which Glasgow had eulogized in her early novels was no longer gracefully departing; it was being rapidly eliminated as much by a new morality as by industry. During this period, Glasgow's own life was saddened by deaths in her family and by a broken engagement, indirectly caused by the events of war. No longer a young woman rebelling against a set of social mores, Glasgow shared with many southern writers the advantage of that double vision of the South's past and future, whereas before she had been for the most part concerned with the past. As Glasgow reveals in *A Certain Measure*, such a vision provided her with the detachment she needed both to observe the "loss of charm" in the South and to "brood over the fragmentary world" that the South was becoming.[24] Of her four great novels of this period, three treat the southern belle directly, by giving the reader this double vision for observing the belle: the traditional belle of the nineteenth-century South and the modern belle of the 1920s. These novels are *The Romantic Comedians* (1926), *They Stooped to Folly* (1929), and *The Sheltered Life* (1932), which comprise her trilogy about life in the city of Queenborough, Glasgow's name for Richmond.[25]

The first of these, *The Romantic Comedians*, whose title is borrowed from John Esten Cooke's nineteenth-century plantation novel *The Virginia Comedians* (1854), encapsulates one of Glasgow's favorite motifs: all the world is a stage, on which the players act their assigned roles, determined usually by society. The protagonist is the aging Judge Gamaliel Honeywell, surrounded by three belles and the memory of a fourth. Glasgow handles deftly the interplay between society's shaping of their personalities and their attempts to express their own personal desires.

Amanda Lightfoot is the last of the great beauties of the 1880s; her name (aristocratic ladies being renowned for their small feet) suggests the lineage that made her the reigning belle of Queenborough. When Gamaliel jilted her to marry her best friend, Amanda's dignity and reserve permitted her only to suffer in silence. Amanda embodies all the traditional feminine virtues of "patience, gentleness, moderation, reserve."[26] Glasgow's imagery associates Amanda with the delicate canaries she keeps in a gilded cage, lovely but fragile birds that cannot be exposed to chilling breezes from the outside world. When the Judge presents her with flowers for a dance, he selects lilies of the valley, a flower whose purity and fragility symbolize Amanda's.

Unable to admit that she even has any desires, Amanda tells Annabel, who is trying to decide whether she would be hurting Amanda by marrying Gamaliel, that she is perfectly happy with her life and not at all angry with Gamaliel for jilting her years ago. The imagery suggests, however, that Amanda is acutely hurt and lonely; when Annabel asks whether she is unhappy, "A shadow as swift as the flight of a bird darkened the stainless enamel of Amanda's face" (p. 146). Like the perfect lady she has been taught to be, however, she lies beautifully and replies that she feels she has had a full life. Annabel, a modern woman, deplores Amanda's advice that she must exercise "good taste" even in unhappiness; when a young boyfriend jilted Annabel, she told everyone of her pain. Amanda admonishes her that self-control is the chief of a woman's virtues, but Amanda responds that she "should have died of pain" had she repressed her feelings of anger. Annabel concludes from the interview that "there was little help to be found in perfect behavior" (p. 150) and subsequently marries Gamaliel.

Annabel is the selfish, charming, beautiful, brown-haired belle of the new era, as captivating as the traditional belle but with none of her restraint. Even her body, as supple as "rippling water," contrasts with the more "queenly" style of figure, represented by Amanda. Annabel's personality is overt, intrusive; Gamaliel gives her gardenias for the dance, a flower as pungent and insinuating as Annabel herself. Of a new generation, she believes that men as well as women should exercise virtue, that women like Amanda allow men to become "morally flabby" because they do not protest the double standard or speak out when a man's behavior hurts them. However, she is not a flapper; she does not smoke or drink and has an earnest personality. She wants love and happiness, but, having failed to capture the young man she wants, she marries Gamaliel. Her reason for marriage is innocently crass; she asks her mother, "Do you suppose he'd pay all our bills?" (p. 129). For her, marriage is a monetary bargain, an odd throwback to nineteenth-century views of marriage. Glasgow's considerable contempt for this girl is mitigated, however, by the light satiric mode she has chosen for the novel.[27]

Gamaliel, the main consciousness of the novel, continually compares Amanda and Annabel. He believes that it is the Great War that has created such bold women as Annabel, although he cannot say just why this is so. He notices that young women tend to regard his divorced sister, Edmonia, as some sort of heroine: "They treated her scarlet letter less as a badge of shame than as some foreign decoration for distinguished service" (p. 84). When he is blinded by his great attraction for Annabel's vivacity and youth, he forgets that she too is part of this new generation, and he projects onto her qualities of docility, timidity, and submissiveness, none of which she possesses. She constantly asserts, "I want to make something of my life" (p. 89), and "If I cannot have love, I'd rather to die" (p. 288); yet Gamaliel sees her as submissive and restrained, the "true woman" of his memories.

He is reinforced in these illusions by Annabel's mother, who is the villain of the novel. Appropriately named Bella, as her daughter is named Anna*bel*, she is another type of belle, a shrewd woman who manipulates the Judge into marrying her daughter by appealing to his sympathy. Annabel has been "crushed," she tells Gamaliel, by her erstwhile lover; Annabel is helpless, and only the Judge can make her happy again. In rare moments of insight, Bella regrets that she herself has never learned any useful skills, so she must resort to marrying her daughter to the most available rich man. The most extreme example of the destructive mother in Glasgow's fiction, Bella panders her own daughter.

In marriage, Annabel responds with the coolness and lack of demonstrativeness that indicate her lack of passion for a man old enough to be her grandfather, but which Gamaliel pathetically interprets as the "reserve" of a "good woman." He filters all his perceptions through a set of principles acquired forty years earlier. Annabel is pure desire, pure id, and when a new, younger lover presents himself, no conventional restraints can prevent her from leaping out at him: "If I cannot have love, I'd rather to die" (p. 288). "You were all afraid of life," she says, "and you called your fear virtue" (p. 297).

Glasgow grants that Amanda's generation was a "mixture of fortitude and hypocrisy" in which suffering was elevated to an art, and that Annabel is correct in refusing to learn it.[28] But Glasgow criticizes Annabel harshly, because her passions and her candidness destroy the happiness of others, and she has no regard for anyone else's right to love but her own. The new generation of belles, Glasgow implies, in throwing off tradition to fulfill their desires, uncover only the cool, consuming fire of selfishness, not the warmth of tenderness and affection.

In *They Stooped to Folly: A Comedy of Morals*, Glasgow writes about what she calls "the almost forgotten myth of the 'ruined' woman,"[29] rediscovering, she believes, the seduction motif that was part of both pagan and Christian tradition. In *A Certain Measure*, she traces the motif through *Clarissa* and the English Romantic novelists, but believes that the "myth of woman as inspiration" in the Victorian era displaced the seduction motif for a time.[30] World War I, bringing universal disenchantment with ideals that had not prevented war, also brought back the notion of greater freedom for woman, of woman as an obstacle to man—the myth of woman as temptress to whom "ruin" in the Victorian sense was a badge of honor. By choosing World War I as a setting for this novel, Glasgow creates a "background of forsaken standards"[31] against which her ruined women of the old order and the new can stand out in relief. Glasgow realized, as feminist critics have recently pointed out, that the myth of the ideal woman and the myth of the temptress who seeks to be "ruined" stem from the same root—men's fear of women, a fear illustrated in this novel in the weak Martin Welding, a typical Glasgow male who is paradoxically fascinated and repulsed by women. As much a prey to the myths of woman as any of the southern gentlemen of the previous generation, he is eventually destroyed by his own fears.

Glasgow presents belles of several generations to illustrate the changing mores of her society. Aunt Agatha, a belle of the 1870s, gave in to her desires and lost her virginity to a Civil War colonel. For her "crime" she was banished by public opinion to her room, where she has more or less remained for the last forty years. In her isolation, her desire for love overwhelms her entire personality. She attempts to satisfy this need by eating banana sundaes and attending lurid movies such as *Passion in the Purple* and *A Scarlet Sin*. Agatha is a victim of her own impulses, which impel her to defy society's taboos, but she is also a victim of society, which demands that she atone for her mistake by sacrificing her whole life. Her colonel, meanwhile, "lost three wives but never missed a Christmas cotillion."[32] The double standard worked effectively to give him a life unaffected by the incident in their youth.

Milly Burden, a modern belle, rebels against the inherited social order by having sexual relations with Martin and bearing his child, but unlike Agatha she refuses to be ruined; instead, she becomes a secretary. She asserts, like Annabel, "I want to feel free . . . I want my life. I have a right to my life" (p. 231). Perhaps Glasgow could have made Milly another Gabriella, stoically renouncing the "trap" of love to become a successful career woman. But Glasgow's interest in Milly is limited; Milly repeats her assertions about her desire to "live" without ever defining what this means.

Milly is an undeveloping character who seems somnambulistic. She never convinces the reader that her stance is valid or attractive; if this is the result of folly, it is certainly to be avoided. Thus Milly's life is no more preferable than Aunt Agatha's. Glasgow's indifference to this character results from a number of factors. First, she needed a modern foil for Agatha and for Amy Dalrymple of the past generation; she also needed a foil for another modern belle, Mary Victoria, discussed below. Second, Glasgow admitted that she preferred to write about old people because they have a "finality the young do not"; the young are too changeable, "enveloped in emotion," in flux, whereas the old experience the peace that only stasis can present. "Life is not the inalienable property of the young," she reminds her readers.[33] Thus Milly's comments on life have no authority; they are the invalid emotional responses that Glasgow feels victimize youth. Milly is as much a victim of her own emotions as Agatha is of tradition.

Milly's contemporary, Mary Victoria, who marries Martin to "save" him from Milly, clearly follows the nineteenth-century ethic that it is woman's task to inspire and reform a man who has gone astray. Far from seeing Martin as Milly's seducer, she is certain that Milly has lured Martin into sin. Mary Victoria actively perpetrates the dual myths of woman as ideal or fallen. She joins the Red Cross so that she can act as the ministering angel, part of the ideal stereotype. However, her aggressive self-righteousness smothers her husband. She is incapable of loving him or even seeing him as he is; her desire "to curb the lower nature of man" (p. 12) reveals her fear of human passion.

Mary Victoria's mother, Victoria, has taught her that womanly purity is the highest necessity, but in this case Glasgow is, uncharacteristically, far more sympathetic to the mother than to her daughter. Victoria, like Amanda in *The Romantic Comedians*, is associated with a caged canary, sheltered and fragile. Her father-in-law confided to her on her wedding day: "Thank God, Victoria, that my son is marrying a true woman; for pure womanhood is the only thing that stands between man and the jungle" (p. 81). But Victoria feels she has missed something in her life, and she dies disillusioned, cheated by a tradition that has caused in her a "natural frigidity," as her husband calls it, and has robbed her of something that she is too repressed even to identify. Victoria and her daughter are not ruined women in the conventional sense; yet, Glasgow points out, the traditions they live by ruin them, preventing them from becoming tender, warm, and honest, feelings that seem to them to be akin to passion.

In this book only Amy Dalrymple thrives as a fulfilled woman, a victim neither of tradition nor desire. As another "ruined" woman, she flees to "the fleshpots of Europe" where, rather than becoming the pathetic wreck that Agatha is or the wooden mannequin that Milly is, she learns to express her emotions toward both men and women, to see human frailty clearly, and, ironically, to become more charming than she was in her heyday as a belle of the 1890s. Virginius, Victoria's husband, attributes Amy's triumph to the war: "We have lost our way in the universe . . . It is as if the bottom dropped out of idealism" (p. 5). When the war was over, "he discovered that Mrs. Dalrymple's indiscretion had diminished in size. New and perhaps ignoble standards had emerged from the conflict. For the decadence of Europe was slowly undermining Virginia tradition, and even the Southern gentleman, he told himself, was beginning to suspect that the ruined woman is an invention of man. Was it possible . . . that there was something wrong with the past? . . . Was the ideal of pure womanhood infested with moth and decay?" (p. 5). While Amy is not totally admirable—believing as she does that for "a Southern lady of reduced circumstance and with an impaired reputation, love is the only available means of increasing an income" (p. 101)—at least her honesty frees her from the hypocrisy of tradition and the insensitivity of youth. She shows that one need not be a victim.

Both Amy and Virginius's brother, Marmaduke, believe that the so-called virtues of the old-fashioned woman are hypocritical and deceptive, allowing men immunity from sin by reason of their animal natures. Virginius recalls that their father was more dismayed by the uttering of the word *adultery* than the performing of it. Marmaduke accuses Virginius and his generation of forcing an "artificial conformity" on women because "their whole philosophy of life is rooted in the fear of women," and asserts that women know "nothing of freedom because they have embraced sacrifice as an ideal" (p. 130). As with Mary Victoria, freedom to a woman is "an extended area of reform." Mary Victoria, he concludes, is ultimately narcissistic, for "she craves . . . complete domination of the world within reach . . . the wider her sphere of influence, the more flattering it is to her vanity" (p. 130).

The Queenborough novels differ from Glasgow's earlier novels, even from *Barren Ground*, in that there are no truly admirable modern young women in them. If older belles are pathetic anachronisms, the younger belles are either sad copies of their self-sacrificing mothers or selfish seekers after love and pleasure. Both types of belles are essentially narcissistic, seeking gratification only for self, the one by presuming that her opinions and high standards should be adopted by the world, the other by asserting that she is the only person in the world whose feelings are important. Each has an egocentric orientation to life that prevents her from being able to love. Like spoiled children, their aggressive need for love can be associated with the motto "You will love me because I say so." As Karen Horney points out, such demands characterize women who so fear not being loved that they demand love without offering anything in return.[34]

Jenny Blair Archbald in *The Sheltered Life* (1932) is the epitome of the destructive narcissist. She is sheltered not only from the world but from the knowledge of her own sexual drives. Indulged in every way by her widowed mother, flattered by her family into believing that beauty is the most important attribute a woman can possess, Jenny Blair is selfish and expects people to love her for her beauty. Because she has been shielded from any knowledge of sexuality, her repressed sexual desire blossoms in an elaborate fantasy world which she creates and then confuses with reality.

Jenny's narcissism pervades her life, even its most mundane details. She cannot even pass a mirror without admiring herself: "I'm glad I'm pretty I'm glad people love me because I'm pretty."[35] Her sense of her own uniqueness and its attendant privileges begins as early as age nine; she comments disparagingly on the female characters in *Little Women* (which her mother has had to pay her to read): "I'm different. I'm different. I'm alive, alive, alive, and I'm Jenny Blair Archbald" (p. 4). It is her beauty, she believes, that gives her special privileges and excuses her from following society's dictates, a conviction supported by what limited experience her environment offers her. Her Aunt Etta, who as a young girl had eloped with a colonel, now suffers headaches and a persistent rash. Not an attractive woman, she is a "mistake of nature," as her family calls her, in a society that worships beauty. Jenny Blair observes Etta's misery, comparing it to what she believes is the happiness of the lovely Eva Birdsong, her idol.

The structure of the novel reveals that Jenny Blair's childhood and youth, described in the first and third sections of the novel, are controlled by her fantasy world: "The Age of Make-Believe" is quite the same as "The Illusion." Like so many Glasgow belles, Jenny Blair has no father; as a child she fantasizes about him continually, keeping a lock of his hair in her locket. Her best friend in childhood is not another child but George Birdsong, the handsome young husband of Eva. When Jenny Blair enters the forbidden part of town where blacks and factory workers live and sees George at the home of Memoria, his mulatto mistress, he swears her to secrecy; to Jenny Blair this is a magic secret that allows George to enter her fantasy life. George tells her she is a beauty and extracts her promise to guard his secret: "With her enraptured gaze on his face, she nodded as vacantly as a doll, because she felt her heart would burst if she spoke a single word" (p. 60). The scene is one of Glasgow's finest pieces of writing. Jenny Blair does not realize that George has been physically unfaithful to Eva, and Glasgow's use of irony at this point makes it clear that George has visited his mistress but preserves our impression of Jenny Blair's childhood innocence. Jenny Blair will become corrupted by that innocence because it mutates into a blind refusal to "see" life as it is. The narrator's attitude in the scene is gentle toward Jenny Blair and respectful toward Memoria, but severe toward George, who has begun Jenny Blair's corruption.

When Jenny Blair grows into womanhood, she has no interest whatever in eligible young men near her age. She is also "not interested in character"; like many Glasgow belles, Jenny Blair has observed that in romantic novels, which feed her fantasy life, character and integrity in a person often interrupt the love story. More important is her now blatant Electra complex: "I like older men best," she says, because they are more romantic. John, a young man, keeps reminding her of unpleasant realities like the chemical factory nearby, whose noxious fumes are intermingling with the sweet magnolia scents in her neighborhood. John accuses her of not caring for the poverty of the plant's workers nor for the encroachment of the industrial machine in the Edenic gardens of the South, but only for herself:

"You are like every other young girl who has grown up without coming in touch with the world. You are so bottled up inside that your imagination has turned into a hothouse for sensation" (pp. 338–39).[36] The metaphor of Jenny Blair's inner garden and its pollution coalesces Glasgow's mythic and psychological insights: corruption comes from within. The serpent lies within the inner garden of each of us. No longer a determinist, Glasgow adopts the more classic sense of character as fate.

The Sheltered Life is a tour-de-force demonstration of irony, Glasgow's forte. The closeted life, part of southern tradition and designed to produce the pure, ideal woman, in fact results in a belle who becomes increasingly corrupt. Jenny Blair's passion for George becomes an obsession; she must see him every day. She has no will at all to refuse his furtive kisses; she has never been taught, in fact, to exercise her judgment. She is prey to her sexual instincts without benefit of intellect or reflection to curb them.

In contrast to Jenny Blair, Eva Birdsong is the belle of the nineties. Like the canaries owned by Amanda and Victoria, she has a lovely singing voice. She is the last remnant of the past, a legend even in her life; Jenny Blair's grandfather is certain that even in death, Eva's "skeleton will have beauty" (p. 188). As a young belle, Eva believed that love was all-important and, in her one moment of passion, eloped with the virile but dissolute George, whose unfaithfulness becomes a constant source of suffering to Eva. The last champion of the code that she symbolizes, she suffers silently, shields George, and worries obsessively about her waning beauty. She must undergo a disfiguring operation for an unnamed disease and believes that she will then lose her beauty, the one attribute that keeps George with her.

Eva is associated with a once lovely garden, now overgrown by weeds and mold: "All Mrs. Birdsong had meant, the charm, the spirit, the blossoming wildness, could be measured by the blight that had fallen on the place" (p. 349). Eva needs the care and attention of a faithful gardener, which George is not. Like a statue of "carved ivory," she smiles hysterically even when in pain from her illness or from George's behavior. As a work of art, she has fulfilled her role as woman on a pedestal, but the reader sees her utter misery as she struggles to continue in it, becoming increasingly disoriented until her speech rambles incoherently. The southern Eden, Glasgow implies, is overgrown and diseased because of the self-indulgence of its men. In Eva, Glasgow presents her most complete portrait of the deterioration of the nineteenth-century southern belle and, indeed, southern traditions.

As Eva weakens, Jenny Blair, whom Glasgow describes as a small feral animal waiting to pounce on a wounded bird, becomes more bold. She visits the Birdsongs, purportedly to see the ailing Eva, and is able to avoid guilt over her half-conscious attraction to George by denying to herself that she intends any wrong. When she thinks of George, "that glow, that flame that ecstasy . . . beat over her in waves" (p. 354). She is impelled to make a physical overture, seeing him as "the victim of some mysterious power which made her the stronger" (p. 354). As George embraces Jenny, the imagery again suggests the sexual ecstasy that has characterized her fantasies: "Once more the shower of light rained through her being. Once more the sky fell, and the last sunbeam crashed and splintered over the red lilies" (p. 334).

Glasgow handles the imagery of Jenny Blair's depravity with surgical precision: Jenny Blair's sexual impulses seize her with "vulture-like claws," which she uses to clutch George in Eva's own house. It is a splendid scene, Glasgow's best in all her work, an ending worthy of Greek tragedy. George enters carrying beautiful wild ducks he has killed, exulting over his kill. Jenny Blair embraces him, and Eva enters to witness the scene. In her swan song of belledom, Eva does the only thing she has been trained to do: she pretends not to have seen them. Jenny's lust having been revealed, she stands ashamed and then runs out "like a small animal looking for a hole" (p. 391). Eva grasps George's rifle and kills him. When Jenny returns and sees George lying among his ducks, she "began to scream with the sharp cry of an animal caught in a trap" (p. 394). As her grandfather comforts Jenny Blair in the sheltering arms of the old order he represents, she repeats hysterically, "I didn't mean anything in the world" (p. 395).

Jenny's selfishness has brought about Eva's insanity and George's death. She is reckless, irresponsible, and annihilating. She is the last of the belles Glasgow depicts in her fiction, and the worst of them. In Jenny Blair Glasgow unites her two major themes that define the southern belle in fiction: the nineteenth-century belle as the victim of tradition and the modern belle as a victim of her own narcissism. Jenny Blair combines both motifs, for her sheltered childhood has given rise to the sexual fantasies that pervert her. She is ultimately as perverse as Temple Drake in William Faulkner's *Sanctuary* (1931),

for, like Temple, she is a force of destruction in the lives of the innocent people around her. After *The Sheltered Life*, the admirable women
in Glasgow's novels are no longer belles but middle- and lower-class
women, as in *Vein of Iron* (1935) and *In This Our Life* (1941). With
Jenny Blair, Glasgow strips away the glittering facade of the southern
belle to reveal a soulless specter of death. *The Sheltered Life* is her
most bitter indictment of southern tradition.

8

William Faulkner and the Destruction of Narcissus

In the fiction of William Faulkner, the southern belle recurs as an unforgettable character. Her beauty, her status as the daughter of a local aristocrat, and her fallen innocence comprise her central characteristics in Faulkner's works and in those of many other authors of the Southern Renaissance. But unlike most authors of the 1920s and 1930s, who use the belle figure in only one or two novels, Faulkner creates a comprehensive vision by portraying an abundance of belles who live in both the nineteenth and the twentieth centuries. Moreover, Faulkner's belles are unique because he realizes that the relationship of narcissism, repression, and masochism, qualities that previous writers had emphasized separately, forms the controlling matrix of the belle's personality. And Faulkner's belles represent the most self-conscious and comprehensive culmination of the long tradition of associating the belle and all her faults with the South.

Faulkner's method in accomplishing these tasks is that of a historian; he studies the belle as an institution in southern society. If we look at the belle figure in Faulkner's works chronologically—that is, according to the period in which the novel is set, not the date it was written—we discover a complex critique of the vacuousness of southern values and an identification of the forces that led to the degeneration of southern ideals. Drusilla Hawkes in *The Unvanquished* (1938) is a belle during the Civil War. Caroline Compson in *The Sound and the Fury* (1929) lives through World War I until at least 1928. The most important events in the life of Candace Compson, Caroline's daughter, take place from about 1900 to 1910, before World War I. Cecily Saunders, in *Soldier's Pay* (1926), is a belle in the years immediately after World War I. Narcissa Benbow's activities in *Sartoris* (1929), *Sanctuary* (1931), and "There Was a Queen" (1932) span the period 1920–30. *Sanctuary* (1930) and *Requiem for a Nun* (1951) follow Temple Drake from approximately 1930 to 1938.

Definitions: Cecily in *Soldier's Pay*

In his first novel with a belle character, *Soldier's Pay* (1926), Faulkner defines the belle's stereotyped personality traits by exaggerating them. He particularly notes that the narcissism of the belle can lead her to become a cold, self-involved young woman whose obsessive craving for attention has injurious effects on the men around her as well as herself. Cecily Saunders seems conventional enough; she dresses in white, she has idle, useless hands and a character "as graceful and insincere as a French sonnet."[1] Her one concern is obtaining the attention of men, a condoned pastime, to be sure. However, Cecily's flirtatiousness is exaggerated and compulsive. She is engaged to one man and in love with another; she flirts with any and all men, including her father.

Faulkner carefully defines the core of narcissism in the belle by showing three main manifestations of it. First, Cecily concentrates on developing only the traits of coquettishness, to the exclusion of all other qualities in her character. Second, she cannot form loving relationships with men. Third, she is essentially passionless and asexual, and she attempts to preserve her body, on which her sense of self is based, from the changes that might be wrought by sex and pregnancy. These qualities are typical in women who have become fixed in the childhood phase, when excessive self-love is normal. Moving beyond this phase was not encouraged for southern girls; the beauty ethic discouraged it, and the development of a personality that would win a man was the psychic priority.

Cecily is the successful end product of such an upbringing. Her fragile, slim body governs her sense of self-esteem. Her room is dominated by a "triple-mirrored dresser," and Cecily often lies on her bed, "running her fingers lightly over her breasts, across her belly, drawing concentric circles upon her body beneath the covers" (pp. 142–43). But, as Karen Horney writes, a narcissist is never content unless she has the admiration of others as another type of mirror in which to admire herself,[2] so Cecily craves masculine attention and develops her abilities to manipulate men. She has been able to practice these skills from girlhood, her main audience being her father, the oedipal object of her attentions at age five. In young adulthood, she manipulates him with a seductiveness that has lost its girlish innocence. When her father attempts to reprimand her, for example, she poses seductively on her bed, and he quickly forgets the point of his lecture.

Skimpily dressed even in public, Cecily incorporates the postwar morality of the flapper, "the cult of boldness in women" (p. 76), as the narrator calls it, as a useful variant of traditional coquetry. She speaks as provocatively as she dresses, shocking one young man by saying, "You intend to kiss me and yet you are going to all of this damn trouble about it." In spite of her forwardness, he soon realizes she has no intention of yielding to him, the correct behavior certainly for a belle. When the young man calls her a bitch, she taunts, "It's funny how few men know that women like to be talked to in that way" (p. 78). Ironically, however, Cecily essentially follows her community's injunction that belles be flirtatious but pure; she conforms to the traditional mores. She is not "sexually insatiable," as Maxwell Geismar claims.[3] On the contrary, she is properly repressed and essentially remote toward men, wishing only for them to worship her.

Her need for the admiration of others to reinforce her sense of worth explains her revulsion at the disfigurement of Donald, her fiancé. It is as though she sees in his face a hideous reflection of herself. Because her narcissism is based on her body, she is anxious about anything that would alter it; any change in her body would entail an adjustment in her sense of self. Like a "slim, jeweled" animal, a cat or a tiger, like a "flower stalk or a young tree," she is solely "a body created for all men to dream after," not for maternity or love but "a thing for the eye and the mind" (pp. 142–43). While Cecily represents the romantic illusions of the novel's men—who wish her to be a work of art, as Sally R. Page writes in *Faulkner's Women*—she is also prey to her own illusions.[4] As she caresses her body in a fashion suggesting masturbation, she wonders "how it would feel to have a baby, hating that inevitable time when she'd have to have one, blurring her slim epicenity, blurring her body with pain" (pp. 142–43). Thus, while Cecily embodies the qualities of beauty and charm that her community prefers in women, these qualities result in her rejection of sexuality because of her narcissistic desire to preserve the body on which she bases her sense of self. Cecily appears as an idealization in the eyes of men who are so captivated by her appearance that they ignore her inner emptiness.

Narcissism and Destruction: Narcissa in *Sartoris*

After the garden, the most important and ubiquitous symbol in southern literature is the mirror. It is not the mirror of the eighteenth-century Enlightenment, which was the symbol of the artistic mission of reflection or imitation of nature, as noted by Meyer Abrams. The mirror in southern literature refers to images of one's self, self-portraits in the pool of Narcissus. The self-love and vanity of that beautiful young man, his indifference to the world except as it reflected himself, his infantile impulse to kiss the lovely reflection, and his death powerfully inform southerners about their own pride in their civilization, their indifference to the world at large, their impulsiveness, and their fall. Narcissism so pervades the culture that its embodiment in the southern belle character is only one of many manifestations—but the most important of them, because symbolically the fall of Narcissus is linked to the fall of man.

Pride and vanity are ancient sins of Eve. Genesis does not specifically mention vanity—that is, pride in personal beauty—as the Edenic sin, but the desire to take on God's attributes would include beauty; and the sin of the Fall bespeaks a resentment that God possesses these qualities and humans do not. Another tale like those of Eve's jealousy and Narcissus's vanity is the story of Snow White and the wicked Queen. The Queen was the most beautiful in the land and consulted her mirror daily, so vain that she could not tolerate the thought that any other mortal should be as lovely. As Bruno Bettelheim writes in *The Uses of Enchantment*, the rage the Queen feels, and her command to kill Snow White, reveal the deep amoral center of the narcissist, who might like Narcissus destroy herself, but who treats others with equal destructiveness.[5] The world, if it is not an admirer, is a threat, a rival to be eliminated. Hence the narcissist-belle who is intolerant at best, murderous at worst, becomes a possible characterization for the author who is dissecting the belle character. Myth and fairy tale embody the psychological reality of narcissism.

Narcissa Benbow in Faulkner's *Sartoris* (1929) envies and destroys as effectively as any belle in literature. Faulkner's portrait is subtle; he builds from a conventional description of a pretty, innocuous girl to show her true self, as if in a mirror that reflects her character as well as her body. Narcissa is described as a conventional belle; she has violet eyes, wears a white dress, and possesses a face as serene as the "tranquil repose of lilies."[6] Unlike Cecily in Faulkner's earlier *Soldier's*

Pay, she is oddly calm and withdrawn, not at all like the flappers of the 1920s, the era in which she lives. Her brother, Horace, incorrectly interprets this quietness as serene purity.

Narcissa has adopted a pose of serenity for a number of reasons. First, she wishes to conceal her fear of all men (except her brother). Second, she wants to avoid thinking or feeling, and she uses books as a narcotic; as she reads, "she again held her consciousness submerged deliberately, as you would hold a puppy under water until its struggles ceased" (p. 133). The only warmth she allows herself is directed toward her brother, with whom she has a "crippling and morbid relationship," as Robert Penn Warren has pointed out,[7] for she cannot love any man but him. His attention must be hers exclusively; he is her mirror and whatever deflects his attention from her she is compelled to destroy.

Wishing to fulfill Horace's illusion of the purity of womanhood, Narcissa tries to maintain what Olga Vickery calls her "illusion of her own innocence."[8] She also wishes to avoid feeling altogether in order to anesthetize the pain caused by the death of her fiancé. When Bayard, her fiancé's brother, courts her, she responds hysterically: "The Beast, the Beast."

Because Narcissa denies and represses the sexual side of her nature, her interest in sexuality emerges in a perverted form. She passively participates in a bizarre sort of violation; when she receives anonymous obscene letters from a bank cashier, Byron Snopes, instead of telling her brother about these letters she hides them in her bureau with her lingerie. She struggles to reconcile her illusions of her own purity with her sexual fantasies: "her nature torn in two directions and the walls of her serene garden cast down and she herself like a night animal caught in a beam of light and trying vainly to escape" (p. 24).

In a scene in which imagery suggests a rape that never physically occurs, Byron use a long pole to climb onto the balcony, slashes the screen door with his knife, enters Narcissa's room, lies down on her bed, and writhes and moans as if he were raping her. He then removes the letters from her drawer and buries his face in her underclothes. Although violence is only suggested, the scene implies that the class system of the South, which prevents Byron from being able to court and marry Narcissa, has brought about a situation in which daughters of the gentry are available to working-class men only through violent rape. Narcissa has in a sense participated in the "rape" by not contacting the police about the letters, not destroying them, not telling anyone but her Aunt Jenny about them, by placing them with her lingerie, and by absolutely enjoying the masculine attention that the letters represent. While she is not a coquette, and while she is afraid of her sexuality, she nevertheless finds masculine attention in any form to be flattering. Jenny Du Pre, her aunt by marriage, perceives the reality of the situation: "Just like a young fool woman, to be flattered by a thing like this . . . . We are all convinced that men feel that way about us and we can't help but admire the one that's got the courage to tell us, no matter who he is" (p. 70). Narcissa's only concern is that other people might read these letters. She sees no hypocrisy in her outrage over a scented letter that Horace carries, a letter from Belle Mitchell, a woman of whom she disapproves: "You've got the smell of her all over you. Oh, Horry, she's dirty!" (p. 167).

In *Sanctuary* (1931) Narcissa is unmasked as the selfish, hypocritical woman that her name implies. Now a widow with a ten-year-old son, Narcissa is shocked that her brother wishes to help Ruby Goodwin, an unwed mother. "You're just meddling," she cries, and then lashes out at him for all his "offenses": "When you took another man's wife and child away from him I thought it was just dreadful . . . when you just walked out of the house like a nigger and left her I thought that was dreadful too."[9] Narcissa implies that she tolerated these faults because Horace committed them in another town. When he returns to open their house in Jefferson, she is aghast that he could have scrubbed it himself with "all the town looking on." To take Ruby into her house, however in need Ruby might be, is the sort of moral action that a woman concerned only with appearances cannot perform. As Jenny explains to Horace, "Do you think Narcissa'd want anyone to know that any of her folks could know people that would do anything as natural as make love or rob or steal?" (p. 115). Narcissa's concern for social appearance precludes her acceptance of human sympathy, warmth, or natural desires. Thus Faulkner expands his notions of narcissism. Narcissa is as obsessed with social appearance as Cecily in *Soldier's Pay* was obsessed with physical appearance.

When a murder is committed, Narcissa decides that Lee Goodwin, Ruby's common-law husband, is guilty; when she learns that Horace will be the defense attorney at Goodwin's trial, she rebukes Horace: "Anybody but you would realize it's a case of coldblooded murder" (p. 134). In order to preserve her reputation and his as members of a refined, genteel family, she cooperates with the district attorney to be certain that her brother will lose the case. She cares neither for Horace's feelings nor for Goodwin's right to be defended and judged fairly. Ironically, she has aligned herself with the same "good people" of the town who eventually lynch Goodwin. Her concern for her public image and that of her brother is the externalization of her narcissism; she wants to control the reflections that people see of her—in other words, she tries to control the mirror.

Narcissa's behavior results not from what Sally Page calls "childishness"[10] but from her obsessive attempts to conform to the set of traditional characteristics of the belle. In the short story "There Was a Queen" (1932), Faulkner finally reveals Narcissa as the opposite of the genteel southern lady she pretends to be. In this story, Narcissa lives with Jenny Du Pre at the Sartoris estate ten years after the action in *Sartoris*. Mimicking the qualities of chastity and spirituality a lady is required to embody, Narcissa dresses only in white. The reader learns that Narcissa did indeed marry Bayard without loving him; she wanted simply to obtain his money and to console herself for the marriage of her brother to Belle Mitchell.

Devoid of warmth, kindness, or integrity, Narcissa will pay any price to preserve her appearance in the eyes of society, which is still her chief concern in life. When she learns that the letters from Byron, which could damage her image as a lady, are in the hands of a Yankee lawyer, she pays for them by having sexual relations with the lawyer. Thus, her ultimate hypocrisy: she willingly becomes a whore to maintain her image as a lady. Elnora, a black servant in the house, is undeceived by Narcissa's facade of gentility; Elnora calls Narcissa "town trash" compared to Jenny, whom Elnora describes as "quality." Another servant, Isom, remarks, "Look to me like Miss Narcissa good quality as anybody else. . . . I don't see no difference." Elnora replies, "Born Sartoris or born quality of any kind ain't *is*, it's *does*."[11] Narcissa, by her actions, has rejected the inner qualities deserving of admiration and has substituted for them a set of appearances. Narcissa is willing to see an innocent man lynched, to prostitute herself, and to marry for money, in order to conform to societal codes that place reputation above morality. The hollowness of these codes is revealed in Faulkner's stark critique of the degeneration of southern values.

Narcissism cripples nearly all of Faulkner's belles. In the short story "Elly" (1934), our first glimpse of Elly occurs as she stands before her mirror. Her room is scattered with cosmetics and dance programs, trophies of her ability to conquer men. She paints her face to prepare for her evening trysts with a variety of boyfriends. But, true to the code of repression, Elly never allows sexual intercourse. She pursues men, however, and finally succumbs to one of them, Paul, because she wishes to hurt her grandmother; when she learns that Paul may have black ancestry, she exults, "A nigger. A nigger, I wonder what she would say if she knew about that."[12]

When her grandmother observes her lying in the bushes with Paul, Elly assumes that she will expose her to her parents, but she assumes too much and blurts out her guilt. Elly believes that something is wrong with her and that her grandmother, "whose sight nothing escapes," knows in some mysterious way of her inner depravity, or can "see" within her. What seems to be a commonplace adolescent anxiety is revealed to be a guilty obsession.

When Elly has sexual relations with Paul, she believes, in her naive way, that he is a man of honor who will marry her afterward. As a narcissist she wants to see only positive reflections of herself in others and to have others respond only to the facade she has adopted as her "self." Believing that she is inwardly evil for indulging in sexual behavior, she projects onto her grandmother her own self-condemnation. Her grandmother may indeed be a representative of a harsh social expectation, but Elly's delusions—that her grandmother "sees" all—make her yearn to eliminate this imagined threat. In the final scene, Elly seizes the wheel of Paul's car and causes the deaths of Paul and her grandmother. Even as she lies injured, she seems unremorseful and concerned only with herself; she whimpers, "They [the passing motorists] won't even stop to see if I'm hurt" (p. 224). In this story the narcissism of a belle leads both to the destruction of her ability to distinguish reality from illusion and to the destruction of others. No inner ethical system and no capacity for love control Elly's unrepressed sexual desires. Simple freedom from sexual repression is not the answer for the dilemma of a southern belle in the twentieth century.

From Narcissist to Masochist: Temple Drake
in *Sanctuary*

In "William Faulkner and the Myth of Woman," D. E. Brien offers a sociological view of Faulkner's women that can be applied to Temple Drake in *Sanctuary* (1931): "His treatment of the theme [of the spotless southern woman] suggests that as long as men cling to their myth of women, women remain essentially abstractions, objects, things to be used. Until the myth is abandoned, neither men nor women will achieve self-identity. Meanwhile adult, mutual, heterosexual relationships are an impossibility, and society is left with no other option than to continue to pursue its sick and self-destructive course."[13]

Applying this highly suggestive approach to Temple Drake reveals that she is indeed a product of a society that has programmed her to conform to the feminine stereotype of the coquette, and her resulting narcissism impels her inevitably to adopt the behavior patterns of masochism. The child who is treated as a beautiful object begins to define herself as a beautiful object. As Simone de Beauvoir has pointed out, when a woman's self-image is that of an object, not a person, she can expect others to treat her accordingly.[14] According to Karen Horney, the coquette who sees herself as an object may develop masochistic patterns of behavior in which she seeks out those people who will use her as an object.[15] This syndrome, readily observable in Temple's behavior, explains a good deal of this behavior, which has baffled some critics.[16]

Temple has been reared in accordance with her society's emphasis on feminine beauty. As the only girl in a household of her father and four brothers, she has had ample opportunity to practice her coquetry. She must learn coquetry because her goal in this society is to attract a "suitable" husband but not to lose her virginity until she marries him. Therefore, she represses her sexual desire for men of her own social class; by the time she enters college, she finds she is not attracted to southern gentlemen. When she is stranded at a ruined plantation after an auto accident, however, Temple encounters a group of men who are not governed by the code of chivalry. That the setting for much of the action is a dilapidated plantation is an ironic comment on what has become of the plantation society. The bootleggers who now inhabit the place are oblivious to the belle in their midst; they prefer the frank sexuality of a woman like Ruby Lamar. Temple tries to flirt with the worst of these men, Popeye, on whom she bestows a "grimace of taut, toothless coquetry"; but Popeye ignores her (p. 56).

To the coquette, nothing is more abhorrent than to be ignored. Temple's thirst for attention becomes bizarrely exaggerated; she runs hysterically back and forth in front of the house in a "narcissistic rage," the frenzy or tantrum associated with the narcissist who has exhausted all other means of attracting attention. Since Temple's sense of self is based on attention, her fear of what may happen to her at the plantation is mingled with the anxiety of a person whose basic personality is being severely challenged. And, as Olga Vickery observes, Temple is "caught between her longing for the safety of her own world and her desire to share in the 'adventure' of this new one."[17]

Ruby Lamar correctly identifies the syndrome of the "honest woman" who is really a tease: "Take all you can get and give nothing. 'I am a pure girl; I don't do that' . . . just let a man so much as look at you and you faint away because your father the judge and your four brothers might not like it" (p. 55). Temple's moral sense, as Ruby implies, is acquired, not innate. Her family is her conscience, and in the present situation Temple is without her protectors, without a moral sense of her own, and is thus stripped down to a state of vacuous confusion. Ruby continues, "You have never seen a real man. . . . You're just *scared* of it [sex] . . . if he is man enough to call you whore, you'll say Yes Yes and you'll crawl naked in the dirt and the mire for him to call you that" (p. 57). Ruby realizes that to a coquette, even humiliation from a "real man" would be a type of attention; she thus predicts Temple's subsequent masochistic behavior.

Temple's sense of her own value is measured only by men's reactions to her coquetry. If they ignore her, her fragile ego crumbles, and she becomes hysterical in her attempts to get attention. However, the only value she can acquire as a coquette is the hollow, materialistic value of an object. As Simone de Beauvoir states:

> the narcissist finds it impossible to admit that others are not passionately interested in her; if she has manifest proof that she is not adored, she imagines at once that she is hated. . . . the role of narcissist is played at the expense of reality; an imaginary character solicits the admiration of an imaginary public; a woman infatuated with her ego loses all hold on the actual world, she has no concern to establish a real relation with others. . . . when she talks, she is speaking a part, when she dresses, she dresses a part.[18]

Temple is as constantly concerned with her costume as an actress; her make-up and clothing are repeatedly mentioned. Even when she is waiting to be raped by Popeye, she takes out a compact and fluffs her hair, all the time watching her own face intently (p. 84). The ritual of adornment is preparation for the titillation of men; she prepares for Popeye as she would primp in her dormitory room before a college dance: "The air would be steamy with recent baths, and perhaps powder in the light like chaff in barn lofts. . . . Shoulders smelling of scented soap and the light powder in the air and their eyes like knives" (pp. 181–82).

Temple's narcissism also explains her tendency to watch herself with unusual detachment. At the beginning of the novel, her blank, cold eyes "watched Gowan slip his arm into hers and the fleet revelation of flank and thigh as she got into her car" (p. 33). When she is hysterically running in front of the old plantation, she sees a man watching her and pauses like Cinderella: "For an instant she stood and watched herself run out of her body, out of one slipper. She watched her legs twinkle against the sand, . . . then whirl and run back and snatch up the slipper and whirl and run again" (p. 109). Ironically, the man for whom she is performing is blind.

Even as she waits to be raped, Temple charts her experience; she listens carefully to her heart pounding, feels her nostrils expanding, sees her skin jerking under Popeye's touch. She feels absolutely important: "Now I am. I am now" (p. 260). For Temple the moment of sexual violation creates her as a being; the act that she has anticipated all her life, her initiation into womanhood, has come at last, and she is not about to miss an instant of it. She has been carefully taught to await the lover who will possess her, and as a woman she wants this lover, although he comes to her not with love and understanding but with violence and perversion.[19] Later, Temple even relates the actual rape to Horace Benbow with macabre enjoyment and fascination: "Horace realized she was recounting the experience with actual pride, a sort of naive and impersonal vanity" (p. 259). While she may be horrifying Horace, she is pleasing herself. Once again she is at the center of the stage, captivating her audience as the charming, vivacious coquette.

Temple's narcissism even accounts for her numbed fascination with the immediate result of her defloration, her blood. Sitting in Popeye's car on her way to Memphis, Temple listens "to the hot minute seeping of her blood, saying dully to herself, I'm still bleeding, I'm still bleeding" (p. 163). When Popeye continues to ignore her, hysteria overtakes her pain, and she screams. Popeye—something of a psychologist-sadist—reminds her of her appearance. Temple must maintain her coquettish facade; she immediately stops crying and dabs powder on her face and freshens her lipstick (p. 165). She now begins to exhibit another crucial personality trait, submissiveness. When Popeye hands her a sandwich, she gets in the car "quietly" and eats "obediently" (p. 165). Her wifely, passive submission to Popeye indicates her acceptance of the fact that she now belongs to him.

The narcissist, who has all her life been an object, whose ego has been formed by others, who has been admired from afar, becomes a masochist by submitting herself as an object to be used and disposed of by others. The dynamics of the personality of the masochistic female have long been a topic for the psychoanalytic treatise. Freud's orientation to this topic is biological; he reasons that masochism is the result of woman's anatomical destiny. For the woman, the onset of menstruation as the mark of her womanhood is accompanied by pain. Her first sexual relations are also marked by pain. And the supreme task of woman, to give birth, is nine months of discomfort and pain. Thus, Freud concludes, woman's sexual pleasure is allied so closely with genital pain that the two become inseparable. The female usually accepts this fusion of pleasure and pain; if she does not, she will assert her frustrated desire to avoid all these essential female acts by coveting the phallus. When she discovers that she cannot, she will try to destroy the male.[20]

Karen Horney points out that these theories are not substantiated in the majority of *normal* females; furthermore, the desire for a penis in young girls may be cultural, not part of the innate unfolding of the personality.[21] (She does admit that, while Freud's orientation over-emphasizes the role of anatomy, he is correct when he points out that masochism seems to be more frequent in women than in men in modern society.[22]) Because Temple's behavior conforms to the five traits of the masochist identified by Horney (see chapter 7), heretofore baffling passages in *Sanctuary* become clear. Temple is inhibited in expressing demands and aggression, particularly in regard to her sexual desires. Required by her society to be the virgin-coquette, she punishes herself for having desires that are not consonant with her societal role. Her taunting abuse of Gowan and her demands for attention at the plantation show the inhibition placed on her by society, an inhibition against the normal enjoyment of one's sexuality.

Second, Temple regards herself as a helpless creature, demanding special favors as a result. Throughout her life she has been treated with the deference due a well-brought-up young lady; at the same time, however, she is allowed to make no important decisions by herself. Thus she is convinced that she is weaker than men and must depend upon them. She needs Gowan to take her to Oxford, to protect her at the plantation; when he abandons her, she comforts herself by chanting that her father is a judge, as though verbalizing this dependency will protect her.

Third—just as Temple has been dependent on her father's social position to protect her—she becomes completely dependent upon Popeye. Consequently, she remains at the brothel, at first in an almost trancelike state, passive and meek: "Lying on her back, legs close together, she began to cry, hopelessly and passively, like a child in a dentist's waiting-room" (p. 179). Fulfilling Horney's fourth criterion, she allows Popeye to use and exploit her. Her only reaction to the way he has treated her is crying, which ends her lethargy. Anticipating his arrival at the brothel, she reveals that she is still the coquette: "her movements were jerky; she smoked swiftly, moving about the room . . . spying herself in the mirror. . . . She turned before it, studying herself" (p. 275).

The fifth characteristic of the masochist is "a using of weakness and helplessness as a means of wooing and subduing the other sex."[23] Temple uses helplessness to control the men she encounters. Although she hardly moves from her bed during her first days in Memphis, her sexuality is beginning to develop; after a few days, she not only submits to Popeye but desires him. She calls him "Daddy" (p. 284) not only as a manifestation of an Electra complex but also because she acknowledges his superiority to her, his authority as a man, and her consequent helplessness.

Thus, as a masochist Temple wishes to be made a thing for others' use, "To see herself as a thing, to play at being a thing."[24] Southern society will allow no alternative. Her ego, divided by the dualistic emphasis on coquetry and premarital virginity, is fragile and weak. It is barely capable of supporting a personality and, as interpreted by Allen Tate, is dominated by compulsions beyond her control.[25] Temple's behavior after her rape can be explained by de Beauvoir's observation that "Masochism perpetuates the presence of the ego in a bruised and degraded condition."[26] Thus masochism is also Temple's ghastly defense mechanism against the attitudes with which her society has nourished her. Her violent actions against herself begin long before rape, for even her behavior with Gowan and her other young men seems to indicate a girl with no goals or purpose in her life, who is quite willing to take rides in cars with dangerous people, to court danger, to invite destruction. Away from home perhaps for the first time, she is exposed to a college atmosphere with fairly liberal attitudes toward sex, which contradict her stern upbringing. Her desire for sex, forbidden by society yet so easily available, may cause Temple to feel guilty because she thinks that her desires make her no better than a prostitute, an attitude often observed in young girls of strict backgrounds.[27]

Temple, of course, not only feels like a prostitute but becomes one. Her sexuality, awakened so grotesquely, mutates into the grossest nymphomania. Temple will force others to treat her as a sexual object, not merely by revealing her legs as she gets into a car or by "running her legs off" in the presence of men as she does at the plantation, but by hysterically demanding a man's attentions: "She felt long shuddering waves of physical desire going over her, draining the color from her mouth, drawing her eyeballs back into her skull in shuddering swoon. . . . She began to say Ah-ah-ah-ah- in an expiring voice, her body arching slowly backward . . . her hips grinding against him, her mouth gaping in straining protrusion" (p. 231–32). For Temple to be the perfect carnal object, her ego must be entirely annihilated, her humanness obliterated. And this is precisely what happens. Her eyes grow dark, sink back "into her skull above a half moon of white, without focus, with the blank rigidity of a statue's eyes, . . . saliva running pale over her bloodless lips" (p. 233). She goads—"Are you afraid?"—and finally begs: "Please. Please. Please. Please. Don't make me wait. I'm burning up" (p. 287). She looks and desires as an animal does; now she is totally nonhuman and completely an object, a ghastly statue without a pedestal.

Finally, Temple's masochistic need to be exploited can also account for her perjury at the trial of Lee Goodwin, a man she knows to be innocent. She is quite willing to leave the responsibility for justice in the hands of the men at the trial. She does not acknowledge that saving Goodwin's life is her responsibility, because she has been taught that she is incapable of being responsible for anyone, even for herself. Her father has been the moral authority in her life; and his presence in the courtroom only reinforces this attitude. Temple's "detached and cringing" demeanor at the trial reminds the gallant men in the room that she is too fragile to defend herself. When the district attorney asks her name and she replies inaudibly, he condescendingly entreats her: "Speak out. No one will hurt you. Let these good men, these fathers and husbands, hear what you have to say and right your wrong for you" (p. 341). Ironically, these men represent the source of Temple's "wrong"; the district attorney calls the subject of the trial one of the "most sacred affairs of the most sacred thing in life: womanhood" (p. 340). Completely seduced by the very myths they have invented, the men at the trial assume that Temple could not possibly be at fault; no proper southern woman consents to being raped, to being kept as a prostitute, and to being party to unspeakable perversions.[28]

Faulkner's final portrait of Temple and her father captures in miniature Temple's dehumanization: she sits in "an attitude of childish immobility," like a drugged person, beside her father, personifying all her society's expectations of her as a female, "in shrinking and rapt abasement" (p. 347). Her father is her final torturer, her first and last subduer. As she was acquiescent to Popeye, so she was and is to her father. At the end of the novel, in Luxembourg Gardens, she sits serene, passive, bored, primping in her mirror, studying her face. She is like the music floating in the air, "prone and vanquished in the embrace of . . . rain and death" (p. 380).

The Narcissist as Mother: Caroline Compson and Family Honor

In *The Sound and the Fury* (1929), Faulkner presents a daughter of the gentry who must "save face" for her family at all costs and hence represents the most pernicious aspects of traditional honor. A southern woman traditionally displayed extravagant pride in her family's lineage; the need to uphold the "name" of the family was the sacred trust of women in the South, a society based on honor, not law. As Bertram Wyatt-Brown writes in his comprehensive and definitive study *Southern Honor: Ethics and Behavior in the Old South*, women were the "heroines and arbiters of male honor"; woman's role was to remind her male relatives of their duty to redress wrongs by using physical violence. In this archaic code, individual status depended entirely on the group's opinion.[29]

Caroline Compson, who lives approximately from 1890 to 1929, is of the next generation after Drusilla in *The Unvanquished*, who upheld the code to the letter. Unlike Drusilla, Caroline has never experienced a war, which inspired Drusilla to become a priestess of honor, but Caroline nonetheless conforms to the notion that a woman must be the guardian of her family's good name. Her belief that a lady is chaste, refined, fragile, and must be sheltered and fiercely protected by doting southern gentlemen not only warps her personality but contributes to the destruction of her husband and children.

Her insistence upon the fragile state of her health and her need to be coddled by her family indicate the self-concern that blinds her to the needs and desires of her family and prevents her from responding to them with warmth. As a narcissist she can "see" only herself, not others. She fails to acknowledge or to understand the mental retardation of her son Benjy, who is the antithesis of the physically superior male her society prefers. Caroline denies Benjy's condition; she orders her daughter, Caddy, to take away Benjy's cushion (without which he always cries): "Take that cushion away . . . he must learn to mind."[30] Her insensitivity toward Benjy is matched by her antipathy toward another son, Quentin. Even after Quentin commits suicide, she insists that he did so simply to "flout and hurt" her; otherwise God would never allow such a thing to happen, because "I'm a lady. You might not believe that from my offspring, but I am" (p. 274). It is not surprising that Quentin feels as if he never had a mother. Caroline gives her children the perfunctory, negative attention that often characterizes narcissistic mothers. Many commentators have noted the "emotional withdrawal" of southern mothers; Wyatt-Brown writes of their dependence, in many cases, on the mammy to mother their children.[31] Caroline never hugs her children, with the exception of Jason, who in her eyes is a Bascomb like herself and thus a reflection of herself.

Her hypochondria is a typical symptom of the narcissist, her headaches and spells of weakness obvious bids for attention. Clinically, such symptoms have been defined as hysteria, the term Freud used to describe the extreme conditions of his patients. The term *hysteria* connotes the erroneous pre-Freudian notion that any female's depression, anger, protest, or even sexual desire might be a result of the "womb" disease (the rough translation of *hysteria*). As applied to the belle, the Freudian usage is appropriate, however. The hysterics he treated often displayed a coquettish flirtatiousness that was paradoxically accompanied by a strict, unyielding repression and moral code. The coquettish exterior masks a "cold calculating quality," writes Otto Kernberg in *Borderline Conditions and Pathological Narcissism*.[32] The symptoms that brought such women to the couches of therapists were a panoply of aches, spells, and pains localized in some symbolically significant part of the body.

As a model of womanhood for her daughter, Caddy, Caroline can offer only negative impressions, for she has no maternal or sexual identity. For example, she never picks up her children for fear she will injure her back, and she reprimands Caddy for carrying Benjy: "All our women have prided themselves on their carriage. Do you want to look like a washerwoman?" (p. 77). Caroline embodies the hypocritical elitism of the old order; she even objects to Caddy's calling her brother "Benjy" because "nicknames are vulgar. Only common people use them" (p. 78).

Like the mothers of many of Ellen Glasgow's belles, Caroline has a pernicious effect on her daughter, who eventually becomes a prostitute. Because Caroline believes "that a woman is either a lady or not" (p. 127), she dons black when her daughter first kisses a man, thereby communicating to Caddy that sexual behavior is the behavior of a "fallen woman." Her obsessive adherence to the social code that allows only two roles for women, lady and whore, eventually leads her to reject her own daughter. She is concerned not with morality but with how Caddy's behavior affects Caroline's own reputation in the community; as her husband says, "whether it be a sin or not has not occurred to her" (p. 126). Caroline believes that Caddy's behavior, like Quentin's, has been intended only to hurt her. When Caroline accuses her granddaughter of "vanity and false pride," it is obvious that these qualities are more apparent in Caroline than in the granddaughter and that Caroline projects her own faults onto others.

Caroline's lack of warmth toward her children and her insistence on the purity of women contribute to her coldness toward her husband. In the story "That Evening Sun," Caroline says her husband's name "Like she believed that all day father had been trying to think of doing the thing she wouldn't like the most, and that after a while he would think of it."[33] She has repressed her desire for sex, the desire she associates with fallen women. Her mock illnesses provide her with excuses to avoid having sexual relations with her husband. As her husband becomes an alcoholic, as her children variously reach out to their mammy, Dilsey, and to Caddy for affection, Caroline systematically disregards their individual problems, desires, and needs. Since her sense of self-worth depends on constant reinforcement from other people, she is profoundly anxious to be surrounded only by people who are like herself. Consequently, she cannot love her own family as they are, and her own personality becomes a mere echo of society's codes.[34]

Southern Rebel: Caddy in *The Sound and the Fury*

If a belle has the desire to love and the courage to discard crippling conventions, she defines herself as a rebel who lives outside the code. Her fate is either to reembrace social norms, as Drusilla does in *The Unvanquished*, or to be a pariah. Indeed, if one chooses not to be a "lady," the only other role (the one that includes *all* other behaviors, as Caroline Compson says) is that of a fallen woman. Candace Compson, called "Caddy" in *The Sound and the Fury* (1929) and in the short story "That Evening Sun" (1932), lives from approximately 1893 to 1943—from the period before World War I through the changes in morality of the twenties and into the years of World War II, when she is last seen as the mistress of a Nazi general. Caddy, like Drusilla in *The Unvanquished*, is a girl of unrepressed passion and courage; torn between the alternatives of becoming a "lady" like her mother or becoming a fallen woman, she chooses the latter. Ironically, rebellion against the code is as self-destructive as conformity to it. Women can't win in southern society, according to Faulkner.

Caddy was "doomed and knew it," as Faulkner writes in his 1945 appendix to *The Sound and the Fury*, the victim of her cold mother and her aloof, nihilistic father. In an interview Faulkner calls Caddy a "fatherless, motherless girl" who tries to escape the home "where she has never been offered love or affection or understanding."[35] Caddy tries to be both mother and father to her brothers. As a mother, she hugs and kisses Benjy, is sensitive to his special needs, and wants to protect him from being sent to an asylum. She is courageous, kind, and unselfish with her love. She also tries to be the authority that her father refuses to be; when Jason maliciously cuts up Benjy's paper dolls, Caddy seeks the retribution Benjy is incapable of obtaining himself. She possesses the ability to love because she has been spared her mother's self-centeredness, perhaps because her brothers need her so much. And she has a positive model of adult womanhood to emulate—her black mammy, Dilsey, who shows Caddy affection, warmth, compassion, and courage. But these qualities are not endorsed by her society as "high status" values for women, and they are embodied in a representative of a race of people without power in that society. Bartlett and Cambor show in "The History and Psychodynamics of Southern Womanhood" that a southern girl's maternal and sexual identities were learned, if at all, from her mammy, not from her childlike mother.

When seven-year-old Caddy climbs a pear tree to witness her grandmother's funeral, she is reenacting the powerful story of Eden. Because the scene is so rich in mythic associations, however, it is easy to overlook the psychological information about Caddie that the scene affords. Caddie learns about death, and her brothers learn about desire as they stare up at her muddy underpants. It is at this moment that Quentin begins to feel longing that would later become sexual, Jason to feel a mixture of jealousy at her bravery and anxiety over her failure to obey her elders. But what does Caddy think? Is she altered by this repetition of the Eden myth? Does she feel ashamed, as did Eve? Is she an Eve who brings knowledge of sex and death into the world? While her brothers are forever changed, Caddy is not changed or corrupted by her new knowledge. She has acted out of her innate courage, her curiosity, her disregard for social taboos, and her athletic and graceful physicality, and these qualities remain intact.

The incident suggests that Caddy is not the repressed little girl her society has traditionally approved. She is outgoing, curious, and defiant; all her emotions are natural and uninhibited by social expectations. She refuses to be sheltered and constantly expresses a desire to understand her surroundings. In "That Evening Sun," perceiving the fear of the Compsons' servant Nancy (who is afraid her estranged husband will kill her), Caddy asks her parents, "Why did she [Nancy] want to go home and bar the door?"[36] It is this same desire to know that causes her to climb the pear tree to witness the funeral of her grandmother.

She is trapped, however, in a world that does not reward girls for curiosity and lack of inhibition. Seeking outside her family for the love that has been denied her, Caddy has sexual relations with Dalton Ames. When Ames reveals that he does not love Caddy, her desperate need for love causes her to confuse sex with affection, which she continues to seek with many partners. Karen Horney, on the relationship between culture and personality, points out that when a person's pursuit of love takes the form of "compulsive and indiscriminate" sexual behavior, the cause may be a desire to gain the affection and esteem, not simply of the sexual partners, but of "the original loved person"[37]—in Caddy's case, perhaps the parental warmth she never experienced. If the reader can trust Quentin's report of her account of her sexual behavior, Caddy's compulsiveness is quite clear: "*I didn't let him, I made him*" (p. 166).

Caddy would doubtless agree with the notion that virginity means even more to southern men than to women. The famous passage in the novel concerning female sexuality does not, however, describe her viewpoint, or Faulkner's for that matter, as some critics have maintained,[38] but that of a southern gentleman who is riddled with anxiety about women and is recalling the words of his father: "Women are so delicate so mysterious Father said. Delicate equilibrium of periodic filth between two moons balanced moons he said . . . Liquid putrefaction life drowned things floating like pane rubber flabbily filled getting the odour of honeysuckle, all mixed up" (p. 159). Quentin Compson, Caddy's brother, is the character who reports this speech. As a narrator, he is not reliable because his memory is shaped by his incestuous desires for his sister, his dearth of love from his mother, his insanity, and the southern code of honor, which dictates that he must avenge Caddy's loss of virginity. The speech probably combines Mr. Compson's point of view with Quentin's anxiety. In any case, Caddy is not delicate or mysterious or monstrous. She is strong and straightforward in a milieu that forbids her these traits.

Caddy begins to lose control over her life as the community whose morality she has defied begins to defeat her. Pregnancy compels her to marry a man she does not love. Herbert, her husband, divorces her when he finds she is pregnant. Her mother and family cast her out. She becomes a prostitute, an end that seems ironically correct since it reduces her love to a commercial exchange, her defiant courage to quivering submission to her brother Jason. In one tragic scene, Jason insinuates that Caddy's daughter will become a streetwalker like her mother and Caddy wants to strike him. Torn between her pride and her realization that she must not offend this man to whom she is entrusting her child, "she acted for a minute like some kind of toy that's wound up too tight and about to burst all to pieces" (p. 260). She yields, knowing that she is incapable of taking care of her own child. As Catherine Baum points out in "'The Beautiful One': Caddy Compson as Heroine of *The Sound and the Fury*," Caddy's ultimate tragedy is that her unselfish capacity for love eventually results in her loss of the ability to love.

3 / Myth and Meaning in the Southern Garden

9

The Southern Eve

In *The Land Before Her: Fact and Experience of the American Frontiers,
1630–1860*, Annette Kolodny observes that the search for an American Eve went westward between 1850 and 1860: women writers of
domestic novels reinterpreted the Eden myth as an escape from the
industrialized and polluted Garden of the East to new domestic sanc-
tuaries in the West.[1] The mid-century decade was important. Domestic novelists from the 1820s until 1850 had tried to establish the
southern woman as the American Eve—a woman who would trans-
form the land into a Garden and inspire her husband to be a new,
uncorrupted Adam. But it was difficult to make this fantasy convincing, because the Garden was polluted, not by the corruption of industrialism but by the evil of slavery. The failure of the southern woman
to become the model of competence and femininity, of moral reform
and domestic peace, is recorded in that crucially important novel,
Uncle Tom's Cabin. Marie St. Clare represents the failed southern Eve.
Her selfishness, greed, jealousy, violence, and certainly her lack of
maternal affection epitomize the worst sins of the fallen Eve: she refuses to be a helpmate to her husband and thus contributes to his de-
generacy; she gives up her sacred trust, the care of her daughter, to
the kindnesses of slaves like Tom. Out of vanity and jealousy that
there is another more fair, like the wicked queen in "Snow White,"
she orders the beautiful slave Rosa to be whipped and, the reader is
given to understand, raped by the torturer.

The best sort of Eve the South could produce was Marie's daughter, Eva, whose name is no accident but rather the evidence of Stowe's
deliberate use of the Eden archetype. Eva performs the roles that are
incumbent on the Ur-mother of all living persons; she nurtures blacks
and whites alike; she inspires, charms, yet has a hard-headed prac-
ticality. But the Garden is already too diseased for such a person to
exist. The incipient Eden and incipient Eve, Stowe implies, are no

match for the wickedness within the Garden itself; Eva is too frail and never reaches full womanhood.

No wonder, then, that with the official death of the southern Eve in *Uncle Tom's Cabin* in 1852, novelists turned to a new Garden, the western frontier. The South's image as an untouched frontier disappeared with the Civil War, after which the South in the popular imagination was a defeated wasteland. After the turn of the century, thousands of southerners migrated to the West along with northerners, especially during the World Wars. Only in the 1970s has the sunbelt South reclaimed public esteem.

Many writers, notably David Brion Davis in *The Problem of Slavery in Western Culture* (1966) and Annette Kolodny in *The Lay of the Land* (1975), argue that the urge to imagine the New World as the Garden of Eden was powerful and inevitable.[2] The "possession" of "virgin" land by its male conquerors set up an inexorable metaphor: the land was a female to be conquered, subdued, and owned. In the South, colonists looked out over vast forests of untouched land, contrasting with the booming cities of the Northeast. The great size of the region discouraged the forming of urban centers and the accompanying "vices" of cities: pollution, congestion, starvation, and houses of gambling and prostitution. The South through the 1700s to 1865 was not entirely free of these; as Catherine Clinton reports in *The Plantation Mistress*, southern gentlemen might have to travel to Memphis or New Orleans, but they were away from home so often that they must have felt the trips worthwhile. And the South had its own unique vices—ignored until 1830 and then rationalized—involving the use of black female slaves for the recreation of white males.

But on the physical surface of things the land was green and fresh, fertile and new. Just as the colonists saw "the land as female," as Kolodny says, so too they saw the female as the land. Southern woman, even before the romantic idealizations in the historical novels of Reconstruction authors, was fantasized as a southern Eve in "the highly stylized garden in the wilderness,"[3] the plantation. The pastoral myth obtains its power to shape daily lives because it acts as a fantasy by which one can actually live one's life; it can, says Kolodny, "shape and structure experience." Applied to the South, this theory has profound implications.

Emma Dorothy Eliza Neville Southworth (1819–99) realized late in the 1840s that she was blessed with initials that could identify her with one of her novels' main motifs. Her early novels used her full name or parts of it; her many novels written after 1849 showed her name as E.D.E.N. Southworth. While varied in setting and theme, a number of them systematically offer up the southern plantation as an Eden and its mistress as a latter-day Eve, or at least as close to Eve as a mortal woman can hope to become. In *Retribution: Or, The Vale of Shadows* (1849), plain, orphaned Hester Grey marries her guardian within the first twenty pages of the novel. Southworth struggles to present Hester and her new plantation home as the seat of bliss: the plantation is located in a perfectly circular valley, the mansion itself at the very center of the valley. Her new husband, Colonel Dent, is a Virginia gentleman who has created a paradise in which the "servants" are happy and even educated—all of them can read and write. Colonel Dent has been 'a successful American Adam indeed, who now needs only an Eve with whom to share his paradise. Southworth's version of the American Adam is not the isolate that R. W. B. Lewis notices in the fiction of male authors such as Cooper; he is a courageous artist who creates a happy place out of the raw materials God has given.[4] Hester Grey says, upon her arrival in the valley, "Surely Eden was not more beautiful."[5]

To Southworth, the corruption of the Garden comes not from an evil system that exploits humans, nor from any flaw in the southern Eve herself, but solely from the invasion of a satanic creature: a dark-haired, Italian, Roman Catholic female, Juliette Sommer, whom Hester befriended in the orphanage. Juliette is the wrong sort of woman, a Dark Lady, a beautiful seductress, "a Sinister and inviting Coquette" with "a mesmeric spell" in her eyes (p. 13). Southworth's version of the Dark Lady is not very different from the versions of Hawthorne or James; the stereotype of the seductress holds constant, it seems, for male and female writers, with but one caveat: Mrs. Southworth is absolutely aware of her use of the seductress as Satan. In order to seduce Colonel Dent, Juliette Sommer insinuates her way onto the plantation under the guise of visiting Hester, who loves and trusts her with the intimacy that Lillian Faderman has identified as commonplace among women in the nineteenth century.

Southworth attempts to explain how Juliette became evil, and she finds the Eden archetype suited to probing the mystery of evil. Even as a child in the orphanage, Juliette's "soul resembled . . . summer clime and genial soil, rich in fragrant shrubs; but, springing in the midst, appeared a tiny sapling, that, as it grew, cleared and charred a wide space around it; sweet shrubs withered, bright flowers faded,

. . . and fruit fell unripe and blighted from the vines, destroyed by the poisonous breath of the tree; and the name of the Upas in her soul was Vanity" (p. 9). This rich passage reveals Southworth's belief that all children are good and pure, but that vanity about one's beauty is a female's cardinal sin, one that, if left unchecked by the careful education of an attentive mother, can grow to destroy the good qualities within a little girl. The term *Upas* in the above quotation refers to a type of tree with poisonous juices—here, the tree of vanity that brings evil to one's internal garden, turning a potential Eve into what Southworth later calls "a diabolical agency," "a demon," and a "Satan," whose evil passion consumes the garden with "fire" (p. 56). In this case the home goes up only in figurative flames, and Mrs. Southworth is to be commended for not actualizing the metaphor; in southern literature plantations often burn, from Poe's Usher to Mitchell's Twelve Oaks.

Juliette easily succeeds in her seduction because, Mrs. Southworth informs the reader, Colonel Dent—whose name suggests he is flawed—is virtuous but "untried." Although early in the novel he priggishly lectures the utterly selfless Hester about the moral advantages of not being a beauty, Southworth shows that such self-righteousness does not bring immunity from temptation nor the strength to resist it. What begins as a dalliance ends "with the fire of passion." Hester is spared the knowledge of this by dying in childbirth, shattering Colonel Dent's hope for a life of tranquility.

Years later, Colonel Dent returns from travels with Juliette on the depraved continent of Europe. Juliette's end is appropriately fiery; after her life of abandon in Europe, the reader gets a final glimpse of her as she prays to her lord, Satan, beseeching him to allow her to be able always to inspire love but never to feel it. Like Mr. Rochester in *Jane Eyre*, Colonel Dent is a broken man; having left the source of peace and strength, his home, he has become as dilapidated as the plantation. What was during Hester's time a "clean, cool, quiet, fragrant" well-kept house with rose bushes and arbors has become a wreck with broken windows, dank grasses, and weeds (p. 105). One hope remains: Hester's daughter is as good and lovely as her mother, suggesting that the southern Garden might yet produce an Eve to curb the wayward, uncontrolled lusts of its men.

In a novel written in 1852, the same year as *Uncle Tom's Cabin*, Southworth uses the Fair Maiden and Dark Lady quite overtly. In *Virginia and Magdalene; or the Foster-Sisters*, Southworth examines the mystery of how a girl becomes a seductress. Her answer is essentially that the pattern is already set at birth; for example, the baby Magdalene is described by her mammy as looking wicked, like a vampire. Little Virginia, however, is soft and white and good. These innate propensities are magnified, says Southworth, by upbringing and education. Magdalene is reared by her cruel father, who alternately whips and neglects her; this pain and suffering heighten Magdalene's evil. Also influential in the process is Magdalene's preference for inappropriate and even evil knowledge. She loves books, storms, the sea, epic poetry, astronomy, and all that is strong, powerful, and heroic. Virginia, on the other hand, admires flowers, birds, children, dancing, riding, botany, geology, and picturesque scenery, all that is small, precious, and part of domesticated nature. Virginia learns housekeeping with a passion, and several pages are devoted to formulas for good housekeeping; Magdalene, as might be expected, hates housekeeping. Thus can the incipient seductress be spotted: like Eve she seeks forbidden knowledge, wants to possess a God-like power over the stars, is Byronic in her tastes, and, worst of all, despises housekeeping. In this novel, however, she does not cause anyone's downfall but actually reforms, mostly because of the steadfast love of her friend, Virginia.

As these brief selections show, novelists who used the Eden archetype had to address several aspects of the story: What were Adam and Eve figures like before the Fall? Who was responsible for the Fall? What were Eve's motives? What was the nature of the "sin"? What were the consequences of the Fall? Why does evil exist in a good creation? Another novelist who provided comprehensive answers to these questions was Caroline Lee Hentz.

Hentz often employed the Eden motif, with ubiquitous references to plantations as Eden in her early novels. By the 1850s, she was identifying the source of evil in the Garden—a conventional one: a dark-haired villainess whose slanderous tongue, like Satan's, turns the hero away from the heroine. In *The Victim of Excitement; The Bosom Serpent*, the "parlour serpent," as the villainess is called, has learned the art of slander, "whose ancestral venom is derived from the arch reptile that lurked in the bowers of Eden."[6] Another belle, Ellen Loring, has learned her wicked ways because, as a "daughter of fashion," she "lives without God in the world" (p. 114). She sits in front of her mirror, dresses in immodestly tight dresses, and plots her conquests. A third belle in this overpopulated novel is the worst of the lot; Rosamond desires the beau of the virtuous Eugenia: "'Why should she imagine her(self) to be his wife', whispered the bosom serpent, subtle as its arch prototype in the bowers of Eden" (p. 199). Hentz as narrator then gives the correct and conventional response for the reader: "There is no greenness or fragrance for thee—better that thou hast died" (p. 199). For Hentz, envy and vanity are the key components of female evil.

Hentz joins Southworth in selecting an evil female as the threat to Eve, but she adds some interesting variants. In *Linda* (1850), Hentz uses the "Snow White" fairy tale, in which the wicked stepmother threatens the innocent heroine. When Linda's father remarries, he unwisely chooses Mrs. Walton, a woman who is efficient but mean. The stepmother whips not only the black servants but Linda, separates her from the servants (whom she regards as her friends), isolates her in a small room, and loads her down with tedious needlework. These cruelties are overshadowed by her greatest evil: she wants Linda to marry her son Robert, a self-indulgent, spoiled fellow whom Linda regards as a brother—thus Mrs. Walton urges the innocent maid to incest. The nineteenth-century audience had a horror of incest, but it was practiced often enough. As Wyatt-Brown reports in *Southern Honor*, first-cousin marriage was quite common and some kinship tie influenced as many as 45 to 60 percent of southern marriages.[7] Hentz is decrying a fairly standard practice, not so much because it is incestuous but because the stepmother wants to join two fortunes, not two people. Her suggestion to Linda is made with a "soft, hissing" voice; she moves like a "serpent" who "glides" into Linda's room.[8]

And that is the point: Robert cannot be Adam to Linda's Eve because he is corrupt; as the narrator says, his heart is an "unweeded garden, so long left to rank and poisonous luxuriance" (p. 55). The southern gentleman here is identified not as being evil per se but as being inadequate to the task of cultivating the southern Garden because he is interested only in money and pleasure. An Adam worthy of Eve appears and rescues Linda and her father in a carriage accident; Roland Lee seems to be a buckskinned backwoodsman—as Linda calls him, "Nature's nobleman." However, since noble savages are admirable but not suitable mates for a cultivated person, the reader is relieved to learn that Roland is also the son of a gentleman, and that he and his mother live in a snug and charming log cabin. When Roland and Linda finally marry, they have experienced many separations and hardships so that they are truly purified by their trials. Among the most important of these for Linda is her stay in the wigwam of Tuscarora and his wife, who, like the seven dwarfs, shelter Linda and protect her from being found by her wicked stepmother. These Indians are absolutely kind, though dark, says the narrator—noble savages who provide role models for marriage based on love, not money.

In the last scene, Linda and Roland, like Adam and Eve, are strolling through their plantation garden among the flowers and orange groves. They are met by Tuscarora, whose wigwam has been conveniently relocated at the edge of the plantation, and he lays the game bagged in the day's hunt at Linda's feet. This gesture of fealty to the lady of the manor bespeaks Hentz's vision of harmony of man and nature, of the correct and harmonious arrangement of light- and dark-skinned people. Like the dwarfs in "Snow White," Tuscarora and his wife are invited to live in the palace with the hero and heroine and all live happily after.

By 1852, the southern Eden was no longer a possibility. In *Uncle Tom's Cabin*, published that year, the descriptions of the plantation and its Eve differ remarkably from those of a few years earlier. The plantation house of Augustine St. Clare is of Moorish design, with arches and arabesques, galleries and exotic trees, silvery fish in marble fountains, walkways decorated with mosaics—a place more characteristic of Spain, says Stowe, than America. This exotic garden hasn't the freshness or the straightforwardness of the plantations in Southworth's early novels. And its adult female guardian, Marie St. Clare, is not only indolent and vain but, even worse, a terrible housekeeper. Such a failing in a woman was among the worst imaginable to the reader whose own life centered around daily drudgeries and who was accustomed to reading novels that also provided recipes and household hints. Because Marie refuses even to supervise the kitchen servants, her northern visitor Ophelia exclaims, for all outraged readers, about the shiftless management, waste, and confusion of her household. The only shiftless person on the plantation is Marie. Since she abnegates her role as Eve just as St. Clare refuses to be Adam, their daughter Eva is the only hope for restoration of the southern Garden. Indeed, Eva wants to "Christianize" the slaves, to teach them to read and write—sentiments shared by many southerners in the 1840s and '50s. But Eva's body is too frail; she weakens and dies. With Eva, Stowe demonstrates the inefficacy of those whose humanitarian sentiments are mere whispers of protest against the system of slavery that has enervated its men and made its women vain and lazy.

Leslie Fiedler in *Love and Death in the American Novel* (1966) perceptively observes that nineteenth-century male authors feared the adult female and so depicted the "best" women as nonthreatening, sexless, "white ladies," preferably preadolescent or postmenopausal. Female authors such as Stowe cater to white male anxiety about black men desiring white women (for example, by making Uncle Tom so devoutly Christian and Eva so young); but they generally use the myth differently than men writers do because they are concerned with female fantasies, in this case the settling and cultivating of the South as a second Eden—a real possibility to authors between the 1820s and the 1850s. The obstacles to the incarnation of this dream were too pervasive and insidious; slavery and its effect on personality prevented the South from becoming the promised land. As novelists realized the South would never be home to Eve, they began to show the potential Eves in the novels as flawed—like Marie St. Clare—or too weak and ineffectual to make changes—like Eva. Thus both Eva and Marie represent the impotence and disease of southern society.

Hentz was among the first of the southern novelists to respond to Stowe's indictment of slavery as the evil in the New World Garden. However, she never abandoned her belief in the South as the epitome of civilization, sidestepping the issue of slavery even in the novel written in response to Stowe, *The Planter's Northern Bride*. She wrote this novel in 1850 and revised it in 1854 after the 1852 publication of *Uncle Tom's Cabin*, adding obliquely that "Even in the Garden of Eden, the seeds of discontent and rebellion were sown; surely we need not wonder that they sometimes take root in the beautiful groves of the South."[9] Hentz's style invites the reader to identify with the narrator, who uses "we" frequently, which was common in novels of the time. But she does not identify the direct cause of human discontent as slavery and its attendant evils.

ANTEBELLUM novels had presented the reader with an ideal image of southern woman—chaste, beautiful, lively, domestic, and devout. The young woman of the upper class was held up as a paradigm of earthly virtue whose central task was to correct the innately wayward men whose flaws—gambling, drinking, and abusing the institution of slavery—threatened the seat of Victorian bliss, the home. As Catherine Clinton documents meticulously in *The Plantation Mistress*, the reality of antebellum life was that even the most privileged woman labored on plantations as manager, nurse, and teacher. Diaries and letters reveal that most plantation women experienced profound levels of anxiety caused by well-justified fears of death in childbirth, by marriages to unloving husbands who were often away on long trips, by the ambiguous relationship between the races in which the husband's white and mulatto children played side by side, and by a longing to be better educated.[10] These circumstances contradict the popular image of the southern belle's indolence and life of ease. Her gowns and laces, much emphasized in antebellum novels, were rare sights in reality; for the most part the southern belle turned her dress like everyone else.

While the Civil War brought an end to the old order, it only exacerbated the discrepancy between the myth and the reality of southern women. Woman's role in the war years is well documented; historians agree that as in most wars, women "manned" the plantations in their fathers' and husbands' absences. In addition to their already numerous domestic activities, women entered new realms: they milled grain, plowed fields, and planted cotton; they cared for the wounded and suffered the loss of their men.[11]

Yet when we investigate the image of southern woman in the postbellum novel, we find an increasingly idealized portrait that not only preserves and exaggerates the antebellum ideal but also transforms it. In the antebellum novel (especially those written by women, but even in Kennedy's *Swallow Barn*) the belle was an actor; she had an innate confidence and control over her own life. She was to these novelists the Eve who helped Adam, side by side, equal and strong. Her main duty in these novels is to find her Adam. In the postbellum novel, the belle is acted upon. She is the receiver of action and of attitudes; onto her are projected qualities that betray the profound anxiety of the southern gentleman who has witnessed the demise of the old order that rewarded him exclusively. Most of these novels were written by men, for whom the loss was most acute. Women novelists, by 1852, had given up trying to fantasize the South as Eden; ironically, this fantasy became the province of male writers whose need for a symbol of lost honor led them once again to the Eden and Eve archetypes.

Two groups of novelists who use the belle as a central character emerged in the postbellum period. The Edenics wrote historical novels that place the belle in an antebellum setting, perpetuate the notion that she is an ideal woman, and, most important, present her as a symbol for the lost Garden of the antebellum South.[12] The Lapsarians locate the belle in a postbellum setting, usually Reconstruction, and represent her as symbolic of the South, but place her in destructive situations that parallel the chaos of the South during Reconstruction; these authors present a darkening image of the fallen world in which the belle lives.[13] There is some overlap between these groups, since both are working with the central metaphor of the South as Eden.

Nostalgia for the lost home of the prewar South characterizes the writings of many male authors. The idealization of the Old South in their works has been frequently noted.[14] Lucinda H. MacKethan's essay on the works of Thomas Nelson Page contends that his purpose was "to fashion for the South a definitive version of the dreams of Arcady."[15] In fact, all such studies focus on one idea—that a powerful myth-making impulse was at work after the Civil War. Conditions for the creation of myth were propitious: a myth was needed to preserve the pride of the defeated southerner, to explain how the disaster had come about, and to offer solace for his loss. Since myth presents reasons for "how a reality came into existence, be it the whole of reality, or a fragment of reality,"[16] the urge to mythicize was strong in the South.

The most appropriate cluster of mythic themes and characters that served this need was that of the archetypal Garden—Arcady or Eden, the perfect home lost to us all. The Eden archetype allowed the southerner, particularly the male, to focus on a place that symbolized everything he as a southerner (not simply as an individual) had lost: the plantation. The plantation was not an analogue but a symbol of Eden, powerful enough in its cognitive and emotional associations to invoke the cultural myth of the Garden. The plantation as Eden myth, as it appears in fiction after the Civil War, envisions an ideal society of genteel, distinguished landowners, gracious and lovely wives, pure and winsome daughters, and faithful, industrious blacks, all working harmoniously in a bucolic setting of well-kept rose gardens and white-pillared mansions. Southern pride after the Civil War defeat could be preserved by asserting the superiority of this lost civilization, particularly as it contrasted with the corrupt, materialistic North. At the center of this prelapsarian world were the southern gentleman and lady, Adam and Eve archetypes. The superiority of these character types is a pervasive motif in postbellum literature written by men, and the loss these characters experience accounts for the mournful tone of postbellum essays and fiction alike. Women writers had given up the idea of woman as Eve before the war; thus, the postwar myth-making reflects distinctly male preoccupations.

One postwar codification of the southern Eden and the increasing importance of the female character at the center of the myth is George W. Bagby's *The Old Virginia Gentleman and Other Sketches* (1884). Bagby laments that there has been "a slight falling away from those grand models of men and women who really existed in Virginia, but whom we have come to look upon almost as myths."[17] Bagby rails at the "slander" that misrepresents some of these ladies as "luxurious, idle, cruel, and tyrannical" (p. 21); Bagby may well be referring to the notorious Marie St. Clare of *Uncle Tom's Cabin*, who apparently lives on in spite of the myth, and who accounts for Bagby's exaggerations. Bagby's impressions of the belle in the following quotation are freely borrowed from idealized portraits of women in the plantation novels (he read John Pendleton Kennedy's 1832 plantation novel *Swallow Barn*, in which the southern belle appears in literature for the first time); from comparisons of the South to the Golden Age of Athens; and from stereotyped descriptions of the youth and beauty of belles before the war.

> She was young—not more than eighteen—rather above the medium height; of round and perfect figure; her hair was golden and her eyes were blue; her complexion pure as light itself, fresh as the dew, and glowing as the dawn. She must have felt the many eyes feeding on her cheek and brow, for she turned presently, and how instantly the impatient little foot disappeared, how archly modest the smile that illumined her lightly blushing face! I could read her character at a glance. She was warm, and tender, and true; good, wise, merry, healthy, happy, sweet-tempered, willing, patient, loving, tidy, thrifty, and sincere. [p. 111]

Thomas Nelson Page, in *Social Life in Old Virginia Before the War* (1897), echoes Bagby's remarks on the beauty and personality of the belle by expanding them to show that she occupied "by a universal consent the first place in the system. . . . She was incontestable proof of their gentility . . . a creature of peach-blossom and show; languid, delicate, saucy. . . . She was not versed in the ways of the world, but she had no need to be; she was better than that; she was well bred."[18] Page's and Bagby's idealized portraits, charming though they are, had the seductive power of altering reality, of rewriting history; their dreams of the Old South made potent "a myth that has itself shaped many realities and outlasted many others,"[19] as Lucinda MacKethan writes. Real life for the southern woman was difficult at best. And even antebellum literature, while depicting the belle as an ideal, did not portray her as the delicate, will-less creature of Page's description: Bel Tracy, in Kennedy's *Swallow Barn* (1832), was athletic, a talented horsewoman; Eoline, in Caroline Lee Hentz's 1852 novel of the same name, left home and got a job. Moreover, Page had read Frederick L. Olmstead's anomalously realistic *The Cotton Kingdom* (1861) and had apparently forgotten Olmstead's remarks debunking the southern belief in the aristocratic bloodlines of the gentry (although Olmstead concedes that "the traditional 'old family', stately but condescending, haughty but jovial, keeping open house for all comers on the plantation, is not wholly a myth").[20]

Page and Bagby are presenting the myth, not the reality, of the southern belle. Their choice of imagery in particular indicates their mythic associations with the belle, as in Page's *Social Life*: "For all its faults, it was, I believe, the purest, sweetest life ever lived. . . . It christianized the negro race . . . maintained the supremacy of the Caucasian race, upon which all civilization seems now to depend . . . produced a people whose heroic fight against the forces of the world has enriched the annals of the human race—a people whose fortitude in defeat has been even more splendid than their valor in war. It made men noble, gentle, brave, and women tender and pure and true" (p. 104).

Having set down in nonfiction the paradigm for southern men and women, Page fleshes out his character types in his stories and novels. In *Red Rock* (1897) he reveals an awareness of the myth-making task he has undertaken; one character observes that the hills and gardens of the Red Rock plantation make him feel the "Garden of Eden" must be situated nearby.[21] Of woman's role during the war, Page reports: "Wherever a Southern woman stood during those four years, there in her small person was a garrison of the South, impregnable."[22] The belle in this novel, Blair Cary, is conventionally portrayed—long passages are devoted to her beauty, and she tries to inspire her weak-willed beau to give up "drink and gambling." Her life history is the conventional one for the belle in sentimental plantation novels; she begins the novel as a lively coquette and eventually becomes more sober and marries, thus ending her career as a belle and as an interesting character in the story. Page repeats another conventional plot device by having a northerner and southerner marry, a prescription for healing the break between North and South that had been advocated before the war by influential authors such as Harriet Beecher Stowe and Sarah Josepha Hale, editor of *Godey's Lady's Book.*

For Page the serpent in this southern Eden was represented by the rapacious northern carpetbagger and his protégés, the "insolent" blacks. Worst of all is the direct threat to southern women from the latter; one black in *Red Rock* boasts, "I'm jest as good as any white man, and I'm goin' to show 'em so. I'm goin' to marry a white 'ooman."[23] In this novel, an assault of a white woman by a black man does occur, but the hero shows up immediately and the assailant is punished in the course of the plot. Evil, in the form of white northerners and blacks, begins to enter the southern Eden, a theme that will recur (see chapter 11 for a discussion of the rape of the belle).

Another metaphor Page uses to describe the South personifies the region as a defenseless woman before a judge: "It was to this that the Southerner owed her final defeat. It was for lack of literature that she was left behind in the great race for outside support, and that in the supreme moment of her existence, she found herself arraigned at the bar of the world without an advocate and without a defence."[24] The passage echoes the conclusion of the Edenic myth when Adam and Eve were brought up before God as their ultimate judge, with no defense available to them. But, more literally, the passage reveals a feeling among southerners that the war had been lost for the lack of a convincing literary advocate for the South. The North had had its *Uncle Tom's Cabin,* but there was no southern equivalent. Page earnestly attempted to fill this void with sentimental essays, novels, and short stories, and he was amazingly successful; few readers today recall the wicked Marie St. Clare of Stowe's book, but most can imagine a blonde belle, standing in her immaculate gown before her father's plantation portico. Page's images, not Stowe's, occupy the popular imagination.

Who is the serpent to be blamed for the Fall, both of Eden and the South? Two answers to this question were offered most frequently after the war: the first, as we saw above in Page's *Red Rock,* held northerners and blacks accountable. A second explanation was that woman herself was flawed and therefore responsible for the end of bliss. John William De Forest in *The Bloody Chasm* (1881) introduces Lotharinga Fitz James as the foil to the belle. As her name implies, she is an amoral seductress who attempts to lure Harry away from the virtuous Virginia. The novel's name suggests that the South, like a woman, has been ravaged by the North, has been torn and injured—an image of bloody sexual violation. As in *Miss Ravenel's Conversion*, De Forest is not willing to relinquish the conventional passionlessness of the belle figure; he equates feminine passion with depravity. Virginia is so virtuous, in fact, that she will not have sexual relations with her husband (whom she marries to save her home) because he is a northerner. De Forest is so aware of the implications of his allegory that he writes that her refusal to "live with" her husband is like the South's "refusing to recognize an accomplished fact" (p. 276). This novel ends with the reconciliation of lady and gentleman, South and North, the bloody chasm of the title healed.

The image of woman as seductress and destroyer of potential happiness persists as a undercurrent in southern literature. This image recalls Lilith, the apocryphal first companion of Adam; at the same time, the idea of a chaste belle and an immoral one reflects the widespread concept that there were two types of women, good and bad, angels and whores. Leslie Fiedler in *Love and Death in the American Novel* (1960) writes that a woman in fiction is either a sexless White Maiden with fair hair, who is no sexual threat to the hero and inspires him, madonna-like, toward the spiritual life (a safer dwelling place than the sexual); or a Dark Lady, the bitch-goddess, the mysterious seductress who embodies the double threat of sex and death, the archetype of the Eve or Lilith who brings evil into the world.

By the 1920s southern women authors were entirely aware of the double image of women and used it to criticize the illusions of southern men. Ellen Glasgow's portrait of Annabel in *The Romantic Comedians* (1926) is a good example of the classic bitch-goddess who is not perceived as such because southern gentlemen cannot "see" that a woman of virtue—that is, one who does not yield her virginity before marriage and is passionless in marriage—can be just as lusty and even as amoral as her opposite. "Though he married in the post–Civil War period, he still thought in primitive terms of a world which, like the Garden of Eden, was unaware of its own innocence."[25] Focusing on the central southern myth of the South as Eden, Glasgow extends the image brilliantly by using Annabel as a Lilith-like seductress.

Annabel, though a virgin at marriage and throughout it, nevertheless is not an innocent. She is the serpent in the garden of Gamaliel's thoughts, an exotic bloom whose sensuousness, like that of Rappaccini's flowers, is too exciting for Gamaliel to bear: "As she drifted toward him with her loosened hair, her geranium mouth, and her winged eyebrows, which brooded over the virginal mystery of her gaze, his longing to put his hands on her was so sharp that he drew back as if he had been stung by her beauty" (p. 203). The hypnotic gaze of the Mona Lisa, ambiguous symbol of the Eternal Feminine, who embodies innocence and sexuality, marks her face. Gamaliel cannot touch her, for to him she is pure desire; she burns with a hard, gemlike flame, the "fire at the heart of an opal," which pierces Gamaliel with a "sudden anguish, that she was a symbol, not only of his lost paradise, but of all the burning desire of youth" (p. 238).

William Faulkner also uses the Eden motif in his portrait of Caddy Compson. Caddy is not merely a modern belle destroyed by outmoded convention; she also symbolizes the innocent curiosity that led Eve to try the forbidden fruit. That Caddy lives in a world after the Fall is symbolized by her boldly climbing the pear tree to spy on her grandmother's funeral and learn the "forbidden knowledge" of death. And, as her brothers stare up at her muddy underpants, they seem to learn symbolically the forbidden knowledge of sexuality. Death and sex having entered the lives of these children, Faulkner proceeds to show how their fates resemble that of the South. Many critics have commented extensively on the parallel; as Robert Penn Warren observes, the novel shows how the old order "held the seeds of ruin in itself."[26] But it is not female sexuality per se, or knowledge of it, that brings about the Fall; it is society's denial of its women's strength, curiosity, and sexuality that causes Caddy's damnation. If Caddy does represent the South, then with Caddy, Faulkner is contending that the South destroyed itself because it denied the attributes of its women: their desire for knowledge, their passion, and their strength.

An exception to the historical novels of the Agrarians, Caroline Gordon's *The Garden of Adonis* (1937) presents her version of a modern southern belle in the Garden. Like so many belles in fiction, Letty Allard is motherless and overindulged by her doting father. At twenty-three, she is spoiled and narcissistic and spends her time contemplating her hazel eyes and dark hair in mirrors and enticing numerous beaux. Engaged to a young man of her own age—her fourth engagement—Letty finds that she is not at all physically attracted to him; sitting thigh by thigh in a sagging hammock with her fiancé repulses her. As he kisses her, she feels "prisoned by his arm" and thinks only that the lawn needs mowing. She wonders how she will be able to bear his touching her after the marriage when now his kisses repulse her.

Like Katharine Faraday in *The Hard-Boiled Virgin*, Letty prefers an older, married man, Jim Carter, a dissipated son of an aristocratic family who married his wife only for her money. Letty is aroused by the danger of kissing a man who is so experienced and kisses her as she has never been kissed by her suitors. Gordon employs a setting to reveal the nature of Letty's relationship to Jim. When she and Jim stroll near her father's plantation, they come upon an Indian burial mound where two skeletons have been discovered, one of a man and the other of a woman, with their knees bound and drawn up under their chins. The bound skeletons metaphorically suggest the destructive ties between Jim and Letty, who are both narcissistic and self-indulgent. They lie down upon the mound in a bed of dry leaves for their sexual embrace, but the imagery of drought and death suggests that the heat of their passion is not tempered by friendship, respect, or love. The Garden has become a hot, dry place, a place of death instead of life.

The sterility of Jim and Letty's relationship is associated with the title of the novel, derived from Frazer's *The Golden Bough*, to which Gordon refers in the epigraph: "the garden of Adonis in mythology was filled with flowers and grains planted in shallow pots which in eight days withered because they had no root. These were then carried 'with the images of the dead Adonis and flung with them into the sea or into springs'."[27] Letty, like one of these flowers, is bright and hot, but without any inner resources. Indifferent to qualities of character in others, she seeks a man who is as shallow as herself, as if she narcissistically seeks for her own image in another.

Thus by the 1930s, the image of the fragrant, fertile garden had disappeared: in its place was a dry, barren wasteland.

10

White Anxiety

Before the Civil War, novelists like Caroline Lee Hentz and Mrs.
E.D.E.N. Southworth tried to present the belle as a southern Eve, although they acknowledged that the inadequacy of southern gentlemen to be suitable Adams (being constantly tempted by avarice or by
Dark Ladies) might prevent the fantasy from becoming a reality.
Nonetheless it was a common fantasy until after the Civil War, when
the realization of such a fantasy was no longer possible. Novelists no
longer presented to their readers the possibility of attaining bliss by
becoming the mistress of a plantation. This was now impossible in
the war-ravaged South, and ceased even to be a fantasy in fiction. As
Annette Kolodny points out in *The Land Before Her*, Eve went west to
look for her Adam. Novelists such as Page and Bagby, writing about
the South, wrote postmortems in which they lamented the loss of the
Garden. In the Reconstruction period, a new element found its way
into the Eden archetype novelists used; the source of evil in the Garden was no longer a cruel father or a corrupt woman but another
agent: the black.

If white women were supposed to be pure, cool statues, black men
and women were thought to be the opposite. Generations of white
men and women considered blacks to be like animals, a species apart
from humans, their desires more akin to the instinctual urges of
monkeys than to the controlled passions of humans. The idea of the
libidinous sexuality of blacks became a malicious rationalization for
continuing American slavery, but it was entrenched even before the
discovery of America, as David Brion Davis points out in *The Problem
of Slavery in Western Culture*; compared with Europeans, whose culture
enjoined sexual sublimation, Africans seemed "licentious" and "las-
civious."[1] Europeans and Americans were ignorant of African con-
straints on sexuality; most tribes regulated sexual practices. Girls

were sometimes trained in sexual techniques but they were usually expected to be virgins at marriage; adultery was severely punished. However, polygamy was practiced in Africa and was also endorsed by Islamic law and custom; and other freedoms were permitted that were taboo to Europeans. Davis writes, "to Europeans it was inconceivable that nakedness should be taken as a sign of virginity in a girl."[2] American whites, then, were continuing a long tradition of fantasizing blacks as libidinous and uncontrollable, in contrast to whites and especially white women.

Davis, Catherine Clinton, John Hope Franklin, and other historians have written extensively about the relations of blacks and whites on plantations. A common pattern was the virtual rape of black women by white men; by 1860, of the four million slaves in the United States, one-eighth were mulattoes.[3] White women were expected to tolerate their men's proclivities, since men were popularly thought to be doing their wives a favor by not demeaning them with the sex act. Clinton in *The Plantation Mistress* argues persuasively that whites truly regarded blacks as animals, to the extent that a proper white mistress might very well regard the nakedness of a slave as no more shocking than that of a dog or other household pet. While white wives felt jealousy and anger toward their husbands' mistresses and mulatto children, many wives also were effectively brainwashed by the belief that there was no comparison between sex with a black woman and sex with a white woman.

As for black males, Wilbur J. Cash's insights in *The Mind of the South* (1941) are still current and accurate. Cash asserts that the tendency of the southern white male to require that the southern woman be pure, beautiful, and untouchable was intertwined with southern attitudes toward the black. Because of southern attitudes about white superiority and hence legitimacy of bloodline, the southern woman was isolated from males, both white and black, and indoctrinated with puritanical beliefs that inhibited her sexuality.[4] While the white male performed his dynastic duties with his wife, he sought his pleasure with less repressed black women, thereby contributing to the mixing of the races, which the miscegenation taboo prohibited. The white woman was forced into a role of restraint and passionless tolerance. Male respect for her, says Cash, was a feeble compensation, a method of dealing with the guilt that such a system engendered in its men. This, together with southern notions of aristocracy and chivalry, caused the southern woman to become not simply an ideal for

the South but "a mystic symbol of its nationality in the face of the foe
. . . the shield-bearing Athena gleaming whitely in the clouds, the
standard for its rallying, . . . She was the lily-pure maid of Astolat
and the hunting goddess of the Boeotian hill. And—she was the
pitiful Mother of God. Merely to mention her was to send strong men
into tears . . . or shouts. There was hardly a sermon that did not begin and end with tributes in her honor."[5]

Cash is the first commentator to point out that, far from being only
a character in popular tradition, the southern woman was a symbol at
the core of the southern mind, the objective correlative for southern
ideals. She was the ultimate piece of property, whose possession con-
firmed a man's dominance, often ensured his fortune, and assured the
continuance of the male line. And white men assumed that black men
had but one desire: to rape white women.[6] Cash believes that in the
minds of white men, to violate the southern woman, a symbol of the
South, was to violate the South itself. This belief is the single most
important factor in the southern mythos. It begins to appear in fiction
during Reconstruction and persists well into the twentieth century.

The roots of this belief rest in the Edenic myth, but even more
deeply in the urge to create a myth. Such an urge was strong at the
time of the opening of the New World to Europeans, but in America
it was nowhere and at no time more powerful than in the South after
the Civil War. Allen Tate explains that the South created a unified set
of myths (which became the "imaginative focus" of so many southern novels) out of necessity. The defeated South, unlike any other
region of the United States, had experienced failure and inadequacy.[7]
The political, military, and economic debacle of the Civil War had left
the social order intact, a rankling reminder to the southerner of the
failure of that order when put to the test. To lose in battle is an un-
American experience; we are taught that we are a nation of winners.
As individuals we learn to cope with failure in various ways, but failure in the collective requires a more complicated explanation and
response.

Mircea Eliade in *Myth and Reality* defines a "living" myth as one
that "supplies models for human behavior and by that very fact, gives
meaning and value to life." The South needed to restore the notion
that life had meaning, and creating a myth was the perfect answer to
that need. Myth presents reasons for "how a reality came into existence, be it the whole of reality, or a fragment of reality." Several antebellum beliefs—that the South was founded by aristocrats, that the

South was spiritually and culturally superior to the North, that the South represented a second Golden Age of Greece and southern men and women were thereby the flower of civilization—became codified after the defeat. Eliade says, "Myth narrates a sacred history; it relates an event that took place in primordial Time . . . tells . . . how . . . through the deeds of Supernatural Beings, a reality came into existence."[8] To the southerner, heroic action in the Civil War was the action necessary to preserve a whole way of life. Thus, myth to the South is not simply a narrative of heroic deeds to explain why the South lost but rather, as Allen Tate asserts, "a dramatic projection . . . of heroic action, upon the reality of a society so that the myth *is* a reality."[9]

The characters and plot of the southern myth vary depending upon the teller's level of self-consciousness, from the Civil War veteran for whom the war was a glorious defeat to a Quentin Compson for whom the past is a curse that leads him to schizophrenic fragmentation. Their defeat by northern men and their failure to protect their own land directly challenged the traditional superiority of southern men. To preserve their control and status, they developed myths that provided a feeling of solidarity, power, and pride in the face of encroachments by northerners and by newly freed blacks, formerly the most subordinate group in southern society. For some southerners, myth serves as an escape from time, an escape from defeat, into the legendary past. The hope that "the South will rise again," phoenixlike from its ashes, consoles the defeated, who believe in "the Myth of Eternal Return"[10] by which the future will be a return to the past, thus rendering the inadequacies and disappointments of the present irrelevant and absurd.

We have already seen that the central myth that afforded solace centered around the plantation and the unfallen Eve. Woman's place in plantation society before the war had been that of a moral ideal, but women were subordinate to men in every other way. The one concession to women was their right to chivalrous behavior from men; however, they were expected to be self-sacrificing, totally dependent on men for economic security and social esteem, and unthreatening to men's image of themselves as the rulers of the home. In order to act as the spiritual inspiration of men, a woman could not display sexual feelings, and the married woman was taught to endure the sex act rather than welcome it. A young girl was to be a virgin at marriage, enhancing her value as private property. A mother served as an example of modesty, restraint, and self-sacrifice to her young daughter.

The image of the ideal southern woman caused problems for southern men after the Civil War. As noted above, white women were supposedly aloof, pure, and uninterested in sex, while black women were considered accessible and crude; correspondingly, black men were renowned for their sexual prowess. To preserve and defend the purity of white women became a preoccupation during Reconstruction.[11] The fear that southern women were about to be raped by black men was constant and pervasive. Southern men felt defensive and inadequate as the gallant protectors of southern ideals, including their ideal women.

Blacks, sponsored by the northern invaders, began to hold office and to own land,[12] both traditionally reserved to white society, and then received the vote in 1870;[13] white southerners were appalled and enraged. Hatred and anger toward northerners were displaced onto the blacks, a scapegoat group more accessible and more visibly threatening. As blacks encroached on traditionally white interests, one rationalization for hating them was the belief that black men wished to usurp and possess the supreme piece of white property: the white woman. Added to this anxiety was the fear that black men actually *were* more virile than their white masters.[14] A modern interpretation of this dilemma might be that blacks were unrepressed and therefore threatening to white men, whose morality forbade enjoyment of sex with any but black or lower-class women, and whose inadequacy as warriors paralleled their fear of inadequacy as sexual partners. Jacquelyn Dowd Hall, in *Revolt Against Chivalry: Jessie Daniel Ames and the Women's Campaign Against Lynching* (1979), agrees that the rape complex was a focus or displacement for the economic disruption of Reconstruction. Later, when the "new" caste system took hold—with legal "controls" such as grandfather clauses, withdrawal of the right to vote from blacks, and so on—then lynchings and the anxiety that caused them decreased.[15] Rape most often occurred, as it does today, as an act against women of one's own race. Even under Reconstruction only one-fourth of rapes were interracial, according to both Hall and Susan Brownmiller.[16]

As a result of these interrelated beliefs, southern woman, already an ideal by the time of the Civil War, became the central goddess of the southern mythos by becoming a symbol for the South itself. The theme that began to dominate novels—the threat to white women from blacks and northerners—can be summarized thus: before the Civil War, the South had been an Eden, the southern lady its Eve. But evil entered the Garden in the form of northerners, and in the Civil War the South was raped by the North. Now these northern vultures, as they were often called, selected as their favorites the virile blacks, who would rape southern women as well. White blood would be tainted with colored blood; generations of unbroken patriarchal bloodlines would be lost. After the war, when a southern gentleman paid chivalrous homage to a woman, he was no longer addressing just an ideal homemaker but the chief character of the plantation myth and the sanctuary of values.[17] Thus, in the years of Reconstruction, southerners were united by a desire to preserve white male superiority, to defend the symbol of that superiority, white woman, to keep blacks in their place in the hierarchy, and to punish those who violated the taboos.

Colonel W. C. Falkner, William Faulkner's great-grandfather, published several novels in the 1880s chronicling then-current ideas about southern aristocracy, slavery, and the North—a record in fiction of the myths of the Old South corresponding to Page's and Bagby's imaginative essays. Falkner sensationalizes the threat to the belle's purity after the Civil War; his novels are precursors of twentieth-century drugstore novels. In *The Little Brick Church* (1882), Falkner is explicit about the belle's significance in the minds of southern men. He emphasizes how easy it is for even the purest of belles to yield to the feared seducer. Kate Delroy, Falkner hyperbolizes, is so pure that she has somehow been spared original sin: "her heart had never known sin, her mind had never harbored thoughts of evil."[18] This exaggerated notion of the belle's purity is a Protestant analogue for the inviolateness of the Virgin Mary. Kate is motherless, hence untutored by female influence; her one failing is that she consents to elope with a lover because she has a "romantic mind, as well as many other qualities that are harmless in themselves, but dangerous to the unprotected maiden who has no prudent mother or other female relative to point out the hidden paths that lead to destruction."[19] These "qualities" are her sexual desires; the "hidden path" leading to destruction is sex itself. Significantly, the seducer is not a southern gentleman but a northerner who pretends that he intends to protect and marry her, then jilts her (as in De Forest's seduction plots involving northern men and southern women).

Northerners are totally villainous in this novel. Falkner attributes the southern evil of slavery to northerners: they brought slaves here in the first place, and they sell them. A southerner, Falkner assures the reader, would never sell his slaves or mistreat them. Dunbar, a northern slaveholder, lusts for the lovely slave Tilly, and when Tilly defends her virginity, he whips her. The flogging scene is explicit; Tilly is stripped to the waist, hung from a post, and covered with bleeding stripes. Interestingly, the Quentin Compson–like narrator looks on but does nothing to stop Dunbar. The narrator, who inadvertently represents the moral impotence of southern men, can only stare at the scene, which depicts the sadomasochism of master-slave sexual relations. Too late he runs for help; Tilly dies, and the good southern people flog, brand, and lynch Dunbar.

The seduction of Kate and the graphic portrait of Dunbar's lust and cruelty are unusually salacious and thus differ from prewar novels. These scenes are foreshadowed by similar, though milder, postwar novels. Lilly Ravenel is "seduced" by the dashing but dissolute Colonel Carter just as she is seduced by her own southern sympathies, and Virginia Beaufort in *The Bloody Chasm* feels she has "prostituted" herself to a northerner (worse than a seduction, since she consented), but in these novels both heroines properly married their seducers. Being seduced not because of ignorance (like Lilly) or economic need (like Virginia) but because of an innate flaw was a new trait for the belle. Beginning with this novel, she can be seduced by her own sensuousness. Thus a new motif is introduced: Eve can fall through her own desire; the fear of this idea pervades Falkner's portrait of Kate.

The characters created by Thomas Dixon, Jr., are the flamboyant epitome of the postwar myths about the purity of southern women, the courage of southern men, and the depravity of northerners and blacks. Dixon's most famous novel, *The Clansman: An Historical Romance of the Ku Klux Klan* (1905), later reached an even wider audience as D. W. Griffith's film *The Birth of a Nation* (1915). The purpose of the novel was to show how

In the darkest hour of the life of the South, when her wounded people lay helpless amid rages and ashes under the beak and talon of the Vulture, suddenly from the mists of the mountains appeared a white cloud the size of a man's hand. . . . An 'Invisible Empire' had risen from the field of Death and challenged the Visible to mortal combat.

How the young South, led by the reincarnated souls of Clansmen of Old Scotland, went forth under this cover and against overwhelming odds, daring exile, imprisonment, and a felon's death, and saved the life of a people, forms one of the most dramatic chapters in the history of the Aryan race.[20]

This passage summarizes several themes in post–Civil War fiction. First, the South is referred to as a mother whose children have been vanquished by the predatory North, an image also used in De Forest's *The Bloody Chasm*. The Klan's phoenixlike rising from the dead suggests that its members are divine heroes who will nullify and correct the defeats and losses of the past, a heroic mission that arises out of the mythopoeic impulse. Making the heroes Scottish warriors is similar to W. C. Falkner's frequent references to the heroes in the novels of Sir Walter Scott. Dixon also employs the myth of the dragon's seed, which, when sown in the field of battle, springs up into fierce and mighty warriors.

The Clansman is a compendium of racism, violence, white supremacy, and stereotypes of blacks and whites. The setting is Reconstruction, a period which, Dixon asserts, could have gone smoothly had that great southerner, President Lincoln, been able to institute his programs. (Dixon later wrote a novel on Lincoln and named it *The Southerner.*) In *The Clansman*, Lincoln states that he opposes negro suffrage, that the two races will never be able to live together equally, either politically or socially, that Americans will never tolerate a mulatto citizenship. The "tragedy" of having removed blacks from Africa must be rectified by returning them to Africa. Lincoln speaks as the benevolent northerner, like Mather and Harry in *The Bloody Chasm*, using the metaphor of the union as a marriage, with the South as a straying wife who is still loved, here as a wounded or perhaps raped woman to be helped, not punished: "We fought the South because we loved her and would not let her go. Now that she is crushed and lies bleeding at our feet—you shall not make war on the wounded, the dying, and the dead!" (pp. 54–55).

Reconstruction, however, is administered by Senator Stoneman in Dixon's novel, and becomes a period in which the North "rapes" the South. Dixon depicts Senator Stoneman as the personification of depravity: Stoneman favors the complete mixing of the races; he entertains blacks in his home; he has a black mistress. To Dixon the worst sin is having sexual relations with black people; the women are described as evil and passionate, the men as animals, virile and insolent with the "gleam of the jungle in [their] eyes" (p. 93).

Margaret Cameron, one of the belles in the novel, is tall and stately, with a "subtle languor and indolent grace." She dresses plainly in simple cotton with no jewels, but with a "rose she wore pinned on her breast" (p. 62). Even Phil, a northerner, recognizes her superiority; he says, "The world has never seen the match of your gracious Southern womanhood! Snowbound in the North, I dreamed, as a child, of this world of eternal sunshine. And now every memory and dream I've found in you . . . but for the Black Curse, the South would be to-day the garden of the world!" (p. 151). Dixon thus identifies the belle with the potent symbol of Eve in the Garden before the Fall. Ben, the novel's southern hero, dreams of a new Garden, a new Eden, which is presented as the vision that calls him to be head of the Ku Klux Klan: "Last night I dreamed the South has risen from her ruins. I saw you [Elsie] there. It was our home standing amid a bower of roses you had planted. The full moon wrapped in soft light, while you and I walked hand in hand in silence beneath our trees. But fairer and brighter than the moon was the face of her I love, and sweeter than all the songs of birds the music of her voice" (pp. 150–51). This portrait, with its exaggerated portrayal of the belle, goes beyond the antebellum ideal altogether and enters the realm of myth. It is important to keep in mind that the South's rebirth as a Garden was impossible after the Civil War. While before the war female novelists might have realistically urged readers to consider the South as a potential Eden, male novelists after the war who suggest this are invoking a fantasy, not proposing a reality.

Ben's former sweetheart, Marion, even more than Elsie or Margaret, represents the flower of southern womanhood. Marion has "wistful dreamy blue eyes, shy elusive beauty." The reader first sees her arranging roses in the great house of her plantation. Marion is not at all bitter about Ben's new love; on the contrary, she is delighted to see that he is happy. She is, Dixon asserts, one of the "girls of the South who came out of this war clad in the pathos of poverty, smiling bravely through the shadows, bearing themselves as queens though they wore the dress of the shepherdess" (p. 302).

Juxtaposed to these pure and idyllic plantation scenes are reports of the increasing insolence of blacks and descriptions of their sensuality. "His passions," once aroused, Dixon informs the reader, "are as the fury of the tiger" (p. 293); blacks are most often compared with children, tigers, apes, cannibals, and thieves. Reconstruction and its evil northern originators have unleashed the black tiger. The separate themes of this shrill, disjointed novel meet when Marion's former slave, Gus, bursts into her bedroom: "A single tiger-spring, and the black claws of the beast sank into the soft white throat and she was still" (p. 156). Marion, the pure, sweet rose of the South, is raped by the black demon, the first instance of a rape of a southern belle in a novel. Not having the good fortune to die, Marion washes away the blood, dons a white gown, and throws herself off Lover's Leap, accompanied by her mother. It is a melodramatic but effective scene, designed to arouse the reader's hatred of the black and endorsement of the Klan.

The Ku Klux Klan, Dixon's sole arbiter of justice, must avenge this rape, for northern authorities will not bring Gus to justice. Before Gus is lynched, the Klansmen assemble in the forest and pray: "deliver us from the body of the Black Death. In a land of light and beauty and love our women are prisoners of danger and fear. While the heathen walks his native heath unharmed and unafraid, in this fair Christian land, our sisters, wives, and daughters dare not stroll at twilight through the streets" (p. 319). The Klan is designed to protect women, to embody the patriarchal and chivalric values of the Old South, and to answer violence with violence. The goals proclaimed in the sacred book of the Klan sound lofty: "This is an institution of Chivalry, Humanity, Mercy, and Patriotism: embodying in its genius and principles all that is chivalric in conduct, noble in sentiment, generous in manhood, and patriotic in purpose" (p. 320). Dixon does not perceive the irony of the Klan, which wishes to avenge violence and brutality against whites, using violence as its means. Earlier postbellum authors, including Thomas Nelson Page, do not romanticize the Klan but see it as a disruptive band of hooligans.

Dixon's fear of sexuality and his association of sexual desire with blacks is nowhere more obvious than in his 1912 novel *The Sins of the Father: A Romance of the South*. He devotes the first part of the book to describing the struggle of Norton with the "beast" of sexuality born within himself, a beast aroused by the beautiful mulatto Cleo, whom he blames for arousing him. While Norton despises men who stoop to relations with black women, he hypocritically lusts after Cleo in one hundred pages of titillating temptation scenes. He at last solves the logistical problem by making Cleo his wife's maid, and soon he seduces her.

Dixon, believing that the problem is one of genetics, uses Darwinian theory to support his contentions: "The fact that the negro race have for two hundred years been stirring the baser passions of . . .

men—that this degradation of the higher race had been bred into the bone and sinew of succeeding generations—had never occurred to her [Mrs. Norton's] childlike mind."[21] Discovering that her husband has succumbed to the "Beast," Mrs. Norton is too frail to stand the shock and dies, leaving an infant son, Tom. Norton flees to the safe, white North, where he receives a letter from Cleo revealing that she has given birth to a girl, Helen. Norton packs his mistake off to a boarding school in the Midwest.

Twenty years pass, and Norton returns to the South with young Tom, who soon falls in love with Helen, a blonde, blue-eyed belle in white. Tom, who has been taught "racial cleanness," is in love not only with a mulatto, but with his half-sister. The elder Norton's horrified realization of these bizarre circumstances is his penance for the guilt of his sinful relations with Cleo. Meanwhile, Tom and Helen court by visiting Civil War battlefields, which now appear like gardens. The South has returned to its original state before the Fall; it is "a vast rose garden of light and beauty filled with the odors of flowers and spices and dreamy strains of ravishing music" (p. 246). Dixon seems to be consciously myth-making in this novel, with Tom and Helen the unblemished representatives of the New South, purged of the sins of their fathers.

Norton suffers under the double burden of miscegenation and incest. He suspects it may be too late to break off the romance; he fears that, because of Helen's black blood, the couple may already have had sexual relations. When there seems no possible way of ending this confusion, the deus ex machina descends when Cleo reveals that she has lied, that her own baby died and she stole a white child, Helen. All is well, the guilty punished, the innocent preserved. Dixon concludes, "Nothing is surer than that the South will maintain the purity of her home! It's as fixed as her faith in God" (p. 405). Dixon's content—incest, miscegenation, and guilt and redemption—foreshadows themes in the fiction of the Southern Renaissance, yet his inflammatory tone, offensive stereotypes, and disjointed style confirm that an author's treatment of a topic makes the difference between art and, in this case, propaganda.

White southern men in the postwar period are generally portrayed as requiring the inspiration of pure southern women. Black men and women, on the other hand, are shown as animals who tempt the pure Adams and Eves. The belle herself in the novels of this period continues to possess the characteristics of charm, beauty, modesty, and purity, but she now also speaks against various social causes, such as women's suffrage and northern interference. Often she acts as spokeswoman for the South when she defends slavery. Most important, she becomes a central character in the fantasies of the antebellum South; because of her purity, beauty, and "breeding," she comes to represent the South itself. An act of aggression against her is an act against the South. Her purity must be defended just as the South must be defended against further indignities from northern "vultures" or their proxies, the blacks. Any sensuousness in her is potentially destructive in the extreme.

Paradoxically, the belle's purity, loveliness, and modesty—traditionally the three main components of her personality—are shown to be the ones most harmful to the belle and destructive to others in the fiction of Ellen Glasgow, William Faulkner, and numerous other writers of the Southern Renaissance. The society in which the belle lives, which prevents her personal development beyond childlike dependence on men, is examined and rejected in fiction after 1913. The belle as a symbol of the South's beauty and purity is parodied and inverted so that she represents many of the worst qualities of the South when she appears in the fiction of the Southern Renaissance.

I I

Rape and the Southern Belle

Although the archetype of Eden, with its seducer and lady, is the source of the rape theme as it is used by southern novelists, there are many variations on this theme: the relationship of rape to the narcissism of the southern lady, the Jungian linking of blacks and whites as partners in the South, the devastation wrought on the individual by an act of rape, the identification of the rape of the southern lady with the ravaging of the South, and the recovery of a strong woman from the trauma of rape, which destroys many of the illusions and beliefs created by her conventional upbringing. As mentioned in the preceding chapter, however, the great frequency and variety of rape in southern fiction does not accurately reflect the incidence of rape in real life. Fictional rape thus represents a mythic cultural pattern and is indicative of the position of women in southern society.

Rape stood for ultimate domination and subordination. In a male-dominated society, women were a weaker class. The South's political and economic system had been a squirearchy in which the landed gentry held economic and political power. After the Civil War, however, plantation owners had to adjust to an economic order no longer based on slavery.[1] The patriarchal South had made white men the dominant group in terms of their superior status, their access to lucrative economic roles, their autocracy in sexual roles, and their aggressive temperament.[2] Women and blacks, on the other hand, were deemed subordinate in status, role, and temperament; a woman's status depended upon her father or husband, her economic role was that of a marriageable alliance-maker before marriage and a homemaker after marriage, her sexual role was that of a chaste maiden or faithful wife (so that the legitimacy of the male's line could be preserved), and her ideal temperament was passive, docile, ignorant, and virtuous. As Jean Baker Miller writes in *Toward a New Psychology of*

Women, dominant groups have a variety of ways to convince, cajole, and force subordinate groups to remain so. Subordinates are "said to be unable to perform the preferred roles" because of deficiencies of body or mind, and they are consequently defined in terms of psychological characteristics "that are pleasing to the dominant group," including submissiveness, docility, immaturity, and weakness. "Normal" women have these traits; "abnormal" women show the traits of the dominant group, such as "intelligence, initiative, assertiveness."[3]

Usually these definitions lead to uneasy but functional relations between the sexes; but when these mechanisms fail, the dominant group is in a position of power to take strong measures to reinstate them. Rape as the ultimate act of domination results when the male feels denied the privileges he assumes are his right. The right to copulate with whomever he pleased was long assumed; restrictions placed on him by societal taboos or laws were in no way as severe as those placed upon white women. In fact, for white women, copulation was not a right or a privilege at all but was defined by the dominant group as an odious chore, necessary at best.

The white male's right to copulate, in its most extreme and hideous form, is the basis of rape in southern novels. Black men, part of another subordinate group, do not have that right and must be punished for rape. White women, who do not have any control over copulation at all, are expected to react to rape not only with shame and humiliation, but with suicide. White men who rape do so for good reasons: they were "enticed" or "seduced" by an "abnormal" seductress; or "she deserved it," meaning that the woman was being insubordinate in some way and needed a violent reminder of her proper place; or "she wanted it," meaning that women, passive and submissive masochists, prefer painful, violent sex.

Since white women are not supposed to like sex at all, feelings of sexual desire are at best confusing to a young girl and at worst destructive. In Ruth Cross's *The Unknown Goddess* (1926), Noel Higgins's upbringing shelters her from knowledge about the "unknown goddess" of sexual desire within herself; only fourteen, she is puzzled by the new feelings within her. A handsome doctor vaccinates her, and "Where his fingers closed about her arm a new and dazzling sensation had set in. Like lightning it ran up her armpit, then with a pounding rush to her heart—spread deliciously, tinglingly, to the outermost parts of her body."[4] Noel is pleased and preoccupied with her new body: "There were times when she, like Narcissus, lost herself in the depths of sensuous self-worship. Gazing at her image in a pool or mirror" (p. 17), Noel fantasizes about the young doctor; her fantasies elicit the same shivers of desire she had felt when he touched her arm. The narrator tells the reader, however, that Noel fails to recognize this feeling, for she lives in an era "before the Great Age of Sex in which we more frankly and flamboyantly live" (p. 19), an age when husbands expected their brides to be "unsullied" by knowledge of the grosser matters of life. While Cross mocks the "Age of Sex," she also shows the deleterious effects of innocence upon exuberant but naive young girls like Noel.

When a charismatic revivalist comes to Noel's quiet southern town, she does not realize that the source of her newfound religious ardor is actually her own sexual desire. The preacher, Jarnigan, cleverly manipulates his audience both to take their money and to gratify his desire for power. Noel receives baptism by immersion, a scene so highly sexual in its imagery that it becomes an ironic foreshadowing of Noel's actual sexual initiation. As she stands in the water next to Jarnigan, her dress floats upward about her waist, and Jarnigan presses against her. He is the only person near enough to perceive her partial nakedness: "The white gown clung like calyx to lily as she stood a moment revealed" (pp. 76–77).

In the novel's central scene, Noel and Jarnigan mistake each other's intentions. Jarnigan believes that Noel's vivaciousness is a sexual invitation. As a self-centered product of her upbringing, Noel craves his attention and praise, but she is entirely unaware of the consequences of arousing a man, particularly one who has no respect for the southern code of virginity, which is supposed to protect young girls like Noel. When he begins to kiss her, Noel is shocked, but he replies, "You know perfectly well you wanted me" (p. 97). Noel's knowledge of sexuality is so limited that well into the seduction she has no idea that her virginity is in danger. When Jarnigan begins his physical assault, Noel believes that he means to kill her, unaware as she is of "the awful mystery of the Unknown which threatened" (p. 97). By the time he is finished with her, the narrator tells the reader, "She has been ravished not once, but again and again, by a sex-maddened beast. . . . She no sooner regained consciousness from an attack than her anguish . . . seemed to inflame him anew" (p. 100).

Like Temple Drake in *Sanctuary*, Noel is entirely in the power of her rapist; she yields to his assault and then does not reveal the crime. Her reaction to the rape is to spend the next few months in a state of

withdrawal; symbolically reexperiencing the rape, she hallucinates
that her bedroom is full of cruel, hairy gorillas and menacing ele-
phants with long, swaying phallic trunks. She remains silent because
she is ashamed of what she supposes is her willing participation in
the crime; she believes Jarnigan's assertion that she wanted to be
raped, because she knows that she was attracted to him. Consequently, she begins to believe that the "evil" is not Jarnigan's but her
own, recalling that her mother has taught her that woman's role is to
quell the beast in man.

The rape has left Noel pregnant, and in this misfortune she receives no support from her family. Indeed, her fanatically religious
father is willing to place the entire blame on his own child, rather
than renounce his idol, Jarnigan. Her mother considers her a strum-
pet, and encourages her to despise herself for her "crime." Noel's sister summarizes the opinion of the town: "Nobody nice'll ever have
anything to do with you again and you can't get married and you
might just as well be dead. You're ruined" (p. 128).

Ruth Cross is obviously contemptuous of the southern society that
has manipulated Noel's life, first indirectly causing her rape, by keeping her sheltered and ignorant, and then hypocritically condemning
her for being raped. Cross is no more in favor of the new morality of
the Jazz Age; she tells us that the event in the book occurred "before
the days of flappers and the universal contempt of youth for morality" (p. 129). However, she implies that the traditional morality is
even more odious than that of the present. Not only is Noel ostracized wherever she goes, but she believes herself to be a mon-
strously abnormal person. Cross seems somewhat at a loss about the
best way to end the novel because she avoids the conventional end of
suicide or lingering death for the heroine. The child dies and Noel
becomes a doctor, both respectable stopping places, but Cross permits Noel her revenge. Noel meets Mona, the invalid wife of her seducer; elevating herself to sainthood, Noel sacrifices a beloved fiancé
to care for Mona and her children.

Noel returns home at the end of the novel. Contemplating with her
a bronze statue of a goddess, which has been a favorite ornament in
the house, her former fiancé reflects: "The Unknown Goddess, I call
her . . . she's always stood to me as a sort of symbol of your mother's
consuming ambition to leave her family on a little higher level"
(p. 370). Noel has fulfilled that ambition, not by obtaining wealth or
social standing but by reaching a certain level of spirituality. She is

strikingly similar to Glasgow's Dorinda Oakley or Gabriella Carr; Noel has stoically renounced the flesh and has received the reward of seeing all her enemies brought low by illness or death.

Cross uses a symbolic motif to explain the aspects of Noel's character that motivate her. Sexual desire—the goddess of the flesh—which inhabited Noel in her youth, is depicted as destructive; the bronze goddess of self-sacrifice, which Noel comes to resemble, is preferred. Noel's saintliness is not totally convincing, however, for it seems to be a defense against the men who betrayed her so terribly. Revealingly, Cross as narrator comments that after the rape, "it would take years, a lifetime, perhaps, to disassociate him from the idea of men in general" (p. 101). Such an observation undercuts Noel's religious fervor. Still, she has refused to be the "ruined" woman her society demanded in these cases; she has made a life for herself and has learned to love others.

An interesting treatment of the rape motif appears in *Cinnamon Seed* (1934) by New Orleans–born Hamilton Basso, a journalist for the *New Republic* and the *New Yorker*. Basso's constant theme in his novels is that southern institutions, far from protecting individuals, injure them and warp them. The institution of the southern belle affects white men, white women, and black men, creating suspicion and hatred in white men, fear and feelings of inferiority in black men, and guilt and repression in white women.

Cinnamon Seed opens upon a scene of what the narrator calls an "unreal city" of prostitutes and merchants, housewives and shopkeepers, all lonely and materialistic people living during World War I. The image alludes to T. S. Eliot's Wasteland, a frequent motif in Depression novels of the 1930s.[5] As the narrator surveys this landscape he begins to piece together stories about his southern family—in particular, stories of Ann, a belle of the late 1800s. Ann is first seen in a fragrant, moonlit garden, a contrast to the depraved twentieth-century city at the beginning of the novel. The scene seems conventional; a suitor is on his knees, proposing marriage. Ann's thoughts, however, are ominous: "she was afraid: afraid of herself, afraid of him, more deeply afraid of fear."[6] She refuses him because she feels desire for Sam, a handsome, educated black servant. The author describes the attraction in Jungian terms, implying that these seeming opposites may be incomplete parts of one another.

In a scene that at first suggests the threat of rape, Sam reciprocates this desire. When he enters Ann's empty bedroom, he runs his fingers

over the quilt on her bed. But he is no rapist; unlike Byron Snopes in
Sartoris, Sam does not wish to frighten or hurt anyone. When Ann
discovers him, she is not so much disturbed by Sam's presence as by
the fact that she is attracted to him. She denies her feelings: "It's not
true! . . . It's not true! He never attracted me. He is a Negro. I am a
white woman. It is only in my mind. It is a horrible thing my imagination has conjured up" (p. 81). Tense, ashamed, and tormented by
her guilty desires, she consents to marry the suitor in the garden if he
will take her away from the South. The garden, at first described as a
fragrant and lovely Eden, becomes diseased, as if to reflect Ann's
mental turmoil: "A thin moon ventured into the sky . . . Mosquitoes
swarmed about her in whining droves, assailing her neck, and arms,
giving the heated dark its only sounds save the external exhaustion of
the stream" (p. 82).

The garden has deteriorated not because a rape has occurred but
because society has thwarted natural love between members of different races. This novel represents a sophisticated move away from the
rape motif that began in post–Civil War novels toward a sense of
indictment of the South's social corruption. Basso realizes that the
myths of southern womanhood injure both men and women, because
they create repression and guilt. He resists the easy plot element, a
rape, for it would be an act of violence wrought from the inequities of
southern life toward both blacks and women.

Allen Tate's *The Fathers* (1938) is a powerful, well-crafted novel in
which the characters are enveloped in an atmosphere of tension gen-
erated by the contradictions inherent in the old order. Unlike his fellow Agrarian Stark Young, Tate perceives that the ethic of purity for
southern women conflicts with the coquetry they are also encouraged
to develop.

Jane is the epitome of the submissive woman—exceptionally quiet,
a "normal" girl who attracts men because of her docility. Young Lacy
is attracted to "the lovely insipidity of her docile eyes, the constantly
parted lips, and the languid posture . . . yet . . . a vitality the men
paused to observe, with the remark: 'What a pretty girl!' when she
was not pretty at all. It was doubtless this vitality in the innocence of
a sixteen-year-old girl that made her attractive to men."[7] Although
Jane never does or even says anything vital, men project this attribute
onto her on the basis of her youth and appearance. Actually she is
cool and distant toward Lacy; when he touches her, she responds
only by saying his name. Her innocence is fostered by her sheltered

life; she knows nothing of money, poverty, childbirth, or sex, although she has some idea that she is attractive to men. Though she says she loves Lacy, Jane marries his brother Semmes, because, as she nonchalantly explains to Lacy, "Oh but you didn't ask me. Semmes did—weeks ago" (p. 216).

Jane is convinced that Yellow Jim, a runaway slave, is a threat to her and insists that he has malevolent interest in her. Eventually, in a scene reminiscent of the rape scene in Dixon's *The Clansman*, she is attacked by Jim, who is described as a cat who crouches, springs upon her, and scratches her with his clawlike nails; he is overpowered, however, before the rape can occur. Like Gus in *The Clansman*, Jim embodies the stereotype of the black male as "half-savage" and almost cannibal-like, whose urges are uncontrollable.[8]

Tate's focus on the aftermath of the incident transcends stereotypes. He uses the reactions of various characters to the attempted rape to show the failure of southern codes of behavior. Her sister Susan dons black, as if Jane were no longer a living person. Lacy wants to avenge her honor by killing Jim but hesitates because he is uncertain whether he or Semmes, Jane's fiancé, is the more suitable avenger, a bitterly comic twist to the southern code of honor. George Posey, Susan's husband, is incapable of shooting Jim because Jim is his half-brother (avenging the honor of southern womanhood is more difficult than one might think). Alternating between asking for her dead mother and sitting on her bed in a catatonic state, Jane—as any well-brought-up belle in her situation should—becomes mentally deranged. The priest who sits with her explains to Lacy that there is only one solution for a girl like Jane: "the Mother Superior will come for the young lady at eleven o'clock. There's no other way. The girl can never be the bride of any man" (p. 263).

Only much later in life does Lacy realize that Jane herself is somewhat responsible for the attack, for she was "man's woman . . . but safe only in quiet times; a girl . . . who, in order to create excitement that she could not find in herself, imagined that because Jim was a runaway there was something sinister about him; a girl who could have never been in love and would have thrown herself about, perpetual apple of disorder indefinitely, had not Semmes and, to her, the foolish excitement of war, made marriage interesting" (p. 270). As a narcissist who thrives on the attention of others, successfully enticing but not loving both whites and blacks, Jane did not consciously entice Jim to rape but did create a volatile situation. The reader is not certain whether she is responsible for the attack or whether the assault was motivated more by Jim's unleashed "animalistic" drives. This confusion on Tate's part is admirable in a way. While the racist explanation that blacks are animalistic and the sexist notion that women are "asking for it" are both objectionable, Tate realizes (ahead of his time) that the reasons for acts of rape are many and complicated. Although he does not grasp them all, and while he uses stereotypes as well, he does grapple with the complexities and turmoil that such an action represents. He does not represent the act pruriently, as does Thomas Dixon, Jr., nor attractively, as do writers of drugstore plantation novels. To his credit, Tate avoids the argument that all women wish to be raped, the central rationalization in the most popular novel of the 1930s, *Gone with the Wind,* in which a husband rapes his wife and "she loves it."[9]

One novel offers a well-balanced, normal adulthood as a possible future for a belle who is raped. In *Southern Charm* (1928), by Isa Glenn, the reader is presented with three possibilities for the belle, two traditional alternatives and a third, clearly preferable one. A native of Atlanta where her father had been mayor, and a cousin of the artist James McNeill Whistler, Glenn studied art in Paris until her cousin told her she had no talent. Marrying Brigadier General J. B. Bayard Schindler in 1903, she traveled with him to the Philippine Islands, South America, and the South Seas. In 1925, Glenn studied motion picture producing and writing at Columbia, and then she wrote two fine novels about the southern woman.

Glenn's first novel, *Southern Charm,* opens as Mrs. Habersham is visiting her married daughter, Alice May, in New York City. Mrs. Habersham is a perfect product of the southern code and has reared her daughters similarly. Observing her daughter Alice May's marriage to Roger, a northern businessman, she becomes disturbed. Although Alice May is an "angel," she is selfish, preoccupied with her appearance, and utterly useless except as a household ornament. Alice May is too selfish to consider the wishes of her husband, and Mrs. Habersham realizes that Roger is at a dangerous age when Alice May's fading beauty and childish helplessness will not keep him interested.

Whenever Alice May wants to be indulged, she pleads that she is "not strong," a traditional ruse for getting one's own way.[10] Her husband responds by treating her like a child, by calling her his "cross little girl," his "poor little girl," and his "pet." Like Nora in Ibsen's *A*

Doll's House, Alice May manipulates him to get what she wants; theirs is not a frank relationship between two adults but more like a father-daughter relationship in which Alice May controls her husband by alternating between coquetry and helplessness. Roger is convinced that she is all a woman should be, fragile, childlike, lovely, and ignorant; he brags, "She's never voted, you know. She told me she didn't see what the law had to do with Southern ladies."[11]

Suddenly into their lives comes Mrs. Habersham's other daughter, Laura, who, unlike Alice May, was a chubby, unpopular girl. Years earlier, craving the attention she did not receive from young southern men, she turned to a northern man, who raped her. Her family, like Noel's in *The Unknown Goddess*, blames her for the seduction; her mother pays her to leave town and tells their friends that Laura went to Europe and died of a fever.

To Mrs. Habersham's surprise, however, Laura has not been "ruined" at all but is happy and productive. A career woman, Laura has not married but has many friends, both male and female, and makes it clear to her mother that she has sexual relationships as well. Mrs. Habersham cannot understand why, with such a life, Laura looks chic and elegant rather than dowdy and depraved. She has reared both her daughters to be ladies like herself; Alice May is a lady by traditional standards and Laura is not, yet Mrs. Habersham finds she dislikes Alice May and admires Laura.

How can a girl reared as a belle, then raped and disowned, come to live a happy life? Mrs. Habersham examines the past for an answer. She recalls Alice May's graduation twenty years earlier from the Cassandra Toombs Seminary for Young Ladies, at which Miss Cassandra proffered her annual advice to the girls (the same words Mrs. Habersham had heard at her own graduation): "Always remember, girls, that a lady must be pure. Among common people, women sometimes do awful things. But, when a lady does an awful thing, God punishes her. She is no longer a LADY: she becomes the *Scarlet Woman of Babylon*! Remember that, girls, and guard your good name and fair fame as you would guard pearls of great price. Like a pearl, if your diadem is dropped in vinegar, it is dissolved" (p. 128). Mrs. Habersham realizes that attitudes like this caused her to renounce her innocent daughter. Further, she realizes that she ignored Laura because Laura was not pretty—even thought that she need not worry about protecting the virtue of an unattractive child. Laura pathetically attempted to obtain the attention of young men who were uninterested in a girl who was not pretty; her seducer, like Noel's in *The Unknown Goddess*, was a person outside the southern code of behavior. Twenty years later, Mrs. Habersham struggles to accept the fact that Laura was not responsible for her own seduction. (As Mrs. Habersham exclaims, the term *rape* is used only "in connection to what a Negro man does to a white woman" [p. 247]; *seduction* is used to describe what a white man does to a white woman.)

Laura rejected the code represented by her mother's attitude, realizing consciously that she could live by convention and be ruined and miserable, or find the strength to continue with courage. Forcing her mother to face the truth, Laura now recounts the details of the rape. When her assailant began his attack, Laura's only defense was to repeat pathetically Miss Cassandra's sex lecture to him. Her appeal had no effect on the man; in her sexual ignorance, she believed at first that he was trying to kill her. Mrs. Habersham at last is forced to acknowledge the inadequacy of the values she taught her daughters, an inadequacy that Laura had to face at the scene of the rape.

The novel ends with Roger praising Laura's strength; Alice May realizes that to keep him, she will have to change. Mrs. Habersham accepts the fact that her set of values will not affect the resolution of this triangle: "Alice May and Roger had had a bomb thrown into their placidity of existence, but it was no affair of hers" (p. 300). Mrs. Habersham has learned the deficiencies of "southern charm" from her confrontation with the "new woman" who is Laura. Yet she cannot give Alice May the benefit of her wisdom; Alice May must learn for herself and must change if she can.

12

The Belle on Trial

Authors of the 1930s who indicted southern traditions often used the metaphor of the courtroom trial. This metaphor appeared fifty years earlier in Thomas Nelson Page's writing and reached a climax in William Faulkner's *Requiem for a Nun* in 1951. The trial recalls the Eden archetype; expulsion from Eden is only one of the penalties imposed for transgression—in Genesis Adam and Eve are judged guilty and a sentence imposed. Milton expanded this part of the story in *Paradise Lost*. Particularly in the Southern Renaissance, southern authors acted both as defendants and as prosecutors of their own society; they identified crimes, brought the suspects to judgment, decided guilt or innocence, determined appropriate punishments, and decided who might be capable of redemption.

A literal trial, often with a black rapist as defendant, occurs as a central plot feature, but in all the novels in this group there is a sense of ambiguousness about who is guilty and who is innocent; guilt is usually communal and southern society becomes the real defendant. Moreover, most of the belles in these novels are portrayed as the daughters of judges, who represent the traditions that are on trial (an ironic situation because these fathers are invariably poor judges of how to live and what values to pass on to their daughters). While the belle has always had a close relationship with her father, in books before 1900 her father was a planter-squire. The modern belle's father lives in town and works as a lawyer-judge whose task is to preserve legal tradition—hence the easy analogy with his role as a faded inheritor of the southern past. These authors found this metaphorical cluster appropriate because it provided them with a model for indicting the South and bringing it to trial before the ultimate jury, the reader.

Ward Greene examines the purity of the southern belle in *Death in the Deep South* (1936), a detective novel probably based on the Leo Frank case, which received much attention because of circumstantial evidence against Frank. Because its heroine, Mary Clay, is the daughter of a working-class father and because she is neither pure nor beautiful, she cannot be considered a belle according to the criteria we have defined. However, her community transforms her into a pure and beautiful representation of southern womanhood—but only after she is raped and murdered.

Greene uses the genre of the hard-boiled detective story to present the case of the murder of Mary Clay. Mary is a sixteen-year-old coquette, precociously wearing lipstick, high heels, and stockings to entice boys. Her flirting infuriates one young man, who follows her to the business college where she is taking secretarial courses. One hour later her body is discovered in the elevator shaft at the school; she has been beaten, raped, and strangled with her own silk stockings.

The reader is not told, however, that the young man is the murderer. In fact, as the search for her murderer becomes the focus of the novel, Mary Clay's reputation and character undergo a complete change as the townspeople and the media fabricate a legend. She is remembered as innocent when she was in fact sexually experienced: "The lily child, the innocent, the ewe lamb whose slaughter would cry to millions for atonement."[1] The first suspect is perfect for the script of which Mary is now a part—Tump, the school's black janitor, suspected only because the townspeople believe that all black men desire white women and, if the opportunity presents itself, will rape them.

But Tump is not the only serpent in this Garden. Greene carefully chronicles the assigning of guilt to those who fit in best with the town's expectations. For the object of their vengeance the townspeople finally settle on the northerner, Professor Hale, who teaches at the college. Because Tump has a feeble but reliable alibi, the better suspect seems to be Hale, both because he was at the school on the afternoon of the murder and because he is a northerner. A suitable scapegoat for the town's fears and hatreds, he is called a "foreigner," a "fairy . . . or a communist," all of which in this town are as bad as being a "nigger." Newspapers in the North and South take up opposite sides of Hale's case, arousing the emotions of the townspeople and uniting them as a group. Stating that the South's bigotry is the true criminal, northern papers criticize Hale's arrest and decry his probable conviction. Southern papers describe him as "the New York pervert who goes to trial today for the foulest crime ever perpetrated on an innocent daughter of Dixie in the first flower of her girlhood" (p. 72).

Greene presents the trial in the words of all those people in the town and outside it who either uphold or deny the myth of pure southern womanhood. The radio, the newspapers, the barrooms, the jury, and Hale in his cell provide the panoramic enlargement of the myth. The defense attorney blames the hysterical mood of the town on the depression: "They needed a victim. The times cried out for it. . . . Hatred and fear were the invisible witnesses" (p. 102). Ultimately, the mob judges Hale: they capture and hang him. The apotheosis of Mary Clay is thus an essential part of a societal myth that condones the hatred resulting from the community's fear of outsiders and blacks. Greene ingeniously forces the reader to attend to the psychology of the town rather than simply to discover "who done it," for the reader is never told who actually committed the murder of Mary Clay.

A rape is also the central action in John Peale Bishop's *Act of Darkness* (1935). Bishop, best known for his poetry and criticism and his friendships with Edmund Wilson, F. Scott Fitzgerald, and Allen Tate, uses several traditional belle devices, yet his treatment is among the most insightful and comprehensive of Southern Renaissance authors. The victim is Virginia Crannock, a judge's daughter who once scandalized the town in a rare uninhibited moment by riding astride a horse rather than sidesaddle. Her early exuberance does not ultimately exempt her from a fear of sexuality, which, Bishop implies, is the inevitable result of her society's injunction that a belle be pure. At the opening of the novel, Virginia, at thirty-seven, has never married.

Her seducer, Charlie, is not black but, as the title of the novel implies, the color of the rapist's skin is of no importance; the act of rape itself is what is evil. Although his family is one of the "best" in the community, Charlie has no respect whatever for the code of pure southern womanhood: "I used to wonder about her [southern woman], why she was supposed to be so delicate and so pure. Now I know. She was pregnant all the time . . . You had to protect her, on the chance that she was concealing a couple of children under the crinoline . . . I never saw any sense in this talk about southern chivalry."[2] Charlie represents the deterioration of his family; he gambles, drinks, and is cruel to his submissive wife, whose pregnancies he resents because they prevent him from having sexual relations.

Charlie's contempt for women includes Virginia, who criticizes his treatment of his wife and offers to help pay some of their bills. He raves, "They all try to get you down. And if you put two women together they're both at it. They'll try to twist you . . . There's only one thing you can do to a woman . . . You've got to strip her and take her . . . It's the only relation they understand" (pp. 131–32). His overt misogyny, unique in novels about the belle, is actually a manifestation of the same attitude that usually produces adulation. Katherine M. Rogers in *The Troublesome Helpmate: A History of Misogyny in Literature*, R. W. Hays in *The Dangerous Sex: The Myth of Feminine Evil*, and Karen Horney all contend that anxiety about women has traditionally been handled either by categorizing them as angels or whores, the first too exalted to "stoop" to hurting a man, the second too degraded to be able to threaten a man. Horney asserts that idolization of the female, the most prevalent traditional attitude toward the belle, is really an overcompensation in men who "actually fear and hate her."[3] Thus Charlie's hatred of women is simply the unadorned animosity and fear of his community, which professes to worship women.

When Virginia comes to stay with Caroline, one is reminded of the kitchen scenes in Williams's *A Streetcar Named Desire* as the aging but still lovely Virginia sits in a cool white dress with Charlie. Charlie and Virginia are physically attracted to each other, Charlie because he wishes to dominate this haughty lady, and Virginia because Charlie's sexuality arouses the passion she has repressed since her youth. When they take an early morning walk into a cornfield, Virginia knowingly places herself in a vulnerable situation, and the two have sexual relations. Whether a rape has occurred or not is left to a court, and to the reader, to decide.

Virginia's initial reaction to her first intercourse is like that of Temple Drake in *Sanctuary*; she experiences a dissociated fascination with her lost virginity. She recalls the act by using metaphors; she remembers Charlie lying on her as if he were a heavy "sky that could not rain." He "crushes" her, until "the night comes down in a violent rain" (p. 175), images that suggest an all-powerful sky-god who overpowers her. She believes, however, that she has participated in the act and perversely enjoys the idea that she may have tantalized Charlie; she tells no one of it until two months later when she consults a doctor to see if she is pregnant. She is not pregnant; but the doctor, shocked that a spinster has had sexual relations, persuades her to reveal the name of her lover. Soon afterward, Charlie is arrested for rape.

In court, Virginia's attorney represents her as a noble, pure, southern lady who has been horribly raped by a brutal beast. Like the attorney in Faulkner's *Sanctuary*, Virginia's attorney becomes her chivalrous defender, "the hero whose duty it was to protect Virginia" (p. 213). He makes much of the fact that Miss Virginia, as he calls her, wore a white dress and underclothes and was badly bruised.

The defense emphasizes first that Charlie is from a fine family; as the young narrator of the novel realizes, "it was impossible to convict a gentleman of anything" (p. 271). Charlie's own defense is rather bizarre: as a man, he says, he could not refuse her, even though "hating the woman . . . he shamelessly allowed her to complete his animal rapture . . . he swore he had only maintained a passive prowess. . . . 'I did only what a man must do'" (pp. 246–47). Charlie uses as his defense the belief that a man's passion is uncontrollable whereas a normal woman either feels no passion or is able to control it; hence, Virginia, who is a spinster, is not "normal" but rather lonely and frustrated.

Public opinion ironically condemns Virginia either way: if a rape occurred, she should now be insane with shame; if no rape, then why would a lady assent to the sex act? Ultimately, it is the fact that this tarnished southern lady remains self-contained and does not collapse that convinces the jury to declare Charlie not guilty. Even the prosecution's final appeal to the jury, to "protect and preserve the virtue of its women inviolable, to proclaim to all the world that the virtue and virginity of the women of this community are safe in the hands of a jury" (pp. 269–70), does not convince the jury that a "lady" would have reacted calmly to a rape.

The novel makes it clear that whether the act was a rape or a seduction is irrelevant; more important is the fact that southern beliefs do not provide suitable outlets for natural sexual drives. The narrator recalls the story of Othello and Desdemona, a tale of a society whose "moral disorder" resembles the chaos of this modern southern community. Charlie is not black, and Virginia is not young, but both participate in a dark and violent act, born out of the fear of female sexuality in southern women, shared by southern men and women alike. Leslie Fiedler rightly calls *Act of Darkness* an "inverted parable of rape and the Southern lady,"[4] because "the rapist of white women is black only as the dream of revenge against their emasculating Ladies is black inside the darkness of the white heads of Southern males."[5] In this inversion, Virginia is not (in her mind at least) the virgin her name implies; and, if she represents the State of Virginia, or the South itself, then her ambiguous purity and fading beauty are ironic comments about the South. By inverting the usual pattern of rapist and lady, Bishop shows how a regional myth can corrupt and disorder both men and women.

William Faulkner brings Temple Drake to trial in *Requiem for a Nun* (1951). Is it possible to reclaim a woman so debased as Temple? Is atonement possible in the fallen world of *Sanctuary?* Can Paradise be regained? The novel is set in Jefferson, Mississippi, about 1938, eight years after the Goodwin trial in *Sanctuary*. Only the most painful circumstances permit the suffering and atonement that can save a person who has been as depraved as Temple. When she realizes that she is responsible for the murder of her infant daughter, even though her black servant Nancy actually killed her, Temple at last is able to develop the qualities of unselfishness and love so frequently lacking in the belle. Moreover, the symbolic connection between Temple and the South resonates as an always implied deeper reading of the text.

Our last glimpse of Temple in *Sanctuary* was one of a totally depraved, vacuous woman. At the trial in *Sanctuary*, the district attorney defends Temple as the "sanctuary" or "temple" of southern values. The final tableau of Temple and her father at leisure in the Luxembourg Gardens shows her to be passive, bored, and narcissistic; she holds her mirror in her hand and gazes into it.

Temple does indeed represent southern womanhood, as George Marion O'Donnell's tidy schematization of the novel indicates.[6] More than a mere allegorical figure, however, she also symbolizes the decay of the southern ideals that she, as a belle, is supposed to embody. Because Faulkner shows that the ideals are in themselves destructive, the image of Narcissus is complete in the person of Temple Drake. Lewis P. Simpson assigns an even more cosmic significance to Temple beyond these: "Temple symbolizes the utter end of the dream of the moral regeneration of mankind in the beautiful and fertile garden of the New World."[7] Thus Faulkner finds the character of the southern belle an ideal vehicle for two of his major themes: the fall of the South and the fall of man.

In *Requiem*, Temple attempts to obtain clemency for Nancy by testifying at her trial; thus her own past is examined and she finds herself on trial again, with a second chance to help the actual defendant. At first she evades and rationalizes, but she finally confesses, describing herself as "the all-Mississippi debutante whose finishing school was the Memphis sporting house. . . . Temple Drake liked evil" and knew that "her father and brothers would know evil when they saw it, so all she had to do was, do the one thing which she knew they would forbid her to do."⁸ As Temple speaks, she realizes that she wishes not simply to save Nancy but to save her own soul. Telling the truth about her past becomes an admission that "The past is never dead. It isn't even the past" (p. 92). This statement suggests that, like Temple, the South can atone for its sins by facing the reality of its sins, "so limitless in capacity is man's imagination to disperse and burn away the rubble-dross of fact and probability, leaving only dream" (p. 261).

The three prologues to each of the "acts" of the novel function as Hawthorne's prologue, "The Custom House," does in *The Scarlet Letter*, universalizing the specific actions of the characters. Faulkner's prologues contain descriptions of the genesis of Yoknapatawpha County, not only in the time of man, but before time; the setting elevates the actions of the individual characters to a universal significance. As a result, *Requiem for a Nun* answers the question of how the individual and the society she represents can be redeemed by endorsing the courage to discard illusions, to tell the truth, and to suffer. Thus, Temple Drake Stevens discovers what Faulkner's other belles could not, what Narcissa Benbow, Caroline Compson, and Elly never even tried to discover—that self-centered love leads to repressed and perverted sexuality. Temple's atonement is not a guarantee of redemption, but at least that possibility is open to her and at least the possibility can exist in the modern world.

The modern southern belles in Faulkner's fiction are diminished in comparison to their nineteenth-century counterparts in his fiction; most are doomed by their own narcissism to destroy themselves and other people. Ironically it is Temple, the sanctuary of southern womanhood, and thereby the most destructive and depraved of all of Faulkner's belles, who offers the most hope for the salvation not simply of the fallen South, which she represents, but of the fallen world, which the South itself represents. Thus, the southern belle in Faulkner's fiction is at once a symbol of the Old South and the New, and of the fall of man. And the belle is also a symbol of the regeneration of the individual, of the South, and of humanity. In 1950, when Faulkner accepted the Nobel Prize, he asserted that "love and honor and pity and pride and compassion and sacrifice" are the qualities that enable humanity to "endure and prevail."⁹ In *Requiem for a Nun*, published a year after this address, Faulkner chooses one character from all his past fiction to be the seeker after these qualities. It is Temple, the fallen belle, who is this seeker.

EPILOGUE

After the Fall: The Persistence of the Belle
in Contemporary Literature

A traditional southern—and uniquely American—character, the belle figure has been a perfect vehicle with which to represent the flowering of the Old South in antebellum times, the "rape" of the South during and after the Civil War, and the decay of the South in the glare of modernism in the twentieth century.

But the best writers of the Southern Renaissance do not simply represent the belle as a straw goddess; she is not an allegory, nor a stereotype, in the works of Faulkner, Glasgow, Gordon, and Mitchell. These writers create a character who has her own integrity independent of her mythic significance, because they show southern woman herself as a victim of the myth of southern womanhood. Her oppression by the patriarchy and her repression of emotion and sexuality in order to conform to the myth itself are the themes of the best of these modern writers. Another modern theme is the self-destruction of the belle, encouraged by nineteenth-century society, which required her to be beautiful and thus caused her to be narcissistic. Writers of the Southern Renaissance show that all of these aspects of the belle's environment contrive to make her incapable of dealing with the demands of modern life.

The relationship of the belle to the race issue is yet another recurring concern of the Southern Renaissance writer. In particular, the importance of rape as a southern preoccupation—as a matter not only of violence but also of sexuality and race—is a motif of modern fiction.

The imagery modern writers use when speaking of the belle correlates perfectly with that of nineteenth-century writers. Authors use the pastoral metaphor of the South as Eden to speak about the southern woman as Eve, who must be protected from the satans her society produces. The trial metaphor, in which the southern woman literally goes to trial or is the daughter of a judge, often represents the southern way of life being "put on trial."

While several writers of the Southern Renaissance are better writers than others (for example, Glasgow, Faulkner, and Tate are admittedly superior to Greene, Pope, and Young), it is clear that great writers are always part of a literary milieu and are responding to the same set of traditions and modern influences as less well-known and less talented writers. By studying both kinds of writers comparatively, we can see that our best writers *are* superior because they understand the enormity of their task; the belle can be a stereotype, or she can be used to indict southern tradition, or she can be a fallen Eve. To employ the belle as a symbol and to create a believable character besides are the tasks of the great novelist; only a Glasgow or a Faulkner can do it consistently, although Glenn's Julia and Mitchell's Scarlett belong in the list of splendidly created characters.

The hundred-year span that is the scope of this book marks the stunning transition of the belle figure from a representative of the virtues of southern society to an embodiment of its vices. Her fate and that of the South continue to be themes in literature, but the modern reader is no longer surprised when the belle is less than a lady. In fact, the fallen belle, an astonishing development in the 1920s, has become a new stereotype, a cliché that only the best writer can handle with freshness. The mediocre and the worst of them write popular, often lurid historical romances.

The aim of the popularizers is solely to titillate a reader who is interested in the sensationalizing of the Old South. Plot in their books concerns the rape of the "pure" southern belle by a black; the belle is not a symbol, and the act is not political but is motivated solely by lust—his and hers—and by the sexual inadequacy of white men and by the animal-like virility of black men. This last "motivation" is an ironic return to the stereotypes of writers like Thomas Dixon, Jr. The demeaning notion that all women want to be raped is standard. There is no metaphor of the Garden, nor any other metaphor. What action there is is based on violence—whippings and castrations. The novels of Kyle Onstott, which include *Mandingo*, are the best of this "worst" category, for they are at least thoroughly researched and historically accurate.

The best authors after 1940 have a double self-consciousness when dealing with the belle; they are reacting still to the same myths as writers of the 1920s and 1930s, but they have also read Faulkner,

Glasgow, Tate, and Mitchell. The milieu in which they write has been drastically changed, as much by the core writers of the Southern Renaissance as by World War II. The very self-consciousness of these writers necessitates a different treatment of their works, one that is outside the range and purpose of this study and one that many critics have fruitfully begun. Jane Flanders's essay "Katherine Anne Porter and the Ordeal of Southern Womanhood" contends that Porter's belle figures, especially Miranda, give evidence of the "rigidly circumscribed experience and sexual repression of the white Southern woman . . . by the doctrine, taboos and social realities of a paternalistic culture."[1] Fine criticism has been written on the belles in the plays of Tennessee Williams, although no study has yet fully related them to the continuity of the belle tradition. For example, Amanda Wingfield's illusions about her gentlemen callers in *The Glass Menagerie* (1945) are a common motif in works about the belle, one that appears as early as 1904 with Mrs. Blake in Glasgow's novel *The Deliverance*. Blanche du Bois' sense of propriety in *A Streetcar Named Desire* (1947) clashes with her repressed sexual drives when, like Virginia in *Act of Darkness* (1935), she confronts a man outside the code of southern chivalry, a man whose overt sexuality is simultaneously desirable and repulsive to her. In addition, her narcissistic coquetry induces her to entice the one man who can destroy her. Blanche cannot reconcile her divided personality in the face of the violent passions of the modern world; consequently, she withdraws into a world of illusions and madness. She is thus an anachronistic representative of a moribund social order, whose dictates both cause her internal anxiety and make her unfit to cope with the modern world.

William Styron's Peyton Loftis in his first novel, *Lie Down in Darkness* (1951), repeats a typical situation for the belle in her incestuous attachment to her father. Since Peyton's self-love depends on her father's attention alone, her personality cannot withstand the assaults of sharing his love or of being removed from it. And, as with Temple Drake and Alabama Beggs, Peyton's narcissism prevents her from being able to love her husband or any other man. Sexual relations with her husband and other men become futile, guilt-ridden attempts to obtain the affection that Peyton wishes to receive from her father. Her withdrawal into a schizophrenic fantasy world leads eventually to her suicide, her symbolic flight from reality back to her father's arms.

Thus Styron's first novel develops traits that make the belle a figure of tragedy. His most recent novel, *Sophie's Choice*, places the belle in the mainstream of human life. While not the protagonist, the belle is a counterpoint to Sophie, in the ghostly presence of Maria Hunt, the young woman whose suicide is the genesis of Stingo's novel. Styron's plot and several other aspects of *Sophie's Choice* both blur and clarify the tension between autobiography and fiction in a way that few modern novelists have dared. *Inheritance of Night*, Stingo's book, is the obvious fictional analogue of Styron's own *Lie Down in Darkness*. The doom that enshrouds Peyton Loftis is parallel to that of Sophie: the internal torment of a beautiful, young, privileged woman whose father committed vast injustices in the service of a society gone berserk. The tendency of these women, so caught up with their fathers' love yet so repelled by their fathers' crimes, is to seek out punishment and fulfillment with men who are catalysts to help them achieve self-destruction.

Styron as Stingo is conscious of these parallels, as evidenced by passages comparing the American South with prewar Poland—physically, in descriptions of landscapes; and in the shared experience of defeat and occupation by hated enemies, with the consequent hatred of scapegoat groups (blacks and Jews) as modes of compensation. How a young, sensitive woman is molded within such a social order is the focus of both novels. The reader of *Lie Down in Darkness* can readily perceive the Faulkner parallels, the Oedipal innuendos, the failed myths of decayed aristocracy, southern gentleman, and belle; but *Sophie's Choice* challenges us to look at *Lie Down in Darkness* through several darker glasses, to blur our demythologized perception so as to see the myths once again.

The novels of Shirley Ann Grau, in particular her Pulitzer Prize–winning *The Keepers of the House* (1964), show the belle in relation to the blacks on the plantation as well as to the whites—perhaps the favorite modern variant of the kind of belle who was established in fiction by 1939. Possibly as a result of the renewed commitment in the late 1950s to the civil rights movement, novels about the belle after this date emphasize sexual relations between blacks and whites. Grau's aim in her novels, however, is to develop a character, not to titillate readers. While the issue of race and sex in the South is potentially sensational, she treats it compassionately.

Other valuable recent contributions are the works of Margaret Walker and Alex Haley. Walker's *Jubilee* (1966) is told from the point of view of a courageous young black woman, not the traditional protagonist for such novels. The tone of the novel is one of compassion toward the belle and the slave, who are both victims of a dehumanizing institution. Alex Haley's *Roots* (1976) is the history of a southern black family, from their origins in West Africa to the present. While an oversimplified and romantic account, in which the blacks are too good and the whites are too evil, the book is nevertheless historically based and is quite moving. Haley has created a new surge of interest in the Old South that may result in more authentic fictional treatments.

The fate of the belle in a modern twentieth-century setting also continues to be a topic in fiction and nonfiction. In Willie Morris's novel, *The Last of the Southern Girls* (1973), Carol Honeywell's charm and beauty become her chief weapons in games of political intrigue and power in the nation's capitol. Carol searches for sexual fulfillment as she tries to discard the taboos her southern upbringing has taught her. Essays and articles about the belle stereotype abound in popular magazines—for example, those of Florence King, author of *Southern Ladies and Gentlemen* (1975), Barbara Howar, and poet Rosemary Rogers. A psychoanalytic case study of a woman called "Belle" appears in Dr. Robert L. Stoller's *Sexual Excitement* (1979).

The best of the contemporary-belle authors is Gail Godwin. In short stories and novels, she refers steadily to the work of Ellen Glasgow, prolific novelist of the Southern Renaissance. Godwin and Glasgow both write about young southern women, and their work is similar in theme and characterization. In particular both Glasgow's and Godwin's central focus is the pervasively difficult relationship between mothers and daughters, difficult because the mothers so often embody the ethic of self-sacrifice and denial that characterize traditional southern mores. The daughters attempt to realize themselves as autonomous women of action and to do so must reject these mores—hence reject the women who represent them, their mothers. This deep psychic separation is not easy for the Glasgow daughter, and especially those in *Virginia, Life and Gabriella*, and the Queenborough trilogy. Godwin quite directly refers to the isolated state of her contemporary young women, whose independence is purchased at the price of severed relationships with their mothers. To Godwin mothers are also the repository of restrictive structures for southern women, but she moves beyond Glasgow's rather gloomy prognosis for contemporary women. In *Glass People* (1972), *The Odd Woman* (1974), and *A Mother and Two Daughters* (1982), the young women return to the South, to the heritage they have rejected, and to their mothers, and find that within their pasts are values that console, sustain, and inspire them. Godwin's work both imitates art and is enriched by art, for she finds in Glasgow her creative and psychic mother, whose writing can be cherished and employed to inspire new directions.

As a literary phenomenon, the southern belle is a fascinating vehicle for cultural and psychological motifs. In the hands of an unskilled author, she is merely a stereotype; for a Faulkner or a Glasgow, however, she can be both a poignant, complex individual and a multifaceted symbol of an entire society. And even though most authors acknowledge the role of belle as anachronistic and injurious, they continue to paint her portrait in their works. Perhaps her fascination is ultimately that she represents a human ideal, now regarded as antique, but at once eliciting a paradoxical nostalgia and serving as a warning for the present. As a role model for contemporary women, the belle should be avoided. As one of the most complex images of woman in literature, her day is certainly not over.

NOTES

Full publishing information may be found in the bibliography.

Introduction: The Goddess in the Southern Pantheon

1. Bagby, *The Old Virginia Gentleman*, 16.
2. Faulkner, *Sanctuary*, 231–32.
3. Gaines, *The Southern Plantation*, 1–17.
4. Putnam, *The Lady*, 296.
5. Eliade, *Myth and Reality*, 72.
6. Wertenbaker, *Patrician and Plebeian in Virginia*. See also Owsley, *Plain Folk of the Old South*. Recent histories continue to debunk the stereotypes. The two best on southern women are Anne Firor Scott's *The Southern Lady: From Pedestal to Politics, 1830–1930*, and Catherine Clinton's *The Plantation Mistress*.
7. Discussions of the southern mythos include Frederick J. Hoffman's *The Art of Southern Fiction*, 1–28. Hoffman's first chapter is a particularly succinct summary. The essays in Louis D. Rubin and Jay B. Hubbell's *The South in American Literature: 1607–1900* offer fine analyses as well.

Francis Pendleton Gaines's *The Southern Plantation*, published in 1924, is the paradigm for such studies. Gaines separates the popular conception of the plantation from the actual historical plantation, and he presents three types of plantation characters who have occupied the literature and legends of the South: the planter, the belle, and the black. W. J. Cash's *The Mind of the South* also furnishes much general material for understanding southern myths. The southern cavalier and the South's tradition of aristocracy have been exhaustively studied by William R. Taylor in *Cavalier and Yankee*. Shields McIlwaine's *The Southern Poor White from Lubberland to Tobacco Road* investigates this figure in modern southern literature. The myths of southern history and of the Civil War have been examined by Thomas J. Wertenbaker, *The Old South*; C. Vann Woodward, "The Irony of Southern History," in *Southern Renascence*; and Bertram Wyatt-Brown, *Southern Honor*. The myth of the New South after the Civil War has been studied by Paul M. Gaston, *The Old Creed: A Study in Southern Mythmaking*, and George Tindall, *The Emergence of the New South Creed: 1913–1945*. The black as a subject of myth and as an inhabitant of the South has been, since

Thomas Nelson Page's *The Negro*, a continuing topic of study for the critic and scholar.

Yet in all these studies the belle is either ignored or receives only partial treatment. Francis P. Gaines identifies the southern belle as a character in the popular tradition of the southern plantation, not an artistic tradition—a character from popular culture who happens to appear in literature. The belle, as he describes her, is "one of the delights of popular fancy. She is the Juliet of our National romance; not even the war could alter sentiment concerning her, for many a Northern soldier married the Southern girl. Beautiful, graceful, accomplished in social charm, bewitching in coquetry yet strangely steadfast in soul, she is perhaps the most winsome figure in the whole field of our fancy. The loveliness of her costume is a part of the image" (16).

Gaines is the first commentator to point out that the belle's predominant virtue is chastity, "a spotlessness in thought and act," which he compares with the literature of the twenties in which "the Magdalen has eclipsed the Madonna" (176). Not satisfied with simply presenting the image, Gaines looks for the reality of the belle, as he does with all the plantation characters, finding a woman who was "the boast and idol of masculine society . . . [and yet] the pathetic victim of society" (180). She is utterly dependent economically, she is restricted by excessive chaperonage (which, Gaines implies, inhibits authentic relationships), and she is forced to marry men who hold to a double standard of morality, compelling her to tolerate her husband's black mistresses (181). These aspects of southern plantation life are carefully excluded from the idyll in nineteenth-century fiction.

The first book-length study of the southern lady in literature is Marie Fletcher's 1963 dissertation, "The Southern Heroine in the Fiction of Representative Southern Women Writers, 1850–1960." Unfortunately the boundaries of this study exclude male writers who also depict the southern belle, and Fletcher's definition of the belle includes the middle-class and lower-class southern woman, when in fact the belle figure must properly be defined as an unmarried young aristocratic lady. As a balanced overview, Fletcher's study is commendable because, like so many first studies in uncharted areas, it describes many works without trying to mold each to fit a central hypothesis. She concludes, however, that the southern woman emerges in the fiction of the Southern Renaissance as "an independent, capable, yet pretty woman who attains her status not by birth or wealth but by her inner worth," who takes the place of the "pure and beautiful lady" of prior literature (iv). This optimistic conclusion does indeed apply to the lower- and middle-class women in many of the novels, such as those of Caroline Gordon and Eudora Welty. Dorinda Oakley in Ellen Glasgow's *Barren Ground*, who works for her living in spite of the distractions of men, her "nerves," and her sexual drives, certainly conforms to the pattern Fletcher describes. Her study does not, however, account for the portrayal of the southern belle in fiction of the twenties and thirties. For example, Katharine Faraday in Frances Newman's *The Hard-Boiled Virgin*, far from being self-reliant, becomes self-deluded, artificial, a victim of a rigid code that robs her of the potential implied in the title's egg image; hers becomes a petrified, toughened personality. Certainly Fletcher's thesis does not account for Temple Drake, Blanche du Bois, Scarlett O'Hara, or Peyton Loftis.

The only work that attempts a study of these modern belles is a 1975 dissertation, "Myth and Agony: The Southern Woman as Belle," by Anne W. Lyons. Lyons hypothesizes that the belle was an artistic invention of the nineteenth-century sentimental novelist who wished to create colorful descriptions of heroines and hence used sets of unrelated physical features and personality traits in grammatical "parataxis," producing a superficial character through a faulty aesthetic; in the hands of a Faulkner, a Capote, or a Williams, however, the belle becomes not a stereotype but "genuinely real and humanly sensitive," no longer a vehicle for other concerns that authors tend to project upon her. Lyons finds "no evolution of the character" from her first appearance to the present, since authors merely move the scenery around her and retain the stereotype. For example, according to Lyons, Blanche du Bois in Tennessee Williams's *A Streetcar Named Desire* is the same belle as Bel Tracy in John P. Kennedy's *Swallow Barn*, an 1832 plantation novel regarded as the first successful novel in that tradition. Blanche is merely placed in a new environment in which—a credit to Williams's aesthetic—she cannot live, either as a stereotype or as a human being.

Lyons's study contributes most to the topic when it emphasizes the nineteenth-century aesthetic requirements for the novelist. To maintain that the belle functions as a mere literary stereotype, however, is to ignore her centrality in southern mythology and her significance as a cultural ideal. Furthermore, such a thesis resists finding any consistent pattern within both the traditional belle and the modern belle. In short, the sociology of the culture that produced her and the psychology of the character herself are deemphasized, since Lyons sees the belle as a literary stylization placed in different settings.

Anne Goodwyn Jones's *Tomorrow Is Another Day: The Woman Writer in the South, 1859–1936* does much to begin to analyze the tension created within the southern woman trying to conform to psychologically contradictory ideals. Her book explores the biographies of seven southern women writers and shows how their major works—indeed, the fact that they wrote at all—allowed these authors to remove the masks that their society had encouraged them to wear. Jones's purpose, however, was not to describe or analyze the belle figure created by male and female authors; hence the diverse manifestations of the belle remain to be reconciled.

8. Beauvoir, *The Second Sex*, 137–38.
9. Gilbert and Gubar, *Madwoman in the Attic*, 12–14.

Chapter 1: The Belle as an Antebellum Ideal

1. Mitchell, *Gone with the Wind*, 7.
2. Kennedy, *Swallow Barn*, 85.
3. Papashvily, *All the Happy Endings*.
4. Kennedy, *Swallow Barn*, 109.
5. Houghton, *The Victorian Frame of Mind, 1830–1870*, 341–92.
6. Ibid., 252.
7. Ibid., 385.
8. The actual facts of the matter were forgotten. Frederick Law Olmstead, writing

in 1861, points out that the names of the "old families" of the plantations were not those of cavaliers but of "tinkers and tailors, poacher and pickpocket, indentured servants bound for Virginia" (*The Cotton Kingdom*, 335).

9. Of the authors studied, only Kennedy was aware that Bel's patrician snobbery is pretentious at best, based on illusion rather than verifiable reality. Bel herself is unaware of the fantasy in which she lives, as she seeks to have her gentlemen conform to her image of them as knights. They respond both by sheltering her from the fact that she and they are not aristocrats and by using the ruses of medieval courtly love, thus reinforcing her fantasy. Ned's "love disease" resembles that of Troilus himself; his behavior is wild, melancholy, and erratic, his hair grows too long, his clothing is unbrushed. See Kennedy, *Swallow Barn*, 192.

10. Taylor, *Cavalier and Yankee*, 146.
11. Gaines, *The Southern Plantation*, 19.
12. Taylor, *Cavalier and Yankee*, 147.
13. See Scott, *The Southern Lady*.
14. Dew, "On the Characteristic Differences between the Sexes," 495.
15. Ibid., 498.
16. Ibid., 499.
17. Ibid., 501.
18. Bartlett and Cambor, "The History and Psychodynamics of Southern Womanhood."
19. Hale, *Sketches of American Character*, 104. While Hale was a northerner, her work was widely read in the South; moreover, at this early date, the regional identification of North and South was less pronounced than it was to become by the 1840s.
20. Ibid.
21. Hale, *Northwood*, II: 146.
22. Ibid., I: 19.
23. Ibid., I: 31−32.
24. Hentz, *Linda*, 8.
25. Ibid., 104.
26. Fiedler, *Love and Death in the American Novel* (1966), 12.
27. Hentz, *Eoline; or Magnolia Vale*, 304.
28. Ibid., 22.
29. Ibid., 161.
30. Ibid., 251.
31. Stowe, *Uncle Tom's Cabin*, 209.
32. Ibid., 218.
33. Ibid., 220−21.
34. Ibid., 237.
35. Ibid., 278.
36. Hentz, *Marcus Warland*, 7.
37. Phelps, "Southern Housekeepers," 189.
38. Ibid.
39. Ibid., 193.
40. Hentz, "The Beauty Transformed," 277−78.

Chapter 2: The Belle as the Fallen South

1. De Forest, *Miss Ravenel's Conversion from Secession to Loyalty*, 64. Subsequent references in this chapter are cited in the text.

2. De Forest, *The Bloody Chasm*, 28. Subsequent references in this chapter are cited in the text.

3. Several parallels to Scarlett O'Hara's situation in *Gone with the Wind* (1936) are evident; certain characters, situations, and even dialogue correspond to those in Margaret Mitchell's novel. This novel was probably an influence on Mitchell's work.

4. See Coulter, *The South During Reconstruction*, 65, 385–91, for a discussion of the attitudes of the New South.

5. Eggleston, *Dorothy South*, 338–39. Subsequent references in this chapter are cited in the text.

Chapter 3: The Southern Renaissance

1. John M. Bradbury, *Renaissance in the South*, 7.

2. Stewart, *The Burden of Time*, 94–95.

3. Cash, *The Mind of the South*, 282.

4. E. Scott, *Migrations*, 228.

5. Cash, *The Mind of the South*, 293.

6. Bradbury, *Renaissance in the South*, 8.

7. O'Neill, *The Woman Movement*, 80.

8. A. Scott, *The Southern Lady*, 166–67.

9. Quoted in Anthony and Harper, eds., *History of Woman Suffrage*, IV: 97.

10. A. Scott, *Southern Lady*, 126.

11. Tate, "The Fugitive, 1922–1925," 83.

12. Rubin, "Southern Literature"; Holman, *The Roots of Southern Writing*; Bradbury, *Renaissance in the South*.

13. Rubin, "Southern Literature," 33.

14. Geismar, *Writers in Crisis*, viii.

15. Dollard (in *Caste and Class in a Southern Town*, 9) points out that this feeling persists into the twentieth century.

16. Stewart, *Burden of Time*, 96.

17. The novels of F. Scott Fitzgerald blend the figure of the flapper with that of the belle, a complex portrait that requires an entire study of its own. Since he is not a southern writer who is part of the Southern Renaissance, his works are not included in this chapter (see note 27 for this chapter). The career woman appears continuously in fiction, often as a single woman, hence as the stereotypical old maid. See Deegan, *The Stereotype of the Single Woman in American Novels*.

18. Gaines, *The Southern Plantation*, 176.

19. "Southern Letters," 214.

20. Haardt, "The Southern Lady Says Grace," 57. Subsequent references in this chapter are cited in the text.

21. Quoted in Kunitz, *Twentieth Century Authors*, 1253.

22. E. Scott, *Narcissus*, 3. Subsequent references in this chapter are cited in the text.

23. Horney, *The Neurotic Personality of Our Time*, 270.

24. Pope, *Not Magnolia*, 28. Subsequent references in this chapter are cited in the text.

25. Z. Fitzgerald, *Save Me the Waltz*, 38.

26. See Horney, *Feminine Psychology*, 229.

27. Z. Fitzgerald, *Save Me the Waltz*, 40. Subsequent references in this chapter are cited in the text.

Scott Donaldson has studied the belle figure in Scott Fitzgerald's short stories; see his "Scott Fitzgerald's Romance with the South." Donaldson contends that Fitzgerald's progressively negative portraits of belles are based on his deteriorating relationship with Zelda Fitzgerald. Fitzgerald's use of the literary archetype of the belle, however, in works such as *The Great Gatsby* and, indeed, in most of his fiction, merits fuller treatment than Donaldson's biographical interpretation. A recent view is found in C. Hugh Holman's essay, "Fitzgerald's Changes on the Southern Belle: The Tarleton Trilogy."

28. Horney, *New Ways in Psychoanalysis*, 91.

29. Horney, *Feminine Psychology*, 229.

Chapter 4: Frances Newman

1. Donald Davidson, "Review," 27.

2. Ibid.

3. Ibid., 28.

4. West, *The Strange Necessity*, 328.

5. Ibid., 333.

6. See Horney, *Feminine Psychology*, 230, on the sort of society that fosters neurotic masochism.

7. Newman, *The Hard-Boiled Virgin*, 29. Subsequent references in this chapter are cited in the text.

8. Karen Horney points out that segregation of a young girl from men can result in anxious relationships with men later in the girl's life (*Feminine Psychology*, 128).

9. Newman, *Dead Lovers Are Faithful Lovers*, 32. Subsequent references in this chapter are cited in the text.

10. Adrienne Rich, *Of Woman Born*, 290.

Chapter 5: Historical Novels of the Depression

1. Pertinent discussions of the literary climate of the 1930s are Leslie Fiedler's "Afterword: John Peale Bishop and the Other Thirties," in *Act of Darkness*, by John Peale Bishop, 305–19; and Louis D. Rubin, Jr.'s essay "Trouble on the Land: Southern Literature and the Great Depression," 96–113.

2. *I'll Take My Stand*, xxvi. Subsequent references in this chapter are cited in the text.

3. Lawson, "Portrait of a Culture in Crisis," 150.

4. Gordon, *Penhally*, 180.

5. Young, "Not in Memoriam, But in Defense," in *I'll Take My Stand*, 348–49.

6. Hackett, *Fifty Years of Best Sellers, 1895–1945*, 69. In this same year, Carl Carmer's paean to the South, *Stars Fell on Alabama*, containing his descriptions of the persistence of present-day belles, was number three on the best-selling nonfiction list.

7. Bradbury, *Renaissance in the South*, 49.

8. Young, *So Red the Rose*, 55. Subsequent references in this chapter are cited in the text.

9. Faulkner, *The Unvanquished*, 167. Subsequent references in this chapter are cited in the text.

10. See Wyatt-Brown, *Southern Honor*, 173.

11. Hackett, *Fifty Years of Best Sellers, 1895–1945*, 74.

12. Mitchell, *Gone with the Wind*, 3. Subsequent references in this chapter are cited in the text.

13. Horney, *Feminine Psychology*, 126.

Chapter 6: Memory and Illusion

1. Hackett, *Fifty Years of Best Sellers, 1895–1945*, 20.

2. Auchincloss, *Ellen Glasgow*, 14.

3. Glasgow, *The Deliverance*, 198. Subsequent references in this chapter are cited in the text.

4. Pope, *Old Lady Esteroy*, 84.

5. Greene, *Weep No More*, 284.

6. Glasgow, *Virginia* (1929), viii.

7. Glasgow, *Virginia* (1913), 22. Subsequent references in this chapter are cited in the text.

8. Glenn, *A Short History of Julia*, 25.

9. George Cary Eggleston, *Dorothy South*, 423. Subsequent references in this chapter are cited in the text.

10. Scott, *Migrations*, 3. Subsequent references in this chapter are cited in the text.

Chapter 7: Ellen Glasgow's Belles

1. Glasgow, *The Miller of Old Church*, 130–31.

2. Auchincloss, *Ellen Glasgow*, 46. Several other studies of Glasgow's fiction have useful comments on her belle figures. Those most helpful to this study, besides the ones already mentioned, are Frederick P. W. McDowell's *Ellen Glasgow and the Ironic Art of Fiction* and Joan Foster Santas's "Ellen Glasgow's American Dream."

3. John Edward Hardy in "Ellen Glasgow" contends that Glasgow's ladies are stereotypes, but they are more complicated. Nor are they only symbols of repression, as Maxwell Geismar contends in *Rebels and Ancestors*, 281.

4. Glasgow, *A Certain Measure*, 11.

5. Ibid., 13.

6. Ibid., 21.

7. Glasgow, *The Battle-Ground*, 86. Subsequent references in this chapter are cited in the text.

8. Clinton, *The Plantation Mistress*, 28.

9. Glasgow, *The Deliverance*, 481. Subsequent references in this chapter are cited in the text.

10. Horney, *Feminine Psychology*, 227.

11. In this study I do not treat the character of Marie Fletcher, who is not a belle because she is not the daughter of landed gentry. Consequently, Glasgow asserts, she is prey to her own "rustic temperament," that is, sexual passion, when she sees the tanned and muscular Christopher. In later novels Glasgow confronts the notion that an upper-class woman could also be swayed by physical desire.

12. Glasgow, *The Woman Within*, 104.

13. Ibid.

14. Cabell, "Two Sides of the Shielded," in *Some of Us*, 52.

15. Horney, *Feminine Psychology*, 230.

16. Ibid., 229.

17. Glasgow, *The Ancient Law*, 49. Subsequent references in this chapter are cited in the text.

18. In contrast, another character, Emily Brooke, is always placed in a lovely garden, a setting that indicates her naturalness.

19. Glasgow, *The Romance of a Plain Man*, 183. Subsequent references in this chapter are cited in the text.

20. Overton, *The Women Who Make Our Novels*, 32–33.

21. Glasgow, *Life and Gabriella*, 30. Subsequent references in this chapter are cited in the text.

22. Wagner, *Ellen Glasgow: Beyond Convention*, 19.

23. Glasgow's own personal life, fraught as it was with painful love relationships, might account for her propensity for this sort of ending in her novels. It is significant that she begins this pattern in *Life and Gabriella*, written in 1916, several years before her fiancé deserted her for the Queen of Romania. Thus, the ending of *Barren Ground* is probably not merely a result of the trauma of her broken engagement but a deeper hostility, perhaps toward a distant or absent father, as is often the case in such fantasies, Horney points out. Perhaps this is why Gabriella has no father. The deaths of these men are analogous to the castration complex Horney describes (as opposed to Freud's theory of penis envy), in which the girl is angry with the father when she realizes she cannot have him as the object of her infantile sexual desires, nor can she have his child as proof of his love for her (*Feminine Psychology*, 48). A child whose father is dead, like Gabriella, also feels angry with him for deserting her.

24. Glasgow, *A Certain Measure*, 150.

25. *Barren Ground*, while thematically related to these novels and to *Life and Gabriella*, does not contain the young woman of genteel origins that I am defining as a belle. Similarities between Dorinda and other Glasgow belles, however, have been noted when appropriate.

26. Glasgow, *The Romantic Comedians*, 56. Subsequent references in this chapter are cited in the text.

27. See my article "The Comic Male: Satire in Ellen Glasgow's Queenborough Trilogy."

28. The narrator's ironic stance encourages the reader to believe that Glasgow shares the views of her narrator.

29. Glasgow, *A Certain Measure*, 234.

30. Ibid., 231.

31. Ibid., 238.

32. Glasgow, *They Stooped to Folly*, 83. Subsequent references in this chapter are cited in the text.

33. Glasgow, *A Certain Measure*, 45–46.

34. Horney, *The Neurotic Personality of Our Time*, 174.

35. Glasgow, *The Sheltered Life*, 344. Subsequent references in this chapter are cited in the text.

36. The symbol of the machine in the South is a variant of the theme discussed in Leo Marx's *Machine in the Garden*.

Chapter 8: William Faulkner

1. Faulkner, *Soldier's Pay*, 71. Subsequent references in this chapter are cited in the text.

2. See Horney, *New Ways in Psychoanalysis*, 89.

3. Geismar, "William Faulkner: The Negro and the Female," in *Writers in Crisis*, 147.

4. S. Page, *Faulkner's Women*, 17.

5. Bettelheim, *Uses of Enchantment*, 203.

6. Faulkner, *Sartoris*, 41. Subsequent references in this chapter are cited in the text.

7. Warren, "Faulkner: The South, the Negro, and Time," in *Faulkner: A Collection of Critical Essays*, 251.

8. Vickery, *The Novels of William Faulkner*, 22.

9. Faulkner, *Sanctuary*, 89. Subsequent references in this chapter are cited in the text.

10. S. Page, *Faulkner's Women*, 83.

11. Faulkner, "There Was a Queen," in *Collected Stories*, 729.

12. Faulkner, "Elly," in *Collected Stories*, 210. Subsequent references in this chapter are cited in the text.

13. Brien, "William Faulkner and the Myth of Woman," 132.

14. Beauvoir, *The Second Sex*, 613.

15. Horney, *Feminine Psychology*, 229.

16. The main questions that have perplexed critics are posed by James R. Cypher in "The Tangled Sexuality of Temple Drake." Why does Temple remain at the plantation when she has ample opportunity to escape? Why does she submit to her captivity at Miss Reba's Memphis brothel? And why does she testify against Goodwin, herself becoming the instrument of his death? Cypher's approach to these questions is psychoanalytic: Temple has been reared by her father alone. She is the victim not of Popeye but of an unresolved Electra complex whereby she transfers her incestuous love for her stern father, and her obedience to him, to a father-surrogate,

Popeye. Her obedience to her father accounts for her testimony at the trial, and her European trip represents the "honeymoon" of Temple and the man she has wanted all along, her father.

Cypher does not ask any questions about Temple's flirtatious hysteria at the plantation, her preoccupation with her own rape, her submission to violent perversion, and her lurid nymphomania. Psychiatrist Lawrence S. Kubie ("William Faulkner's *Sanctuary*"), attempting to explain Temple's motives, repeats the discussion of the Electra complex, although he adds that Temple's fantasies reveal a classic case of penis envy; because of this jealousy, Temple seeks to castrate men by exciting them with flirtatious behavior, though she ultimately never satisfies them.

Kubie's argument still does not account for Temple's passivity after her rape. In "Faulkner's Mythology" George Marion O'Donnell resolves this difficulty by explaining Temple as an allegorical figure: "Southern Womanhood Corrupted but Undefiled (Temple Drake), in the company of Corrupted Tradition (Gowan Stevens, a professional Virginian), falls into the clutches of amoral Modernism (Popeye), which is itself impotent, but which with the aid of its strong ally Natural Lust ("Red") rapes Southern Womanhood unnaturally and then seduces her so satisfactorily that her corruption is total, and she becomes the tacit ally of Modernism. Meanwhile Pore White Trash (Goodwin) has been accused of the crime which he, with the aid of the Naif Faithful (Tawmmy), actually tried to prevent. The Formalized Tradition (Horace Benbow), perceiving the true state of affairs, tries vainly to defend Pore White Trash. However, Southern Womanhood is so hopelessly corrupted that she willfully sees Pore White Trash convicted and lynched; she is then carried off by Wealth (Judge Drake) to meaningless escape in European luxury."

Neither the psychoanalytic nor the allegorical point of view presents complete answers for Temple's motives, because an all-important element has been omitted: the culture that produced her.

17. Vickery, *The Novels of William Faulkner*, 107.

18. Beauvoir, *The Second Sex*, 600–601. Another analogue to Temple's psychosis is R. D. Laing's notion of the schizoid personality. When an individual whose entire personality is constructed on a "false self" is suddenly confronted with a situation in which the "false self" cannot function, the individual may become schizophrenic; the schizophrenia is often accompanied by dissociation from the body. Thus Temple, who has heretofore conformed to the role of the southern belle, finds it inadequate in dealing with Popeye. See Laing's *The Divided Self*.

19. In the most perverse sense, Popeye epitomizes the southern male. (He is not, as O'Donnell says, Modernism, but Property Acquisitor.) In possessing Temple he can "acquire" goods, can become an owner, just as Temple's future husband would have. Like any patriarch, he seeks to possess a sought-after commodity (who is also a woman), yet ironically he has no sexual power with which to establish his ownership; therefore, he substitutes another sort of power, violence, in order to enslave Temple. When Popeye takes Temple to the Memphis brothel, he illustrates Beauvoir's maxim "The surest way to assert that something is mine is to prevent others from using it" (*The Second Sex*, 143).

20. Freud, "Some Psychological Consequences of the Anatomical Distinction between the Sexes," 186–97.

21. Horney, *Feminine Psychology*, 217.

22. Ibid., 224–25. Horney's list of masochistic traits is strikingly similar to the classic traits of the "hysterical personality" of the narcissist, but it is also similar to what previous generations described as the "healthy female." All three types are emotional, excitable, dependent, and unaggressive, accept pain, fear the world, and are seductive. For the full comparison, see Betsy Belote's "Masochistic Syndrome, Hysterical Personality, and the Illusion of a Healthy Woman," 335–48.

23. Horney, *Feminine Psychology*, 229.

24. Beauvoir, *The Second Sex*, 602.

25. Tate, "Introduction," *Sanctuary*, xii.

26. Beauvoir, *The Second Sex*, 613.

27. Ibid., 334.

28. Baughman, *Southern Rape Complex*, 193.

29. Wyatt-Brown, *Southern Honor*, 34.

30. Faulkner, *The Sound and the Fury*, 78. Subsequent references in this chapter are cited in the text.

31. Wyatt-Brown, *Southern Honor*, 136.

32. Otto Kernberg, *Borderline Conditions and Pathological Narcissism*, 238.

33. Faulkner, "That Evening Sun," in *Collected Stories*, 294.

34. Jo Ann Crandall's "William Faulkner and the Myth of Southern Womanhood" contains a thorough discussion of Caroline Compson's conformity to social norms.

35. "William Faulkner: An Interview," with Jean Stein, in Hoffman and Vickery, eds., *William Faulkner: Three Decades of Criticism*, 73.

36. Faulkner, "That Evening Sun," in *Collected Stories*, 303.

37. Horney, *Feminine Psychology*, 246.

38. Faulkner critics have frequently assumed that the words and actions of his characters represent his own opinions. The other trend in Faulkner criticism reduces Faulkner's "women" to one-dimensional representatives of cultural stereotypes and mythic archetypes. Both trends preclude the sustained analysis that has been afforded Faulkner's male characters.

The trend toward categorization was inaugurated by George Marion O'Donnell's essay "Faulkner's Mythology" (1939). O'Donnell's overview of Faulkner's "spiritual geography" was necessary in 1939, to be sure, since until that time critics had emphasized the violence and depravity contained in individual works and had dismissed them as examples of the "cult of cruelty," as Henry Seidel Canby expressed it.

Maxwell Geismar in *Writers in Crisis* (1942) identifies the female and the black as twin "scapegoats" upon which Faulkner projects his hatred of the modern South. He maintains that the destruction of the modern southern woman in Faulkner's works reveals Faulkner's desire to witness the destruction of the modern South. The Faulknerian female, he writes, desires to destroy the Faulknerian male; thus he pigeonholes Temple's behavior as willing degradation, Caroline Compson's behavior as self-serving hypochondria, and Caddy's behavior as sexual weakness. Geismar equates Faulkner's portraits of female depravity with Faulkner's hatred of the southern "Waste Land" and contends that this equation arises from deep psychological conflicts within Faulkner himself, and that Faulkner believes "the female source of life is itself inherently vicious" (180).

Irving Howe, in *William Faulkner: A Critical Study* (1952), continues this thesis, asserting that because women are representatives of evil, they exemplify Faulkner's personal hatred of women. The first premise, however, is much too narrow a view of Faulkner's complex portraits of women; even if it were true, the second part of the hypothesis suggests that one's fiction equates directly with one's personal experiences or psychological make-up, a fallacious and misleading critical viewpoint. Howe not only believes that belles represent corrupt society in Faulkner's works, since these women are the violators of nature and freedom in the novels, but also that the "female malevolence" of the young women in Faulkner's works is so exaggerated that it reveals misogyny in Faulkner himself (141). Thus, for Howe, Faulkner's Cecily is the "young American bitch" and Temple is the "trembling, sexless, ferocious bitch." Only women who are "beyond the age of sexual attraction" are admirable. With such a thesis, Howe cannot adequately explain the personalities of Caddy, Narcissa, or Drusilla Hawks; perhaps this is why he does not mention them.

Criticism of Faulkner's women in the 1960s continued to present them as extreme examples of pairs of archetypes. Leslie Fiedler says, in *Love and Death in the American Novel* (1960), "In no other writer in the world do pejorative stereotypes of women appear with greater frequency" (309). According to Fiedler, Faulkner prefers prepuberty or postmenopausal females; all others are either fertile earth mothers, "mindless daughters of peasants," or "sterile temptresses," sexually insatiable daughters of the aristocracy (1966 ed., 321). He contends that Temple Drake is the epitome of the sexually aggressive Dark Lady, although she is supposed to be a White Maiden. Cecily and Temple are stereotypes that he describes as "cold as [a] nymphomaniac Venus" or the "Good Bad Girl."

David M. Miller in "Faulkner's Women" maintains that Faulknerian women are "either earth mothers or ghosts" (3). Using this classification, Miller places Cecily and Temple in the company of Jenny Du Pre, Judith Sutpen, and Joanna Burden, as sexless ghosts. But Narcissa Benbow joins Lena Grove and Eula Varner as an earth mother! Naomi Jackson divides Faulkner's women similarly into "Demon-Nun and Angel-Witch" (1967), although she is one of the first critics to insist that negative portraits of women in the novels do not represent the point of view of the author but that of other characters in the story. Even a critic such as Cleanth Brooks, who has presented perceptive analyses of individual women in individual novels, flounders when faced with an overview of Faulkner's women. In his introduction to Sally R. Page's *Faulkner's Women: Characterization and Meaning* (1972) he defines the Faulknerian woman as "the goal and end of action" (not herself an actor); as "nature; or she may be the temptress . . . or the life-giving being" (xiv–xv). Maureen Anne Waters separates Faulkner's women into "great Good Mothers" or "Terrible Devouring mothers" in "The Role of Women in Faulkner's Yoknapatawpha" (1975).

The two main premises of these critical assessments are the biographical and the archetypal, and both premises limit the investigation of Faulkner's women severely. One does not assume that Faulkner hates southern men because Quentin Compson is weak and insane, Sutpen is monomaniacal, and Joe Christmas is a murderer, even though these men are as destructive as Caroline Compson, Temple Drake, and Caddy Compson. The reader usually believes that Faulkner intends to show how these men came to be as they are, and that they deserve pity and awe because they suffer and are human. Faulkner himself declared in a 1956 interview: "The opinion that women cause all the trouble is not my own. . . . they have held families together and it's because of families that the race has continued and I would be sorry to think that my work has given anyone the impression that I held women in morally a lower position than men, which I do not" (in Jelliffe, ed., *Faulkner at Nagano*, 69).

The positive assessments of Faulkner's women have been scarce. Karl E. Zink in "Faulkner's Garden: Woman and the Immemorial Earth" uses the archetypal premise to present the ambiguity of the Faulknerian woman rather than to define her as a limited force of good or evil. His argument is that "Faulkner casts the human condition against fundamental processes, the raw common denominator of life on Earth, and it is quite possible that the male's ambiguous fear and hatred and love of woman must be explained in terms of his fear and hatred and love of the old Earth itself, to which woman is so disturbingly related" (149). Woman, he finds, is associated with flowers, the outdoors, sexuality, fertility, and all the timeless cycles of nature; thus Cecily is associated with the inevitability of natural forces, Caddy embodies the natural sexuality of the earth, and Caroline Compson's denial of the natural condition of motherhood brings about the destruction of her family. Because Zink chooses the archetype Earth, which is itself multidimensional, his is a balanced evaluation of the positive and negative aspects of Faulkner's women characters.

The study that partially serves as the necessary corrective to tendencies toward biographical fallacy and reduction to stereotypes is Sally R. Page's *Faulkner's Women: Characterization and Meaning* (1972). The thesis of the study is that "Faulkner's women are too original to be regarded as replicas of other characters or of some stereotyped view of women" (xxii). Page examines Faulkner's imagery in order to show that he regards women as representative of either life or death, of moral order or perversity and decadence. Page sees Cecily, for example, as a representative of the failure of romantic idealism; Caddy is praised for her "warmth and responsiveness, her aggressive courage," and her ability to love. Page asserts that Faulkner shows that man is in need of woman not as a romantic ideal or a pure virgin, but as one who can love. Ilse Dusior Lind argues against Faulkner as a misogynist in "Faulkner's Women," in *The Maker and the Myth: Faulkner and Yoknapatawpha* (1977). Other critics who treat Faulkner's women effectively are Cleanth Brooks in *William Faulkner: The Yoknapatawpha Country* (1963) and Olga Vickery in *The Novels of William Faulkner* (1964); both books offer many fine elucidations of female characters.

Chapter 9: The Southern Eve

1. Kolodny, *The Land Before Her*.
2. See Davis, *The Problem of Slavery in Western Culture*, 8; and Kolodny, *The Lay of the Land*.
3. Kolodny, *The Lay of the Land*, 132.
4. Kolodny, *The Land Before Her*.
5. Southworth, *Retribution; or, The Vale of Shadows*, 30. Subsequent references in this chapter are cited in the text.

6. Hentz, *The Victim of Excitement; The Bosom Serpent*, 58, 80. Subsequent references in this chapter are cited in the text.

7. Wyatt-Brown, *Southern Honor*, 220.

8. Hentz, *Linda*, 103. Subsequent references in this chapter are cited in the text.

9. Hentz, *The Planter's Northern Bride*, vi.

10. The historical realities of life for southern women have been examined by Anne Firor Scott in *The Southern Lady: From Pedestal to Politics, 1830–1930*.

11. Ibid., 81–82.

12. For an early, illuminating discussion of the extravagant glamorizing of the antebellum South in the novels of Eggleston, Page, Joel Chandler Harris, and Thomas Dixon, Jr., see Francis P. Gaines's *The Southern Plantation*, 65–83, 91.

13. A third group writing about southern women in this period is composed of realists such as Kate Chopin and George Washington Cable. Their books differ significantly from those of the other two groups; the setting is always New Orleans and the culture being written about is Catholic, French, and Caribbean. Moreover, the Civil War is not the central event. Consequently, this study does not deal with the young women of New Orleans, for the belle as she is defined here is part of the plantation South. The topic clearly deserves book-length treatment.

14. See, for example, Tate's introduction to *Sanctuary*, by William Faulkner; Hoffman, *The Art of Southern Fiction*, 1–28; the essays of Rubin and Hubbell in *The South in American Literature, 1607–1800*, ed. Rubin and Hubbell; and Lucinda H. MacKethan, "Thomas Nelson Page: The Plantation as Arcady," in *Dream of Arcady*, 36–60.

15. MacKethan, *Dream of Arcady*, 314.

16. Eliade, *Myth and Reality*, 6.

17. Bagby, *The Old Virginia Gentleman and Other Sketches*, 19. Bagby also praises the timidity, spirituality, self-denial, and withdrawal of the plantation matron. Subsequent references in this chapter are cited in the text.

18. T. Page, *Social Life in Old Virginia Before the War*, 51–52. Subsequent references in this chapter are cited in the text.

19. MacKethan, *Dream of Arcady*, 322.

20. Olmstead, *The Cotton Kingdom*, 335.

21. T. Page, *Red Rock*, 29.

22. Ibid., 50.

23. Ibid., 291.

24. T. Page, *The Old South*, 50. Consistent with Page's courtroom image are the images of William Faulkner and John Peale Bishop, who write about the judgment and "fall" of southern belles Temple Drake and Virginia Crannock in, respectively, *Sanctuary* (1931) and *Act of Darkness* (1935). See chapter 12 for a discussion of the trial motif.

25. Glasgow, *The Romantic Comedians*, 203. Subsequent references in this chapter are cited in the text.

26. Warren, "William Faulkner," in Hoffman and Vickery, eds., *William Faulkner: Three Decades of Criticism*, 113.

27. Gordon, *The Garden of Adonis*, frontispiece.

Chapter 10: White Anxiety

1. Davis, *Problem of Slavery*, 468–70.
2. Ibid., 470.
3. Franklin, *From Slavery to Freedom*, 155.
4. Cash, *The Mind of the South*, 84.
5. Ibid., 86.
6. Ibid., 115. See also the cited works of Catherine Clinton, John Hope Franklin, David Brion Davis, among the many commentators on the "Southern rape complex," as Cash called it.
7. Tate, "Introduction," *Sanctuary*, x. See also the discussion of the southern mythos in Frederick J. Hoffman's *The Art of Southern Fiction*, 1–28, and the essays in Louis D. Rubin and Jay B. Hubbell's *The South in American Literature, 1607–1900*.
8. Eliade, *Myth and Reality*, 2, 6, 5.
9. Tate, "Introduction," *Sanctuary*, x.
10. Eliade, *Myth and Reality*, 6.
11. See Dollard, *Caste and Class in a Southern Town*. Dollard, writing about this syndrome in 1937, theorizes that men who have such anxieties "are defending women not only from the sexual thoughts and attention of Negroes but also from their own" (137); that is, white men who cannot accept their sexual desire for white women as natural project their own feelings onto black men.
12. Coulter, *The South during Reconstruction*, 65.
13. Ibid., 60.
14. See, for example, T. Page, *The Negro: The Southerner's Problem*, 84.
15. Hall, *Revolt Against Chivalry*, 131.
16. Ibid., 161; see also Brownmiller, *Against Our Will: Men, Women, and Rape*.
17. The reactions to *Uncle Tom's Cabin* (1852) may indicate that the stereotype of the black rapist of a white female existed prior to the war, since the subplot of Eva and Tom may suggest these stereotypes. These ideas, tacitly part of southern culture before the war, were nourished by postwar developments. See Fiedler's *Love and Death in the American Novel* (1966), 266.
18. W. C. Falkner, *The Little Brick Church*, 26.
19. Ibid., 31.
20. Dixon, *The Clansman*, ii. Subsequent references in this chapter are cited in the text.
21. Dixon, *Sins of the Father*, 124. Subsequent references in this chapter are cited in the text.

Chapter 11: Rape and the Southern Belle

1. See Taylor, *Cavalier and Yankee*, for a complete discussion of the southern squirearchy.
2. This discussion of the components of a patriarchy uses the categories of status, role, and temperament found in Kate Millet's *Sexual Politics*, 47.
3. J. Miller, *Toward a New Psychology of Women*, 6–7.

4. Cross, *The Unknown Goddess*, 7–8. Subsequent references in this chapter are cited in the text.

5. See Fiedler, "Afterword," *Act of Darkness*, 313.

6. Basso, *Cinnamon Seed*, 63. Subsequent references in this chapter are cited in the text.

7. Tate, *The Fathers*, 183. Subsequent references in this chapter are cited in the text.

8. See Frank Lawrence Owsley's essay, "The Irrepressible Conflict," in *I'll Take My Stand*.

9. The many rationalizations about rape are discussed in Susan Brownmiller's *Against Our Will*.

10. Horney, *Feminine Psychology*, 229. Using helplessness as a means of wooing and subduing the other sex is one of the traits of neurotic masochism that Horney identifies.

11. Glenn, *Southern Charm*, 86. Subsequent references in this chapter are cited in the text.

Chapter 12: The Belle on Trial

1. Greene, *Death in the Deep South*, 23. Subsequent references in this chapter are cited in the text.

2. Bishop, *Act of Darkness*, 55. Charlie's family qualifies as upper class in this century because his ancestors had been landed gentry in the nineteenth century. Subsequent references in this chapter are cited in the text.

3. See, for example, Horney, *The Neurotic Personality of Our Time*, 51.

4. Fiedler, "Afterword," *Act of Darkness*, 313.

5. Ibid., 318.

6. O'Donnell, "Faulkner's Mythology," 85.

7. Lewis P. Simpson, "Isaac McCaslin and Temple Drake: The Fall of New World Man," in Stanford, ed., *Nine Essays in Modern Literature*, 101.

8. Faulkner, *Requiem for a Nun*, 116, 135. Subsequent references in this chapter are cited in the text.

9. Faulkner, "The Stockholm Address," in Hoffman and Vickery, eds., *William Faulkner: Three Decades of Criticism*, 348.

Epilogue

1. Flanders, "Katherine Anne Porter and the Ordeal of Southern Womanhood," 48.

Selected

Bibliography

Abrams, Meyer H. *The Mirror and the Lamp.* 1953. Reprint. New York: Norton, 1958.

Anthony, Susan B., and Ida H. Harper, eds. *The History of Woman Suffrage.* Vol. IV. Rochester, N.Y.: Fowler and Wells, 1902.

Auchincloss, Louis. *Ellen Glasgow.* Minneapolis: University of Minnesota Press, 1964.

Bagby, George W. *The Old Virginia Gentleman and Other Sketches.* 1884. Reprint. New York: Scribner's, 1910.

Bartlett, Irving H., and C. Glenn Cambor. "The History and Psychodynamics of Southern Womanhood." *Women's Studies* 2 (1974): 9–24.

Basso, Hamilton. *Cinnamon Seed.* New York: Scribner's, 1934.

Baugh, Hansell. *Letters of Frances Newman.* New York: Liveright, 1929.

Baughman, Laurence Alan. *Southern Rape Complex: Hundred Year Psychosis.* Atlanta: Pendulum, 1966.

Baum, Catherine. "'The Beautiful One': Caddy Compson as Heroine of *The Sound and the Fury.*" *Modern Fiction Studies* 13 (Spring 1967): 33–44.

Baym, Nina. *Women's Fiction: A Guide to Novels by and about Women in America, 1820–1870.* Ithaca, N.Y.: Cornell University Press, 1978.

Beauvoir, Simone de. *The Second Sex.* Translated by H. M. Parshley. 1952. Reprint. New York: Bantam, 1961.

Belote, Betsy. "Masochistic Syndrome, Hysterical Personality, and the Illusion of a Healthy Woman." In *Female Psychology: The Emerging Self,* edited by Sue Cox. Chicago: Science Research Associates, 1976.

Bettelheim, Bruno. *The Uses of Enchantment: The Meaning and Importance of Fairy Tales.* New York: Alfred A. Knopf, 1976.

Bishop, John Peale. *Act of Darkness.* 1935. Reprint. New York: Avon, 1970.

Bogardus, Ralph E., and Fred Hobson. *Literature at the Barricades: The American Writer in the 1930's.* University, Ala.: University of Alabama Press, 1982.

Bradbury, John M. *Renaissance in the South.* Chapel Hill: University of North Carolina Press, 1963.

Brien, D. E. "William Faulkner and the Myth of Woman." *Washington State College Research Studies* 35 (June 1967).

Brooks, Cleanth. *William Faulkner: The Yoknapatawpha Country*. New Haven: Yale University Press, 1963.

_____, and Robert Penn Warren, eds. *Stories from Southern Review*. Baton Rouge: Louisiana State University Press, 1953.

Brown, Herbert Ross. *The Sentimental Novel in America, 1789–1860*. Durham: Duke University Press, 1940.

Brownmiller, Susan. *Against Our Will: Men, Women, and Rape*. New York: Simon and Schuster, 1975.

Bryer, Jackson, ed. *The Short Fiction of F. Scott Fitzgerald*. Madison: University of Wisconsin Press, 1982.

Cabell, James Branch. *Some of Us*. New York: Robert M. McBride, 1930.

Cable, George Washington. *Old Creole Days*. 1879. Reprint. New York: Scribner's, 1890.

Carmer, Carl. *Stars Fell on Alabama*. New York: Farrar & Rinehart, 1934.

Cash, Wilbur J. *The Mind of the South*. New York: Alfred A. Knopf, 1941.

Chopin, Kate. *The Awakening*. New York: Norton, 1976.

Clark, Emily. *Innocence Abroad*. New York: Alfred A. Knopf, 1931.

Clinton, Catherine. *The Plantation Mistress: Woman's World in the Old South*. New York: Pantheon, 1982.

Clopton, Virginia Clay. *A Belle of the Fifties*. New York: Doubleday, Page, 1904.

Coleman, Lonnie. *Beulah Land*. New York: Doubleday, 1973.

Collins, Carvel. "A Conscious Literary Use of Freud?" *Literature and Psychology* 3 (June 1953): 3.

Cooke, John Esten. *The Virginia Comedians: or Old Days in the Old Dominion*. New York: D. Appleton, 1854.

Cooper, James Fenimore. *The Spy; A Tale of Neutral Ground*. New York: Wiley & Halsted, 1821.

Couch, W. T., ed. *Culture in the South*. Chapel Hill: University of North Carolina Press, 1935.

Coulter, E. Merton. *The South during Reconstruction*. Baton Rouge: Louisiana State University Press, 1947.

Cox, Sue, ed. *Female Psychology: The Emerging Self*. Chicago: Science Research Associates, 1976.

Crandall, Jo Ann. "William Faulkner and the Myth of Southern Womanhood: The Aristocratic Women in Faulkner's Early Novels." Master's thesis, University of Maryland, 1970.

Cross, Ruth. *The Unknown Goddess*. New York: Harper, 1926.

Cypher, James R. "The Tangled Sexuality of Temple Drake." *American Imago* 19 (Fall 1962): 243–52.

Davidson, Donald. "Review," *Critic's Almanac*, May 13, 1928. In *The Spyglass: Views and Reviews, 1924–1930*, edited by John Tyree Fain. Nashville: Vanderbilt University Press, 1963.

_____. *Still Rebels, Still Yankees*. Baton Rouge: Louisiana State University Press, 1957.

Davis, David Brion. *The Problem of Slavery in Western Culture*. Ithaca, N.Y.: Cornell University Press, 1966.

Deegan, Dorothy Yost. *The Stereotype of the Single Woman in American Novels*. New York: Columbia University Press, 1951.

De Forest, John William. *Miss Ravenel's Conversion from Secession to Loyalty*. 1867. Reprint. Columbus, Ohio: Charles E. Merrill, 1969.

_____. *The Bloody Chasm*. New York: D. Appleton, 1881.

De Rougemount, Denis. *Love in the Western World*. New York: Harcourt, Brace, 1940.

Deutsch, Helene. *The Psychology of Women: A Psychoanalytic Interpretation*. 2 vols. New York: Grune and Stratton, 1941.

Dew, Thomas R. "On the Characteristic Difference between the Sexes and on the Position and Influence of Women in Society." *Southern Literary Messenger* 1 (May 1835): 621–23; (August 1835): 672–91.

Dixon, Thomas, Jr. *The Clansman: An Historical Romance of the Ku Klux Klan*. New York: A. Wessels, 1905.

_____. *The Sins of the Father: A Romance of the South*. New York: D. Appleton, 1912.

_____. *The Southerner: A Romance of the Real Lincoln*. New York: D. Appleton, 1913.

_____. *The Traitor*. New York: Doubleday, Page, 1907.

Dollard, John. *Caste and Class in a Southern Town*. New Haven: Yale University Press, 1937.

Donaldson, Scott. "Scott Fitzgerald's Romance with the South." *Southern Literary Journal* 5 (Spring 1973): 3–17.

Edel, Leon. *The Psychological Novel*. London: Latimer Trend, 1950.

Eggleston, George Cary. *Dorothy South: A Love Story of Virginia Just Before the War*. Boston: Lothrup, 1902.

_____. *Evelyn Bird*. Boston: Norwood, 1904.

Eliade, Mircea. *Myth and Reality*. New York: Harper and Row, 1963.

Falk, Signi Lenea. *Tennessee Williams*. New York: Twayne, 1962.

Falkner, W. C. *The Little Brick Church*. Philadelphia: J. B. Lippincott, 1882.

_____. *The White Rose of Memphis*. New York: G. W. Carleton, 1881.

Faulkner, William. *The Collected Stories of William Faulkner*. New York: Random House, 1950.

_____. *Requiem for a Nun*. New York: Random House, 1951.

_____. *Sanctuary*. New York: Random House, 1931.

_____. *Sartoris*. 1929. Reprint. New York: Signet, 1964.

_____. *Soldier's Pay*. 1926. Reprint. New York: Liveright, 1970.

_____. *The Sound and the Fury*. 1929. Reprint. New York: Modern Library, 1946.

_____. *The Unvanquished*. New York: Random House, 1938.

Fiedler, Leslie. "Afterword: John Peale Bishop and the Other Thirties." In *Act of Darkness*, by John Peale Bishop. 1935. Reprint. New York: Avon, 1970.

_____. *Love and Death in the American Novel*. New York: Stein and Day, 1960. Rev. ed. New York: Dell, 1966.

Finley, Ruth E. *The Lady of Godey's: Sarah Josepha Hale*. Philadelphia: J. B. Lippincott, 1931.

Fitzgerald, F. Scott. *The Stories of F. Scott Fitzgerald*, edited by Malcolm Cowley. New York: Scribner's, 1951.

Fitzgerald, Zelda. *Save Me the Waltz.* 1932. Reprint. Carbondale: Southern Illinois University Press, 1967.

Flanders, Jane. "Katherine Anne Porter and the Ordeal of Southern Womanhood." *Southern Literary Journal* 9 (Fall 1976): 47–60.

Fletcher, Marie. "The Southern Heroine in the Fiction of Representative Southern Women Writers, 1850–1960." Ph.D. diss., Louisiana State University, 1963.

Forrest, Mary, ed. *Women of the South Distinguished in Literature.* New York: Derby and Jackson, 1861.

Franklin, John Hope. *From Slavery to Freedom: A History of Negro Americans.* 4th ed. New York: Alfred A. Knopf, 1974.

_____. *Reconstruction: After the Civil War.* Chicago: University of Chicago Press, 1961.

Freud, Sigmund. "Some Psychological Consequences of the Anatomical Distinction between the Sexes." In *Collected Papers.* Vol. V. London: Hogarth Press, 1956.

Fryer, Judith. *The Faces of Eve: Women in the Nineteenth-Century American Novel.* New York: Oxford University Press, 1976.

Fulton, Maurice Garland, ed. *Southern Life in Southern Literature.* Boston: Ginn, 1917.

Gaines, Francis Pendleton. *The Southern Plantation: A Study of the Development and the Accuracy of a Tradition.* New York: Columbia University Press, 1924.

Garson, Helen S. "The Fallen Women in American Naturalistic Fiction: From Crane to Faulkner." Ph.D. diss., University of Maryland, 1967.

Gaston, Paul M. *The New South Creed: A Study in Southern Mythmaking.* New York: Alfred A. Knopf, 1970.

Geismar, Maxwell. *American Moderns: From Rebellion to Conformity.* New York: Hill and Wang, 1958.

_____. *Rebels and Ancestors: The American Novel 1890–1915.* Boston: Houghton Mifflin, 1953.

_____. *Writers in Crisis: The American Novel between Two Wars.* Boston: Houghton Mifflin, 1942.

Gilbert, Sandra M., and Susan Gubar. *The Madwoman in the Attic: The Woman Writer and the Nineteenth-Century Literary Imagination.* New Haven: Yale University Press, 1979.

Gilman, Caroline. *Recollections of a New England Bride and of a Southern Matron.* New York: G. P. Putnam, 1852.

_____. *Recollections of a Southern Matron.* New York: Harper, 1837.

_____. *Tales and Ballads.* Boston: William Crosby, 1839.

Glasgow, Ellen. *The Ancient Law.* Garden City, N.Y.: Doubleday, Page, 1908.

_____. *Barren Ground.* Garden City, N.Y.: Doubleday, Page, 1925.

_____. *The Battle-Ground.* Garden City, N.Y.:Doubleday, Page, 1902.

_____. *A Certain Measure: An Interpretation of Prose Fiction.* New York: Harcourt, Brace, 1943. Reprint. Millwood, N.Y.: Kraus Reprint, 1969.

_____. *The Deliverance.* Garden City, N.Y.: Doubleday, Page, 1904.

_____. *The Descendant.* New York: Harper, 1897.

_____. *Life and Gabriella.* Garden City, N.Y.: Doubleday, Page, 1916.

_____. *The Miller of Old Church.* Garden City, N.Y.: Doubleday, Page, 1911.

_____. *The Romance of a Plain Man*. New York: Macmillan, 1909.

_____. *The Romantic Comedians*. Garden City, N.Y.: Doubleday, Page, 1926.

_____. *The Sheltered Life*. Garden City, N.Y.: Doubleday, Doran, 1932.

_____. *They Stooped to Folly*. Garden City, N.Y.: Doubleday, Doran, 1929.

_____. *Virginia*. Garden City, N.Y.: Doubleday, Page, 1913. Reprint. Garden City, N.Y.: Doubleday, Doran, 1929.

_____. *The Woman Within*. New York: Harcourt, Brace, 1945.

Glasgow, Ellen, and James Branch Cabell. *Of Ellen Glasgow: An Inscribed Portrait*. New York: Maverick Press, 1938.

Glenn, Isa. *A Short History of Julia*. New York: Alfred A. Knopf, 1930.

_____. *Southern Charm*. New York: Alfred A. Knopf, 1928.

Godbold, E. Stanley, Jr. *Ellen Glasgow and The Woman Within*. Baton Rouge: Louisiana State University Press, 1972.

Gordon, Caroline. *The Garden of Adonis*. New York: Scribner's, 1937.

_____. *Penhally*. New York: Scribner's, 1931.

Grau, Shirley Ann. *The Keepers of the House*. Greenwich, Conn.: Fawcett, 1964.

Greene, Ward. *Death in the Deep South*. New York: American Mercury, 1936.

_____. *Weep No More*. New York: Harrison Smith, 1932.

Haardt, Sarah. "Paradox." *The Reviewer* 5 (January 1925): 64–70.

_____.."The Southern Lady Says Grace." *The Reviewer* 5 (January 1925): 57–63.

Hackett, Alice Payne. *Fifty Years of Best Sellers, 1895–1945*. New York: R. R. Bowker, 1945.

Hale, Sarah Josepha. *Northwood; A Tale of New England*. Boston: Bowles and Dearborn, 1831.

_____. *Sketches of American Character*. Boston: Freeman Hunt, 1831.

Haley, Alex. *Roots*. New York: Doubleday, 1976.

Hall, Jacquelyn Dowd. *Revolt Against Chivalry: Jessie Daniel Ames and the Women's Campaign Against Lynching*. New York: Columbia University Press, 1979.

Hardy, John Edward. "Ellen Glasgow." In *Southern Renascence: The Literature of the Modern South*, edited by Louis D. Rubin, Jr., and Robert D. Jacobs. Baltimore: Johns Hopkins Press, 1953.

Harrington, Evans, and Ann J. Abadie, eds. *The Maker and the Myth: Faulkner and Yoknapatawpha*. Jackson: University Press of Mississippi, 1977.

Hays, H. R. *The Dangerous Sex: The Myth of Feminine Evil*. New York: G. P. Putnam's, 1964.

Hentz, Caroline Lee. "The Beauty Transformed." In *Courtship and Marriage; or, The Joys and Sorrows of American Life*. Philadelphia: T. B. Peterson, 1856.

_____. *Eoline; or Magnolia Vale*. Philadelphia: T. B. Peterson, 1852.

_____. *Linda; or, The Young Pilot of the Belle Creole. A Tale of Southern Life*. Philadelphia: A. Hart, 1850.

_____. *Marcus Warland: or, The Long Moss Spring. A Tale of the South*. Philadelphia: A. Hart, 1852.

_____. *The Planter's Northern Bride*. 1854. Reprint. Chapel Hill: University of North Carolina Press, 1970.

_____. *The Victim of Excitement; The Bosom Serpent*. Philadelphia: A. Hart, 1853.

Higginson, Thomas Wentworth. *Common Sense About Women*. Boston: Lee and Shepard, 1882.

Hobson, Fred C., Jr. *Serpent in Eden: H. L. Mencken and the South*. Chapel Hill: University of North Carolina Press, 1974.

Hoffman, Frederick J. *The Art of Southern Fiction*. Carbondale: Southern Illinois University Press, 1967.

_____. *The Twenties: American Writing in the Postwar Decade*. Rev. ed. New York: Macmillan, 1962.

Hoffman, Frederick J., and Olga Vickery, eds. *William Faulkner: Three Decades of Criticism*. New York: Harcourt, Brace, 1960.

Holman, C. Hugh. *The Roots of Southern Writing*. Athens: University of Georgia Press, 1972.

_____. "Fitzgerald's Changes on the Southern Belle: The Tarleton Trilogy." In *The Short Fiction of F. Scott Fitzgerald*, edited by Jackson Breyer. Madison: University of Wisconsin Press, 1982.

Horner, Lance, and Kyle Onstott. *Falconhurst Fancy*. Greenwich, Conn.: Fawcett, 1966.

Horney, Karen. *Feminine Psychology*. New York: W. W. Norton, 1967.

_____. *The Neurotic Personality of Our Time*. 1937. Reprint. New York: W. W. Norton, 1964.

_____. *New Ways in Psychoanalysis*. 1939. Reprint. New York: W. W. Norton, 1966.

Houghton, Walter E. *The Victorian Frame of Mind, 1830–1870*. New Haven: Yale University Press, 1957.

Howe, Irving. *William Faulkner: A Critical Study*. New York: Random House, 1952.

Howe, Julia Ward, and Thomas Wentworth Higginson, Lucy Stone, Elizabeth Cady Stanton, and Wendell Phillips. "The Other Side of the Woman Question." *North American Review* 24 (November 1879): 428–46.

Hubbell, Jay B., and Louis D. Rubin, Jr. *The South in American Literature 1607–1900*. Durham: Duke University Press, 1954.

I'll Take My Stand: The South and the Agrarian Tradition. 1930. Reprint. New York: Harper, 1962.

Jackson, Naomi. "Faulkner's Women: 'Demon-Nun and Angel-Witch'," *Ball State University Forum* 8 (Winter 1967): 12–22.

Jelliffe, Robert A., ed. *Faulkner at Nagano*. Tokyo: Kenkyusha Press, 1956.

Johnston, Mary. *Hagar*. Boston: Houghton Mifflin, 1913.

_____. *To Have and To Hold*. Boston: Houghton, Mifflin, 1900.

Jones, Anne Goodwyn. *Tomorrow Is Another Day: The Woman Writer in the South, 1859–1936*. Baton Rouge: Louisiana State University Press, 1981.

Karanikas, Alexander. *Tillers of a Myth: Southern Agrarians as Social and Literary Critics*. Madison: University of Wisconsin Press, 1969.

Kazin, Alfred. *On Native Grounds: An Interpretation of Modern American Prose Literature*. New York: Harcourt, Brace, 1942.

Kennedy, John Pendleton. *Swallow Barn or A Sojourn in the Old Dominion*. Philadelphia: Carey & Lea, 1832.

Kernberg, Otto. *Borderline Conditions and Pathological Narcissism*. New York: Jason Aronson, 1975.

King, Florence. *Southern Ladies and Gentlemen*. New York: Stein and Day, 1975.

Kolodny, Annette. *The Land Before Her: Fact and Experience of the American Frontiers, 1630–1860*. Chapel Hill: University of North Carolina Press, 1985.

———. *The Lay of the Land: Metaphor as Experience in History in American Life and Letters*. Chapel Hill: University of North Carolina Press, 1975.

Kubie, Lawrence S. "William Faulkner's *Sanctuary*: An Analysis." *Saturday Review of Literature* 2 (October 20, 1934): 218, 224–26.

Kunitz, Stanley J. *Twentieth Century Authors: A Biographical Dictionary of Modern Literature*. H. W. Wilson, 1942.

Laing, R. D. *The Divided Self*. Baltimore: Penguin, 1970.

Langford, Gerald. *Faulkner's Revision of* Sanctuary: *A Collation of the Unrevised Galleys and the Published Book*. Austin: University of Texas Press, 1972.

Lasch, Christopher. *The Culture of Narcissism: American Life in an Age of Diminishing Expectations*. New York: Warner, 1979.

Lavender, William. *Chinaberry*. New York: Pyramid, 1976.

Lawrence, D. H. "Introduction." *London Mercury* (July 1930). Reprint. In *Selected Literary Criticism*, edited by Anthony Beal. New York: Viking, 1966.

Lawson, Lewis A. "Portrait of a Culture in Crisis: Modern Southern Literature." *Texas Quarterly* 10 (Spring 1967): 143–55.

Legman, G. *Love and Death: A Study in Censorship*. New York: Hacker Art Books, 1963.

Lewis, R. W. B. *The American Adam: Innocence, Tragedy, and the Nineteenth Century*. Chicago: University of Chicago Press, 1955.

Lind, Ilse Dusior. "Faulkner's Women." In *The Maker and the Myth*, edited by Evans Harrington and Ann J. Abadie (Jackson: University Press of Mississippi, 1977).

Lyons, Anne W. "Myth and Agony: The Southern Woman as Belle." Ph.D. diss., Bowling Green State University, 1975.

McDowell, Frederick P. W. *Ellen Glasgow and the Ironic Art of Fiction*. 1960. Reprint. Madison: University of Wisconsin Press, 1963.

McIlwaine, Shields. *The Southern Poor White from Lubberland to Tobacco Road*. Norman: University of Oklahoma Press, 1939.

MacKethan, Lucinda H. *The Dream of Arcady: Place and Time in Southern Literature*. Baton Rouge: Louisiana State University Press, 1980.

McNeil, George. *The Plantation*. New York: Bantam Books, 1975.

Mailer, Norman. *Cannibals and Christians*. New York: Dial Press, 1966.

Marcus, Steven. *The Other Victorians: A Study of Sexuality and Pornography in Mid-Nineteenth-Century England*. New York: Basic Books, 1966.

Marx, Leo. *The Machine in the Garden*. London: Oxford University Press, 1964.

Meeker, Richard K., ed. *The Collected Stories of Ellen Glasgow*. Baton Rouge: Louisiana State University Press, 1963.

Mencken, H. L. *The American Scene: A Reader*, edited by Huntington Cairns. New York: Alfred A. Knopf, 1965.

Messerli, Douglas. "The Door of the Past: The Plantation Tradition and Historicity." Unpublished essay.

Miller, David M. "Faulkner's Women." *Modern Fiction Studies* 13 (Spring 1967): 3–17.

Miller, Jean Baker. *Toward a New Psychology of Women*. Boston: Beacon Press, 1976.

Millet, Kate. *Sexual Politics*. 1969. Reprint. New York: Avon, 1971.

Millgate, Michael. *The Achievement of William Faulkner*. London: Constable, 1966.

Mitchell, Margaret. *Gone with the Wind*. New York: Macmillan, 1936.

Moore, Katharine. *Victorian Wives*. New York: St. Martin's Press, 1974.

Morris, Willie. *The Last of the Southern Girls*. New York: Alfred A. Knopf, 1973.

Mott, Frank Luther. *A History of American Magazines*. 4 vols. Cambridge: Harvard University Press, 1938–57.

Myers, Robert Manson, ed. *The Children of Pride: A True Story of Georgia and the Civil War*. 1972. Reprint. 3 vols. New York: Popular Library, 1972.

Newman, Frances. *Dead Lovers Are Faithful Lovers*. New York: Boni & Liveright, 1928.

_____. *The Hard-Boiled Virgin*. New York: Boni & Liveright, 1926.

O'Donnell, George Marion. "Faulkner's Mythology." *Kenyon Review* (Summer 1939).

Olmstead, Frederick Law. *The Cotton Kingdom: A Traveller's Observations on Cotton & Slavery in the American Slave States*. New York: Mason, 1861.

_____. *A Journey in the Seaboard Slave States in the Years 1853–1854, with Remarks on Their Economy*. 1856. Reprint. New York: G. P. Putnam's, 1904.

O'Neill, William. *The Woman Movement*. Chicago: Quadrangle Books, 1971.

Onstott, Kyle. *Mandingo*. Greenwich, Conn.: Fawcett Crest, 1958.

Overton, Grant M. *The Women Who Make Our Novels*. New York: Moffat, Yard, 1918.

Owsley, Frank. *Plain Folk of the Old South*. Baton Rouge: Louisiana State University Press, 1949.

Page, Sally R. *Faulkner's Women: Characterization and Meaning*. DeLand, Fla.: Everett/Edwards, 1972.

Page, Thomas Nelson. *In Ole Virginia or Marse Chan and Other Stories*. New York: Scribner's, 1906.

_____. *The Negro: The Southerner's Problem*. 1904. Reprint. New York: Scribner's, 1910.

_____. *Red Rock: A Chronicle of Reconstruction*. New York: Scribner's, 1898. Reprint. Ridgewood, N.J.: Greg Press, 1967.

_____. *Social Life in Old Virginia Before the War*. 1897. Reprint. New York: Scribner's, 1910.

Papashvily, Helen Waite. *All the Happy Endings: A Study of the Domestic Novel in America, the Women Who Wrote It, the Women Who Read It, in the Nineteenth Century*. New York: Harper, 1956.

Parkman, Francis. "The Woman Question." *North American Review* 124 (October 1879): 307–21.

Parrington, Vernon Louis. *Main Currents in American Thought*. Vol. III, *The Beginnings of Critical Realism in America: 1860–1920*. New York: Harcourt, Brace, 1930.

Payne, Leonida Warren, Jr., ed. *Southern Literary Readings*. Chicago: Rand McNally, 1913.

Phelps, Almira Lincoln. "Southern Housekeepers." In *Women of the South Distinguished in Literature*, edited by Mary Forrest. New York: Derby and Jackson, 1861.

Pickett, LaSalle Corbell. *Literary Hearthstones of Dixie*. Philadelphia: J. P. Lippincott, 1912.

Pope, Edith Everett Taylor. *Not Magnolia*. New York: E. P. Dutton, 1928.

_____. *Old Lady Esteroy*. New York: E. P. Dutton, 1934.

Porter, Katherine Anne. *Pale Horse, Pale Rider*. 1939. Reprint. New York: Harcourt, Brace, 1964.

Powdermaker, Hortense. *After Freedom: A Cultural Study in the Deep South*. New York: Viking, 1939.

Putnam, Emily. *The Lady*. Chicago: University of Chicago Press, 1970.

Raper, Julius R. *From the Sunken Garden: The Fiction of Ellen Glasgow, 1916–1945*. Baton Rouge: Louisiana State University Press, 1980.

_____. *Without Shelter: The Early Career of Ellen Glasgow*. Baton Rouge: Louisiana State University Press, 1971.

Rich, Adrienne. *Of Woman Born*. New York: Bantam, 1977.

Richards, Marion K. *Ellen Glasgow's Development as a Novelist*. The Hague: Mouton, 1971.

Rogers, Katharine M. *The Troublesome Helpmate: A History of Misogyny in Literature*. Seattle: University of Washington Press, 1966.

Rouse, Blair. *Ellen Glasgow*. New York: Twayne, 1962.

Rowson, Susanna. *Charlotte Temple: A Tale of Truth*. 1791. Reprint. New York: Twayne, 1964.

Rubin, Louis D., Jr. "Southern Literature: The Historical Image." In *South: Modern Southern Literature in Its Cultural Setting*, edited by Louis D. Rubin, Jr., and Robert D. Jacobs. Garden City, N.Y.: Doubleday, 1961.

_____. "Trouble on the Land: Southern Literature and the Great Depression." In *Literature at the Barricades: The American Writer in the 1930s*, edited by Ralph F. Bogardus and Fred Hobson. University, Ala.: University of Alabama Press, 1982.

_____. *Writers of the Modern South: The Faraway Country*. Seattle: University of Washington Press, 1966 (1963).

_____, and Jay B. Hubbell. *The South in American Literature, 1607–1900*. Durham: Duke University Press, 1954.

_____, and Robert D. Jacobs. *Southern Renascence: The Literature of the Modern South*. Baltimore: Johns Hopkins Press, 1953.

Rubin, Louis D., Jr., ed. *A Bibliographical Guide to the Study of Southern Literature*. Baton Rouge: Louisiana State University Press, 1969.

_____, and Robert D. Jacobs, eds. *South: Modern Southern Literature in Its Cultural Setting*. Garden City, N.Y.: Doubleday, 1961.

Ruitenbeek, Hendrik M., ed. *Psychoanalysis and Female Sexuality*. New Haven: College and University Press, 1966.

Sands, Alexander H. "Intellectual Culture of Women." *Southern Literary Messenger* 28 (May 1859): 321–32.

Santas, Joan Foster. "Ellen Glasgow's American Dream." Ph.D. diss., Cornell University, 1963. Ann Arbor, Mich.: University Microfilms, 1965.

Scott, Anne Firor. *The Southern Lady: From Pedestal to Politics, 1830–1930*. Chicago: University of Chicago Press, 1970.

Scott, Evelyn. *Migrations: An Arabesque in Histories*. New York: Albert and Charles Boni, 1927.

_____. *Narcissus*. New York: Harcourt, Brace, 1922.

Seidel, Kathryn Lee. "The Comic Male: Satire in Ellen Glasgow's Queenborough Trilogy." *Southern Quarterly* (Summer 1985).

Simms, William Gilmore. *The Golden Christmas: Chronicle of St. John's Berkeley*. Charleston: Walker, Richards, 1852.

_____. *Katharine Walton; or, The Rebel of Dorchester*. 1851. Reprint. Chicago: Belford, Clarke, 1885.

Simpson, Lewis P. *The Dispossessed Garden: Pastoral and History in Southern Literature*. Athens: University of Georgia Press, 1975.

"Southern Letters." *Double Dealer* 1 (June 1921): 214–15.

Southworth, Emma Dorothy Eliza Neville. *Retribution: Or, the Vale of Shadows*. New York: Harper, 1849.

_____. *Virginia and Magdalene; or the Foster-Sisters*. 1852.

Stanford, Donald E., ed. *Nine Essays in Modern Literature*. Baton Rouge: Louisiana State University Press, 1965.

Stern, Philip Van Doren. *The Annotated Uncle Tom's Cabin*. New York: Paul S. Eriksson, 1964.

_____. *Dred: A Tale of the Great Dismal Swamp*. Boston: Philips, Sampson, 1856.

Stewart, John L. *The Burden of Time: The Fugitives and the Agrarians*. Princeton: Princeton University Press, 1965.

Stowe, Harriet Beecher. *Uncle Tom's Cabin or, Life Among the Lowly*. 1852. Reprint. *The Annotated Uncle Tom's Cabin*, edited by Philip Van Doren Stern. New York: Paul S. Eriksson, 1964.

Styron, William. *Lie Down in Darkness*. New York: Random House, 1951.

_____. *Sophie's Choice*. New York: Random House, 1980.

Tate, Allen. *The Fathers*. New York: G. P. Putnam's, 1938.

_____. "The Fugitive, 1922–1925. A Personal Recollection Twenty Years After." *Princeton University Library Chronicle* 3 (1942): 75–84.

_____. "Introduction," *Sanctuary*, by William Faulkner. New York: Signet, 1968.

Taylor, William R. *Cavalier and Yankee: The Old South and American National Character*. New York: George Braziller, 1961.

Tindall, George. *The Emergence of the New South Creed: 1913–1945*. Baton Rouge: Louisiana State University Press, 1967.

Vandiver, Frank E., ed. *The Idea of the South: Pursuit of a Central Theme*. Chicago: University of Chicago Press, 1964.

Vickery, Olga. *The Novels of William Faulkner: A Critical Interpretation*. Rev. ed. Baton Rouge: Louisiana State University Press, 1964.

Wagner, Linda. *Ellen Glasgow: Beyond Convention*. Austin: University of Texas Press, 1982.

Walker, Margaret. *Jubilee*. New York: Houghton Mifflin, 1966.

Warren, Robert Penn, ed. *Faulkner: A Collection of Critical Essays*. Englewood Cliffs, N.J.: Prentice-Hall, 1966.

Wasserstrom, William. *Heiress of All the Ages: Sex and Sentiment in the Genteel Tradition*. Minneapolis: University of Minnesota Press, 1959.

Waters, Maureen Anne. "The Role of Women in Faulkner's Yoknapatawpha." Ph.D. diss., Columbia University, 1975.

Wertenbaker, Thomas J. *The Old South: The Founding of American Civilization.* New York: Scribner's, 1942.

_____. *Patrician and Plebeian in Virginia: or the Origin and Development of the Social Classes of the Old Dominion.* 1910. Reprint. New York: Russell and Russell, 1959.

West, Rebecca. *The Strange Necessity.* Garden City, N.Y.: Doubleday/Doran, 1928.

White, Robert L. *John Peale Bishop.* New York: Twayne, 1966.

Whittemore, Reed. *Little Magazines.* Minneapolis: University of Minnesota Press, 1963.

Williams, Tennessee. *The Glass Menagerie.* New York: New Directions, 1945.

_____. *A Streetcar Named Desire.* New York: New Directions, 1947.

Woodward, C. Vann. "The Irony of Southern History." In *Southern Renascence: The Literature of the Modern South,* edited by Louis D. Rubin, Jr., and Robert D. Jacobs. Baltimore: Johns Hopkins Press, 1953.

Wyatt-Brown, Bertram. *Southern Honor: Ethics and Behavior in the Old South.* New York: Oxford University Press, 1982.

Young, Stark. *So Red the Rose.* 1934. Reprint. New York: Ballantine Books, 1975.

Zink, Karl E. "Faulkner's Garden: Woman and the Immemorial Earth." *Modern Fiction Studies* 2 (Autumn 1956): 139–49.

INDEX

Library of Congress Cataloging in Publication Data

Seidel, Kathryn Lee.
   The southern belle in the American novel.

   Includes bibliographical references and index.
   1. American fiction—Southern States—History
and criticism.   2. Women in literature.   3. Southern
States in literature.   4. Plantation life in literature.   5.
Psychology in literature.   I. Title.
PS261.S35   1985   813'.009'9287   85-8519
ISBN 0-8130-0811-5 (alk. paper)